Jay Guy Cisco

HISTORIC
Sumner County, Tennessee

WITH

Genealogies of the Bledsoe, Cage and Douglass Families

AND

GENEALOGICAL NOTES OF OTHER SUMNER COUNTY FAMILIES

BY

JAY GUY CISCO

NASHVILLE, TENNESSEE:
FOLK-KEELIN PRINTING COMPANY
1909

Notice

In many older books, foxing (or discoloration) occurs and, in some instances, print lightens with wear and age. Reprinted books, such as this, often duplicate these flaws, notwithstanding efforts to reduce or eliminate them. The pages of this reprint have been digitally enhanced and, where possible, the flaws eliminated in order to provide clarity of content and a pleasant reading experience.

Originally published
Nashville, Tennessee:
1909

Reprinted by:

Janaway Publishing, Inc.
2412 Nicklaus Dr.
Santa Maria, California 93455
(805) 925-1038
www.janawaygenealogy.com

2007

ISBN 10: 1-59641-142-2
ISBN 13: 978-1-59641-142-5

Made in the United States of America

To the Memory of

My Wife

Mildred Georgie Pursley Cisco

Great great grand daughter of Colonel Anthony Bledsoe

Born in Sumner County, August 2, 1831
Died in Jackson, Tennessee, April 1, 1894

This book is affectionately dedicated

ILLUSTRATIONS

Bate, Senator W. B.	222
Bertinatti, Countess Euginie	226
Blackmore, Hon. James W.	47
Blandford, Marquis of	160
Bledsoe, Clifton	129
Bledsoe, Col. Oscar F.	85
Bledsoe, Oscar F., III	127
Bledsoe, Oscar F., IV	143
Bledsoe, Lulu Aldridge	144
Campbell, Governor W. B.	237
Carmack, Senator Edward Ward	240
Cisco, Jay Guy	Frontispiece
Cisco, Mildred Georgie	148
Desha, Governor Joseph	175
Desha, Miss Mary	179
Donelson, Hon. A. J.	246
Fearn, Dr. Thomas	112
Garth, Hon. W. W.	126
Garth, Mrs. W. W.	113
Guild, Judge Joe C.	250
Gwin, Senator W. M.	253
Hall, Governor William	256
Jones, Mrs. Frederika L.	148
Jones, Frederika Elizabeth	148
Judd, Judge John W.	267
Malone, Mrs. Sarah Shelby Wetherred	148
Peyton, Hon. Balie	288
Pickett, Col. Joseph Desha	opposite 176
Pursley, Mrs. Mary Catherine Malone	148
Shelby, Judge Anthony Bledsoe	110
Shelby, Mrs. Sarah Bledsoe	105
Trousdale, Gov. Wm.	303
Williams, D. Shelby	69

Winchester, Gen. James	308
Bledsoe Spring	99
Bledsoe Graves	73
Bledsoe's Lick	38
Bledsoe Monument	100
Cragfont	29
Emigrants Descending the Tennessee River	19
Home of Gov. William Hall	261
Residence of Judge John W. Judd	285
Home of Hallery Malone	277
Home of the Lauderdales	271
Home of Governor Thousdale	44
Monument to Mexican Soldiers	50
Rock Castle, Home of Gen. Daniel Smith	298
Spencer's Choice	301
Spencer's Tree	13

CONTENTS

Anderson, Gen. Samuel R.................................. 220
Barrow, Hon. Washington................................. 120
Barry, Dr. Redmond D..................................... 220
Barry, Judge Thomas..................................... 221
Bate, Senator W. B...................................... 222
Bell, Judge B. D.. 224
Bell, Gen. Tyree H...................................... 225
Bertinatti, Countess Eugenie............................ 226
Blackmore, George Dawson................................ 228
Blackmore, Hon. James W., address of.................... 96
Bledsoe, Rev. Albert Taylor............................. 58
Bledsoe, Capt. Abraham.................................. 103
Bledsoe, Col. Anthony................................... 55
Bledsoe, Col. Anthony, genealogy of..................... 102
Bledsoe, Col. Anthony, will of.......................... 67
Bledsoe, George... 102
Bledsoe, Capt. Hiram.................................... 58
Bledsoe, Henry Ramsey................................... 106
Bledsoe, Col. Isaac..................................... 165
Bledsoe, Col. Isaac, genealogy of....................... 169
Bledsoe, Senator Jesse.................................. 55
Bledsoe, Katherine Montgomery........................... 167
Bledsoe, Mary Ramsey.................................... 70
Bledsoe Monument.. 71
Bledsoe Monument, contributors to....................... 76
Bledsoe, Col. Oscar F................................... 127
Bledsoe, Col. Oscar F., address of...................... 84
Belmont, O. H. P.. 138
Bowen Family.. 231
Bowie, Col. James....................................... 230
Breckenridge, Hon. W. C. P.............................. 178
Cage Family, genealogy of............................... 191
Cage, Jesse... 200

Cage, Major William	191
Campbell Family	235
Campbell, Governor William B	236
Carmack, Senator Edward Ward	239
Carr, John	244
Cisco, Jay Guy	147
Civil Government	26
Clark, Isaac	245
Dawn of Civilization	12
Desha, Eleanor	172
Desha, Issa	178
Desha, Governor Joseph	170
Desha, Lucius Junius Brutus	173
Desha, Margaret Bledsoe	170
Desha, General Robert	111
Donaldson, General A. J.	245
Douglass, Colonel Edward	202
Douglass, genealogy of	202
Ellis, Capt. H. C.	247
Explorations of Sumner County	4
First Land Owners	33
First Settlement in Sumner County	15
Forts or Stations	18
Fulton, Governor William S.	248
Gaines, Colonel George S.	248
Garth, Hon. W. W.	125
Guild, Judge Joe C.	249
Gwin, Colonel Samuel	251
Gwin, Senator William M.	252
Hall, Governor William	255
Hallum, John	262
Hammond, Judge Eli S.	103
Hatton, Colonel Robert	263
Head Family	264
Historic Sumner County	3
Judd, Judge John W.	266
Killed by Indians	21
Lauderdale Family	269

Contents.

Lindsey, Isaac	276
Long Hunters	8
Malone, Hallery	277
Mansker, Colonel Kasper	279
Martin, Dr. R. C. K.	122
McKendree, Bishop William	280
Morgan, Capt. John	281
Morris, Bishop J. B.	282
Odom, Elliott and Boddie families	283
Parker, Nathaniel	286
Peyton, Hon. Ballie	290
Peyton family	288
Peyton, Hon. J. H.	290
Pickett, Colonel Joseph Desha	176
Pickett, Hon. John T.	177
Pioneer Preacher	311
Read, General Isaac D. B.	184
Rogan, Charles B.	188
Rogan, Hugh	291
Rogan, Captain W. R.	187
Rogers, Judge A. A. C.	292
Rutherford, General Griffith	293
Sanders, Hubbard	295
Sharkey, Judge William L.	295
Shelby, David	104
Shelby, Judge D. D.	136
Shelby, Dr. John	108
Shelby, General Jos. O.	123
Shelby, Sarah Bledsoe	104
Scurry, Richard	186
Scurry, William Read	186
Smith, General Daniel	297
Spencer, Thomas Sharp	300
Sumner County in the War with Mexico	46
Sumner County in War	42
Sumner County, topography of	34
Territorial Laws Relating to Sumner County	39
Trousdale, Governor William	302

Vanderbilt, Mrs. W. H.............................. 138
Walton, William..................................... 303
Weatherred, Frank.................................. 304
Williams, D. S...................................... 155
Wilson Family...................................... 305
Winchester, Major George........................... 306
Winchester, General James.......................... 307
Wynne, Colonel Alfred R............................ 310

PREFACE

DURING the months of September and October, 1907, I published in the Sunday edition of the *Nashville American*, a series of papers called "Historic Sumner County." They were so well received that I determined to rewrite, revise and add new matter and publish the whole in book form. This book is the result. It is not intended to be a history of Sumner county—a work to deserve that name would fill many more pages than are herein contained—but to present some of the most interesting details about the first settlement and the first settlers of the county, not accessible in any other form. My aim has been to give facts and to exclude errors. I have personally interviewed many of the descendants of the pioneers, have examined written and printed records, and have written hundreds of letters, many of which have remained unanswered. It was the original purpose to include genealogies of all the pioneer families, but I have been unable to secure the necessary information, the living representatives of the families either did not possess the facts, or were indifferent to their preservation in this form.

History begins with tradition, narratives handed down from generation to generation. But tradition is not always fact, and much of it is absurd, while it may serve to amuse and entertain, it should not be taken seriously. It is the duty of the historian to sift tradition and retain only authentic facts.

I desire to here express my sincere thanks to every individual who in any way gave me assistance in the way of information for this work, and to hope that all may be satisfied with the manner in which I have presented the facts given me.

J. G. CISCO.

HISTORIC SUMNER COUNTY, TENNESSEE.

PLACE one foot of a compass on a line between Gallatin and Bledsoe's Lick, and about six miles east of the first named place, then draw a circle the diameter of which shall be twenty miles, and you will have within that radius a territory which it would be difficult to find a more beautiful, more fertile, or one richer in historical associations. And, too, it would be hard to find a territory of the same extent in which more men known to fame have had their homes. Within that area was erected the first cabin built by members of the Anglo-Saxon race in Middle Tennessee, and was cleared the first field and planted the first corn west of the Allegheny mountains. Within that circle was the home of Griffith Rutherford, a famous General in the Revolutionary war, a member of the Provisional Congress, and President of the Legislative Council for the Government of the Territory South of the Ohio River, and for whom Rutherford county, North Carolina, and Rutherford county, Tennessee, were named; Gen. Daniel Smith, who made the first map of Tennessee, Secretary of the Territory, United States Senator from 1805 to 1809, and for whom Smith county was named; William Trousdale, General, Governor and diplomat, and for whom Trousdale county was named; William Hall, General, Governor and member of Congress; James Winchester, an officer in the Revolutionary war, a Brigadier-General in the War of 1812, and for whom the county seat of Franklin county was named; Colonel Anthony Bledsoe, member of the Legislatures of Virginia and of North Carolina, a Captain in the Colonial army, a Major in the Revolutionary army, a Colonel of militia in what is now Tennessee, and for whom Bledsoe county was named; Colonel Isaac Bledsoe, explorer, pioneer, Indian fighter, and a Major of militia; David Wilson, Major in the war for independence, Speaker of the first Territorial Assembly of Tennessee, and for whom Wilson county was named; Col. Jas. Lauderdale, who fell at the first battle of New Orleans in December, 1814, and for whom counties in Tennessee, Alabama and Mississippi were named; William B. Bate, soldier, Governor and United States Senator; Senator William M. Gwin, of California; Rt. Rev. John B. Morris, Bishop of the Roman Catholic church; William McKendree, Bishop of the Methodist Episcopal church; Robert Hatton, soldier and statesman; Joseph Desha, Governor of Kentucky; Balie Peyton, orator and statesman; Andrew Jackson Donelson, diplomat and candidate for Vice-President on tht ticket with Fillmore in 1856; William Fulton, Governor of the Territory of Arkansas, and United States Senator from that State; Edward Ward Carmack, the greatest living Tennessean, and many others whose names blaze on the pages of history, have had their homes in Sumner county.

EXPLORATIONS

The first authentic account we have of men of Anglo-Saxon blood visiting Sumner County was in 1765, when Henry Scaggs explored the Cumberland country and fixed his camp at what is now known as Mansker's Lick. The names of his companions are not known.

The next explorer was Col. James Smith, a native of Pennsylvania, who, when a young man, in May, 1755, was taken prisoner by the Delaware Indians and held by them until 1759. His journal was first published in pamphlet form in 1799, and was reprinted in "Drake's Tragedies of the Wilderness" in 1845.

In 1766 Colonel Smith was in Virginia, and, hearing of the negotiations between Sir William Johnson and the Indians for the purchase of the land between the Ohio and the Tennessee rivers, and that there was a large body of rich land in that region, concluded to explore it. Following is an extract from his journal:

"I set out about the last of June, 1766, and went in the first place to the Holston river, and from thence I traveled westwardly in company with Joshua Horton, Uriah Stone, William Baker and James Smith, who came from near Carlisle. There were only about four white men of us, and a mulatto slave about eighteen years of age, that Mr. Horton had with him. We explored the country south of Kentucky, and there were no more signs of white men there then than there is now west of the headwaters of the Missouri river. We also explored the Cumberland and Tennessee rivers from Stone's river down to the Ohio. (Stone's river is a south branch of Cumberland, and empties into it above Nashville. We gave it this name in our journal in May, 1767, after one of my fellow-travelers, Mr. Uriah Stone, and I am told that it retains the same name unto this day.)

"When we had come to the mouth of the Tennessee river, my fellow-travelers concluded that they would proceed on to Illinois, and see some more of the lands to the west; this I would not agree to, as I had already been longer from home than what I had expected; I thought my wife would be distressed and think I was killed by the Indians; therefore I concluded that I would return home. I sent my horse with my fellow-travelers to the Illinois, as it was difficult to take a horse through the mountains. My comrades gave me the greatest part of the ammunition they then had, which amounted to only two and a half pounds of powder and lead equivalent. Mr. Horton also lent me his mulatto boy, and I then set off through the wilderness for Carolina.

"About eight days after I had left my company at the mouth of Tennessee on my journey eastward, I got a cane stab in my foot, which occasioned my leg to swell, and I suffered much pain. I was now in a doleful situation; far from any of the human species, excepting black Jamie, or the savages, and I knew not when I might meet with them. My case appeared desperate, and I thought something must be done. All the surgical instruments I had was a knife, a moccasin awl and a pair of bullet moulds. With these I determined to draw the snag from my foot, if possible. I stuck the awl in the skin and with the knife cut the flesh away from around the cane, and then I commanded the mulatto fellow to catch it with the bullet moulds and pull it out, which he did. When I saw it, it seemed a shocking thing to be in any person's foot; it will therefore be supposed that I was very glad to have it out. The black fellow attended upon me, and obeyed my directions faithfully. I ordered him to search for Indian medicine, and told him to get me a quantity of bark from the roots of a lynn tree, which I made him beat on a stone with a tomahawk, and boil it in a kettle, and with the ooze I bathed my foot and leg; what remained when I had finished bathing I boiled to a jelly and made poultices thereof. As I had no rags, I made use of the green moss that grows upon logs, and wrapped it around with elm bark; by this means the swelling and inflammation in a great measure abated. As stormy weather appeared, I ordered Jamie to make us a shelter, which he did by erecting forks and poles and covering them over with cane tops like a fodder house. It was about 100 yards from a large buffalo road. As we were almost out of provisions, I commanded Jamie to take my gun and I went along as well as I could, concealed myself near the road and killed a buffalo.

"While I lay at this place all the books I had to read was a psalm book and Watts upon "Prayer." Whilst in this situation I composed the following verses, which I then frequently sung:

"Six weeks I've in this desert been,
  With one mulatto lad;
Excepting this poor stupid slave,
  No company I had.

"In solitude I here remain,
  A cripple very sore,
No friend or neighbor to be found,
  My case for to deplore.

"I'm far from home, far from the wife
  Which in my bosom lay,
Far from the children dear, which used
  Around me for to play.

"This doleful circumstance cannot
  My happiness prevent,
While peace of conscience I enjoy,
  Great comfort and content."

This was doubtless the first "poem" ever written in what is now Tennessee.

After eleven months spent in the wilderness, Colonel Smith arrived in Carolina in October.

"When I came to the settlement my clothes were almost worn out and the boy had nothing on that ever was spun. He had buckskin leggins, moccasins, a breech clout, a bear skin dressed with the hair on, which he belted about him, and a raccoon-skin cap. I had not traveled far after I came in before I was strictly examined by the inhabitants. I told them the truth and where I came from, etc., but my story appeared so strange to them that they did not believe me. They said that they had never heard of any one coming through the mountains from Tennessee, and if any one would undertake such a journey surely no man would lend him his slave. They said that they thought that all I had told them were lies, and on suspicion they took me into custody and set a guard over me.

"While I was confined here I met a reputable acquaintance who voluntarily became my voucher, and also told me of a number of my acquaintances that now lived near this place who had moved from Pennsylvania; on this being made public I was liberated. I went to a magistrate and obtained a pass, and one of my old acquaintances made me a present of a shirt. I then cast away my old rags and all the clothes I now had was an old beaver hat, buckskin leggins, moccasins and a new shirt; also an old blanket. Being thus equipped I marched on with my white shirt loose and Jamie with his bear-skin about him. In this way I came on to Fort Chissel, where I left Jamie at Mr. Horton's negro quarter, according to promise. I went from thence to George Adams", on Reedy Creek, where I had lodged, and where I had left my clothes as I was going out from home. When I had dressed myself in good clothes and mounted on horseback, no man ever asked me for a pass; therefore I concluded that a horse-thief, or even a robber, might pass without interruption, provided he was only well dressed, whereas the shabby villain would be immediately detected."

In 1778 Mr. Smith received a Colonel's commission in the Continental army, and made a gallant soldier. After peace had been declared he settled in Bourbon county, Kentucky, and was its Representative in the General Assembly from 1788 till 1799. He died in Washington county, Kentucky, about 1812.

THE "LONG HUNTERS"

There is a story found, with variations, in all the histories of early Tennessee and early Kentucky, about the "Long Hunters," "who remained in the wilderness between two and three years." But no two writers agree as to the identity of the members of the party. In fact, there is room for doubt about the story. That there was a party of hunters, some of whom remained in the wilderness for one year, seems to be well established, but who they were is very uncertain. The following account of the "Long Hunters" is condensed

The "Long Hunters"

from Haywood's Civil and Political History of Tennessee, Ramsey's Annals of Tennessee, Marshall's and Collins' Histories of Kentucky:

A company of over twenty men from North Carolina, from Rockbridge county and from the Valley of New River, Va., including John Raines, Kasper Mansker, Abraham Bledsoe, John Baker, Joseph Drake, Obediah Terrell, Uriah Stone, Henry Smith, Edward Cowan, Thomas Gordon, Humphrey Hogan, Cassius Brooks, Robert Crockett, James Knox, Richard Scaggs and others, each with one or more horses, left Reedy Creek, their place of rendezvous, on June 2, 1769. They pursued their way through what is now known as Powell's Valley to Cumberland Gap; thence to Flat Lick; thence down the Cumberland River, which they crossed at a "very remarkable fish dam which had been made in very ancient times;" thence past a place called "The Bush," near the fish dam. Following it for some distance, then crossing the south fork of Cumberland river, they came to a place since called Price's Meadow, near an excellent spring, in what is now Wayne county, Kentucky, where they made a camp and a depot for their skins and game, which they were to deposit there every five weeks. They continued to hunt to the west and southwest, through a country covered with high grass, but finding no trace of human settlements; though they found many places where stones covered large quantities of human bones.

After being out for some time, how long I do not know, James Knox, Richard Scaggs and four others, whose names are not given, left the main party upon Laurel river because game had become scarce, and starting westwardly, crossed Rockcastle river, and going up Scagg's creek, met a party of Cherokee Indians under the old chief, Captain Dick, who directed them to go to Dick's creek, where they would find plenty of meat, to "kill it and go home," which they did.

In June, 1770, some of the hunters returned home,

having been out one year, while ten of them, including Mansker, Hogan, Stone, Gordon, Baker, Brooks (the names of the other four are not given in any account that has come under the notice of this writer) built two boats and two trapping canoes, laded them with furs and bear meat and proceeded down the Cumberland, down the Ohio and the Mississippi rivers to Natchez, where they sold their cargo, and where some of the party settled, the others returning home through Georgia. Of those who returned home only the names of Mansker and Baker are given.

In the fall of 1771 Kasper Mansker, James Knox, Henry Knox, Richard Scaggs, Henry Scaggs, Isaac Bledsoe, Abraham Bledsoe, James Graham, Joseph Drake, John Montgomery, old Mr. Russell, his son, young Russell; Hughes, William Allen, William Linch, David Linch, Christopher Stoph and others, twenty-two in all, with several horses, came out again. It will be seen that five of this party, Mansker, Abraham Bledsoe, Joseph Drake, James Knox and Richard Scaggs, were members of the first party which had gone out in June, 1770.

This party was so successful in getting skins that they were not able to carry them all back with them, and as their hunt was prolonged they built what they called a "skin house," at a common center, in what is now Greene county, Kentucky. Their hunt extended into the barrens of Greene river. One of the hunters, named Bledsoe, wrote on a fallen poplar tree, which had lost its bark: "2,300 Deer Skins lost; Ruination by God."

Some of the members of this company returned to the settlements in February, 1772, because their ammunition was getting short. "Indeed, all of the company except five, namely, Isaac Bledsoe, William Linch, William Allen, Christopher Stoph and David Linch, returned to procure ammunition and for other purposes." These were left in charge of the camp. One of the Linch men was taken sick "with shingles."

and Isaac Bledsoe went with him to the settlement. The other three men were left in charge of the camp. They were discovered by the Indians, who attacked them and captured Stoph and Allen. Haywood says "Hughes escaped and met the rest of the company returning to camp." As the name of Hughes does not appear in the list of those who were left at the camp, this must be an error, it should have been Linch. It was two or three months before the men who had gone to the settlement returned, and the attack by the Indians must have been made soon after they had departed. The camp was not plundered, there was nothing missing but some meat, which it was supposed the dogs left at the camp had eaten. The dogs remained at the camp, where they were found by the hunters on their return, "but were quite wild, as they had not seen a human being for two or three months."

Soon after returning to camp the party traveled on through the forest to the southwest and fixed their camp at a place to which they gave the name Station Camp creek, which it has retained to this day. There they remained from May, 1772, to August of the same year, hunting and exploring the country. It was from members of this party that several geographical localities in Sumner county took their names. Drake's pond, Drake's creek and Drake's Lick took their names from Joseph Drake. . Bledsoe's Lick, Bledsoe's creek were so named for their discoverer, Isaac Bledsoe. Kasper Mansker gave his name to Mansker's Lick and Mansker's creek.

In July or August, 1772, about twenty-five Cherokee Indians came to the camp in the absence of the hunters and plundered it. The hunters continued there for some time afterwards until their ammunition was about exhausted, when they broke camp and started for the settlements. When they had gone as far as Big Barren river, in Kentucky, they were met by another party of hunters, upon which Mansker and four or five others returned and hunted to the end of the season, then went to their homes in the New River country.

Some writers call any company of hunters who were out for any considerable length of time, "long hunters." L. P. Summers, in his very interesting book, "Southwest Virginia and Washington County," says "the most noted 'long hunters' were Elisha Walden, William Carr, William Crabtree, James Aldridge, William Pitman and Henry Scaggs."

In November, 1775, Mansker and some other hunters, the only names of whom that have come down to us are the Bryants, again visited the Cumberland and encamped at Mansker's Lick. Most of them soon became dissatisfied and returned to their homes, but the brave "old Dutchman," Mansker, and three others, remained for some time hunting and exploring.

DAWN OF CIVILIZATION

Thomas Sharp Spencer and others, whose names are not given, "allured by the flattering accounts they had received of the fertility of the soil and of the abundance of game which the country afforded, determined to visit it. They came in the year 1777 to Cumberland river and built a number of cabins about one-half a mile west from Bledsoe's Lick. There they made a small clearing, and in the spring of 1778 planted some corn. That clearing was the first to be made in the Cumberland country, and that corn was the first to be planted by men of the Anglo-Saxon race in Middle Tennessee, or west of the Allegheny mountains. Most of the party returned to the settlements after planting the corn. Spencer and another man remained in the country till 1779.

Spencer was so pleased with the prospects for further settlement which the situation afforded that he could not be induced to abandon the place and return home, as his companion in vain persuaded him to do. The latter, however, determined to leave the wilderness, but, so the story goes, having lost his knife, was unwilling to undertake the long journey without one with which to skin his venison and cut his meat. With backwoods generosity Spencer accompanied him as far on his way as the barrens of Kentucky, put him on

SPENCER'S TREE

the right path, broke his own knife and gave him half of it, and then returned alone to Bledsoe's Lick, where he made his home for the next six months in a large hollow sycamore tree which stood about fifty yards south of the Lick. The tree was said to have been nine feet in diameter, and being but a shell, made a commodious and comfortable home for the brave hunter.

Tradition says that Spencer and his companion quarrelled, and as a result of that disagreement, "Holliday" determined to leave. But this writer is unable to reconcile Spencer's generosity with this story. He was a peaceable man, kind and generous, as all brave men are, declining personal wrangles and disputes, slow to resent a wrong and quick to forgive. It is more likely that "Holliday" became homesick, and that that alone prompted him to return to civilization and to his family. Spencer remained because he wanted to live with nature, where he could hear the throb of nature's heart.

And right here another doubt arises. The first published account of Spencer's spending the winter in a hollow tree was given by Haywood in his "Natural and Aboriginal History of Tennessee," published in 1823. In that work the name of Spencer's companion is given as "Mr. Drake." But in his "Civil and Political History of Tennessee," published in the same year, he gives the name as Holliday, and this is followed by all subsequent writers. Which is correct, or whether such an incident actually occurred, will never be known.

The story of Spencer and his hollow tree was told and retold around the firesides of the pioneers for more than forty years before it was put in print for the first time in 1823. Tradition does not always correctly transmit either dates, names or incidents. Stories repeated around the camp fires and the fireside are apt to gain or lose by repetition, the narrator often drawing upon his imagination, adding to the facts or omitting them. The name of Joseph Drake appears frequently in the early history of Sumner county, but the name of John Holliday appears in no other connection.

FIRST SETTLEMENT

The curtain of history rises on Sumner county in the year 1779, when a settlement of a dozen families was formed near Bledsoe's Lick. "Isolated in the heart of the wilderness, their only protection from marauding Indians was their undaunted courage and the stockade enclosures around their cabins."

The winter of 1779-80 brought many new settlers. The tide had set in, and it continued to flow, despite the many dangers and hardships which the people had to encounter. The first settlers came chiefly from the Watauga, North Carolina and from Virginia, though a few came from Pennsylvania and South Carolina. Many of these hardy men were fresh from the battlefields of the revolution, and brought with them the rifles and the muskets with which they had helped to win independence for their country. Better than rifles and muskets, they brought with them strong and vigorous minds, strong and healthy bodies, a love of freedom, undaunted courage and a determination to conquer dangers and difficulties and build new homes for their descendants or die in the wilderness. And many did die in the struggle. But their efforts were successful, and we owe it to their memories to mark their last resting places, to keep their graves forever green and to keep in mind their heroic deeds and unselfish sacrifices.

The men who settled Sumner county were for the most part of obscure birth and accustomed to poverty. A few of them were men of wealth, and a small per cent. of them were of aristocratic descent. Some brought with them to their new homes money and slaves. They came to found in the wilderness new homes and greater estates and to find better opportunities for their children. Some of the higher social class who had lost their fortunes in the older settlements came to begin life anew. Some were sons of the older families, young men, who came, purchased large estates, married and founded families. But the greater number were poor men, who saw no opportunities in the older settlements. It was these men who "animated by the twin spirit of chivalry and adventure united," contended with the Indians and laid the foundation of Tennessee. It was their sons that followed Jackson in the Indian wars and fought under his banner at New Orleans, and who fought the battles in the war with Mexico, and who followed Lee, Jackson, Bate and Forrest in the Civil War.

Northern historians grow eloquent when they write about the bloodshed at Lexington and Bunker Hill, but they have little to say about the bloodshed at Alamance, Camden, Cowpens, Guilford Court-House, Eutaw Springs, Charleston and King's Mountain, in which many of the pioneers of Tennessee gained imperishable renown.

The first organized resistance to British tyranny in America was by the people of North Carolina in 1770. The first battle of the Revolution which gave independence to the colonies, and the first blood shed in that cause was on the 16th of May, 1771, when the forces of Governor Tryon, numbering 1,100 men, met about 200 of the "Regulators" at Alamance, in Orange county, North Carolina. In the battle that ensued there was stubborn fighting until the ammunition of the Regulators was exhausted and they were driven from the field. Twenty of these brave men were killed and several prisoners were taken, one of which was hung without trial, and twelve others were convicted of high treason and executed. The loss of the British in killed, wounded and missing were sixty-one men.

North Carolina, the mother of Tennessee, was the first of the colonies to throw the gauntlet of defiance in the face of the British. The battle of Lexington was fought on April 19, 1775, and one month and a day later, on May 20, the Mecklenburg Declaration of Independence was signed at Charlotte, twenty-seven brave men affixing their names thereto. A number of the descendants of these signers found their way to Tennessee, among them the Brevards and the Alexanders, ancestors of the families of those names now residents of Sumner and other counties in Tennessee.

Edmund Burke said: "Wherever slavery exists, in any part of the world, those who are free are by far the most proud and jealous of their freedom—and these people of the Southern colonies are much more strongly and with a higher and more stubborn spirit attached to liberty than those to the northward."

Bancroft said: "We shall find that the first voice publicly raised in America to dissolve all connection with Great Britain came not from the Puritans of New England, or the Dutch of New York, nor the planters of Virginia, but from the Scotch-Irish Presbyterians" of North Carolina, the mother of Tennessee. But the Scotch-Irish were not all Presbyterians, many of them were Methodists, and it appears that large numbers of the early pioneers of Sumner county were of the latter faith.

Gilmore says in his "Life of John Sevier:" "With but one exception, the trans-Allegheny leaders were all native Virginians—Sevier, Donelson, and the two Bledsoes being from the ranks of the gentry, Robertson and Cocke from that of the yeoman class, which has given some of its most honored names to English history. The one exception was Isaac Shelby, who was of Welsh descent, but born and educated in Maryland.

"The over-mountain settlers were not fugitives from justice, nor needy adventurers seeking in the untrodden West a scanty subsistence, which had been denied them in the Eastern settlements. And they were not merely Virginians—they were the culled wheat of the Old Dominion, with all those grand qualities which made the name of "Virginia" a badge of honor throughout the colonies. Many of them were cultivated men of large property, and, though the larger number were poor in this world's goods, they all possessed those more stable riches which consist of stout arms and brave hearts, unblemished integrity and sterling worth. They were so generally educated that in 1776 only two in about two hundred were found unable to write their names in good, legible English."

FORTS, OR STATIONS

There are no positive records as to where the first stockade was built in Sumner county, but it is probable that the one built by Col. Isaac Bledsoe was the pioneer. It was built on the borders of the cleared field before mentioned, near a large spring and about one-quarter mile west from the Lick. The only remaining vestige of that famous stockade and the cabins are a few scattered stones and fragments of broken crockery. Some of the logs of which the cabins were constructed were used in building a stable at the home of the present owner of the place, Mr. Belote.

Col. Anthony Bledsoe built his fort two and one-half miles further north and gave to it the name "Greenfield." It was situated on a beautiful eminence, and in the heart of one of the richest bodies of land to be found anywhere. There were in the original tract 6,280 acres. Besides this, he owned several thousands of acres of lands elsewhere, some on the Holston, and some in Kentucky.

Asher, with some others, built a fort two and one-half miles southeast of where Gallatin was afterwards located. That fort was called Asher's Station.

John Morgan built his fort on the west side of Bledsoe's Creek near the mouth of Dry Fork, about two and one-half miles from Greenfield.

Major James White built a fort about three and one-half miles northeast of Gallatin on the waters of Desha creek.

EMIGRANTS DESCENDING THE TENNESSEE RIVER. (*From an old print*)

About the same time Colonel Sanders built one on the west side of Desha creek, and about two and one-half miles from White's Station.

Jacob Zigler's station, or fort, was one and one-half miles from Cairo, on the western branch of Bledsoe's creek. That fort was taken by the Indians in 1791. There were four white persons killed, four wounded and thirteen taken prisoners and carried to the Indian country.

Capt. Joseph Wilson, ancestor of Judge B. F. Wilson, one of the members of the present Court of Chancery Appeals, built a fort which he called Walnut Field Station, about three miles east from Gallatin.

Kasper Mansker and others built a fort on Mansker's creek, about three hundred yards below the site of Walton's Camp ground. The next year, 1782, Mansker built another fort about one mile east from the one he had previously built.

Hamilton's Station was established at the head of Drake's creek, about six miles north of Shackle Island.

Other settlements were made about the same time, but less is known of them, and there is no positive knowledge of their exact locations.

Elmore Douglass, James McCain, James Franklin, and Charles Carter made a settlement on Big Station Camp creek, where the upper Nashville road crosses the creek. James Harrison and William Gibson settled near the Hall place. William Montgomery settled on Drake's creek.

Among the early settlers, of whom the writer has not been able to collect detailed information are the following families: Alexander, Allen, Bryson, Belote, Bentley, Brown, Baker, Baber, Bowyer, Bracken, Chenault, Cantrell, Chapman, Cryer, Crenshaw, Carter, Cummings, Dickinson, Dunn, Darnell, Duffey, Franklin, Gillespie, Clendening, Hassell, Hargrove, Hays, Hanna, House, Harris, Joyner, King, Lewis, Mitchner, Murray, Montgomery, McCain, Provine, Perdue, Pond, Pryor, Roscoe, Read, Rawling, Robb,

Turner, Tompkins, Mastin, Watkins, Wherry, Witherspoon, Woodson, Walton, Williams, Grant, and others.

From the beginning, the settlers of Sumner county were in constant peril. The men seldom ventured from their homes without arms. They lived in groups of several families, bound together by ties of common interest, exposed to common dangers, and ever ready to hazard their lives for the common good. Most of them had been born and reared on the frontiers of Virginia and North Carolina during the stirring times immediately preceding the Revolution. They grew to manhood and womanhood in the wilderness, where danger lurked on every hand, where Tory, British and Indian foes were liable to be met at every turn. Under such circumstances, where midnight attacks were of common occurrence, where fathers, brothers, husbands and sons, when they went to the clearings in the morning were in danger of being shot from ambush and their scalps torn from their heads before they returned to their cabins. Such men courted danger for danger's sake. They were cool and dispassionate, and fear never entered their souls.

The Cherokees and the Creeks were constantly on the war path. There was no safety for the settlers until General Robertson ordered the destruction of the Chickamauga towns, and that order was successfully executed on September 13, 1794. After that time there was peace and safety. But many homes were in mourning for loved ones who had fallen victims to savage cruelty.

THE KILLED

Following is a list of Sumner countains, who were killed by the Indians, so far as has been obtained. There may have been others, but their names have not been preserved:

George Aspey, killed on Drake's creek.

John Bartlett, Jr., August 31, 1792, near Greenfield.

Richard Bartley, near Walnut Fields Fort.

John Beard, near the head of Big Station Camp creek.

John Benton, near Cragfont, April 11, 1793.

Colonel Anthony Bledsoe, at Bledsoe's Lick, July 20, 1788.

Anthony Bledsoe, Jr., near Rock Castle, April 21, 1794.

Anthony, son of Colonel Isaac Bledsoe, near Rock Castle, April 21, 1794.

Colonel Isaac Bledsoe, near Bledsoe's Fort, April 9, 1793.

Thomas, son of Colonel Anthony Bledsoe, near Greenfield, October 2, 1794.

William Brattan, near White's Station.

Robert Brigham, near White's Station.

—— Campbell, a young Irishman, at Bledsoe's Lick, July 20, 1788.

Benjamin Desha, in the summer of 1790, between White's and Sanders' Stations.

Robert Desha, at the same time and place.

James Dickinson, at the same time and place.

John Dixon, near General Winchester's, July 3, 1792.

John Edwards, four miles northeast from Gallatin, where Salem church was afterwards built.

Samuel Farr, or Pharr, near Walnut Fields Fort, April 14, 1793.

Mr. Gibson, near the Hall place, in the winter of 1788.

John Hacker, on Drake's Creek, May 20, 1793.

James Hall, brother of William, June 3, 1787.

Richard Hall, another brother of William Hall, June 3, 1787.

Major William Hall, father of the two last named, and of William Hall, afterwards Governor. They were killed at the same time about half a mile southwest from the Hall home, while moving to Bledsoe's Fort for better protection from the Indians.

The Killed

Michael Hampton, near the head of Red river.
William Haynes, at the same place.
Robert Hardin, near Fort Blount.
Mr. Hickerson, a young man, near Bledsoe's Lick.
Captain John Hickerson, on Smith's Fork, August, 1788.
Henry Howdyshell, near Walnut Fields Fort, April 14, 1793.
Mr. Jarvis, a young man, near Greenfield, April 27, 1793.
A negro slave, belonging to Mrs. Bledsoe, at the same time.
Benjamin Keykendall, near Sanders' Fort, May 16, 1792.
Nathan Latimore, near Rock Island.
John Lawrence, at the head of Red river.
William McMurray, near Winchester's Mill.
John Montgomery, on Drake's Creek, two and one-half miles below Shackle Island, in the spring of 1788.
Robert Montgomery, at the same place.
Thomas Montgomery, at the same place.
Mr. Morgan, an aged man, the father of Captain John Morgan, at Morgan's Fort, in the winter of 1788.
Armistead Morgan, at Crab Orchard.
Captain Charles Morgan, near the Hall place, in the winter of 1788.
Captain Alexander Neely, near Bledsoe's Lick, in the summer of 1790.
Two sons of Captain Neely, at the same time and place.
Mr. Peyton, at Bledsoe's Lick, said to have been the last man to be killed by the Indians in Sumner county.
John Provine, two miles northeast from Gallatin, in May, 1792.
Mr. Price and his wife, near Gallatin.
Prince, a negro man.
Henry Ramsey, "the bravest of the brave," a brother of Mrs. Anthony Bledsoe, near Bledsoe's Lick, in the summer of 1793.

William Ramsey, brother of the above, at the same time and place.

Two sons of Colonel Sanders, near Sanders' Fort, February 22, 1793.

Thomas Sharp Spencer, at Spencer's Hill, Van Buren county.

Michael Sheaver, at Zigler's Station, in June, 1791. His body was burned with the fort after the Indians had captured it.

Mr. Stawder, near Station Camp creek, May 26, 1794.

John Steel, while going from Morgan's Fort to Greenfield.

Elizabeth Steel, daughter of John Steel, at the same time and place.

Hugh Tenin, on Harpeth, December 20, 1794.

Nathan Thomas, near Hartsville.

Nash Trammel, on Goose creek.

Mr. Waters and another man, whose name has not been preserved, on Bledsoe's creek.

Evan Watkins, near Winchester's Mill, October 24, 1794.

Benjamin Williams, his wife and children, and a negro lad, two and one-half miles north from Gallatin.

Archie Wilson, at Zigler's Fort.

George Wilson, in Davidson county.

Major George Winchester, near the east end of Water street, in Gallatin, August 9, 1794. He was on his way to attend court.

Two negroes belonging to James Clendenning.

Jacob Zigler, at his fort when it was captured June 27, 1791.

On June 26, 1791, Zigler's Station was attacked by a large body of Indians, first in the afternoon, when Michael Shafer was killed, and then at night. The station was defended by thirteen men. Jacob Zigler, Archie Wilson and two others were killed; Joseph Wilson and three others were wounded and escaped; three escaped unhurt; eighteen persons were made prisoners. Mrs. Zigler stuffed a handkerchief into the mouth of one of her children to prevent its cries attracting the enemy, and thus made her escape, while two of her children were captured. Of the prisoners, nine were regained by purchase by their parents and friends. One of the prisoners was Mrs. Joseph Wilson, half-sister to General James White, father of Hugh Lawson White. She was afterwards ransomed by him. Her daughter, who was only nine years of age at the time, was twice redeemed from her captors, but was treacherously kept away from her friends. General White determined to make a third effort to liberate her, and accordingly made a long journey to the camp of the Indians, and for the third time paid a ransom for his niece, and set out on his return home, with the girl seated on the horse behind him. He was soon overtaken by a friendly Indian, who informed him that the Indians had repented of their bargain, and had determined to pursue and kill him and recapture the girl. The Indian offered to guide him by a more secure route, which offer was accepted, and he was soon beyond the reach of his enemies.

After plundering Zigler's Fort the Indians set fire to it, and with it was consumed the bodies of the whites who were killed. Among the captured were four negroes.

The soil of Sumner county is sacred because mingled with it is the dust of heroes and heroines, of martyrs in the cause of civilization; men who fought in the battles of the Revolution; men who wrested this beautiful land from the savage red men and paved the way for empire; men who saw their fathers and mothers, their brothers and sisters, their wives and their children, their friends and companions fall before the rifles of Indian foes, saw the scalps torn from their heads and their mangled bodies left as food for beasts and birds of prey. And the women and children were no less heroic than the men, and, if possible, they suffered more. In those days "heroic action sprang spontaneously from the hearts of the people." Many of the men and women who toiled and struggled and conquered the wilderness now sleep in unmarked graves, which time and the plow have obliterated, and in many instances the sacred spot has been forgotten.

In Doddridge's notes we find this: "Is the memory of our forefathers unworthy of historic or sepulchral commemoration? No people on earth, in similar circumstances, ever acted more nobly or more bravely than they did. No people of any country or age made greater sacrifices for the benefit of their posterity than those which were made by the first settlers of our western regions. What people ever left such noble legacies to posterity as those transmitted by our forefathers to their descendants?"

CIVIL GOVERNMENT

Sumner county was organized under an act passed by the General Assembly of North Carolina on November 17, 1786, and was so named in honor of General Jethro Sumner, of North Carolina, a gallant soldier in the War of Independence. The county as originally formed embraced a much larger area than at present. It was the second county to be formed in Middle Tennessee, the first being Davidson. The first court of Sumner county was held on the second Monday in April, 1787, at the house of John Hamilton at Station Camp Creek, about five miles southwest from where Gallatin now is. The members of that court were General Daniel Smith, Major David Wilson, Major George Winchester, Isaac Lindsey, William Hall, John Hardin, Joseph Kuykendall, Colonel Edward Douglass and Colonel Isaac Bledsoe. David Shelby, son-in-law of Colonel Anthony Bledsoe, was appointed Clerk, and held that position until his death in 1822. John Hardin, Jr., was appointed sheriff, and Isaac

CIVIL GOVERNMENT 27

Lindsey, ranger. "And thus there were associated in that court men of education, sound judgment, good morals, and of great influence in the community. The commendation bestowed upon these gentlemen was that most of them could worthily fill the office of Governor or Chief Justice—"fit for Lord Chief Justice or Governor-General." In those days no man held office as a mere sinecure, nor solely for the sake of the pay. Of how many officers in Tennessee can so much be said today?

On April 20, 1796, the General Assembly of Tennessee passed an act appointing Commissioners and Trustees. The Commissioners so appointed were William Bowen, John Wilson, Isaac Walton, George D. Blackmore and Hugh Crawford. It was made their duty to fix on a location for the seat of government for the county. The Trustees appointed by the act were Henry Bradford, David Shelby and Edward Douglass. It was made their duty to purchase the land selected by the Commissioners, erect a court-house, prison and stocks and establish a town.

Section 3 of the act provided that the town should be called "Ca Ira," which name afterwards became corrupted into "Cairo," and it was so incorporated on November 5, 1815.

On October 2, 1797, the above act was repealed and another one passed appointing "James Clendenning, Kasper Mansker, William Edwards, William Bowen, Captain James Wilson, son of John Wilson; James Frazier, Moro Stephenson, William Gillespie, James White, Wetherel Lattimore and John Morgan, Commissioners, to make choice of a place most convenient in the county of Sumner, to purchase land, erect a court-house, prison and stocks, and establish a town thereon, having respect to the center of said county, which is not to exceed more than twenty-five miles, on a direct line from a ford on Mansker's creek, on the road leading from Mansker's Lick to Bledsoe's Lick."

Daniel Smith, James Winchester and Wilson Cage were named as Trustees. In this act it was provided that the name of the town should be "Ca Ira."

On October 26, 1799, the above act was repealed, Sumner county was reduced to its constitutional limits, and "David Shelby, David Beard, Sr., James Crier, Edward Guinn and Captain James Wilson, son of John Wilson, were appointed Commissioners to purchase sixty acres of land, on some part of which shall be erected a court-house, prison and stocks, and that the town be given the name Rutherford," in honor of General Griffith Rutherford.

On November 6, 1801, an act was passed by the Legislature providing that the "public buildings of Sumner county shall be established and erected at one of three hereinafter named places, situated and lying on the east fork of Station Camp Creek, viz.: On the place known by the name of Dickens, now said to be the property of John C. Hamilton, Esq., or at the place of Captain James Trousdale, whereon he now lives, lying on the road that leads from Major David Wilson's to John Dawson's; or at the place whereon David Shelby now lives."

Samuel Donelson, Shadrack Nye, James Wilson, "Curly, son of Samuel Wilson;" Charles Donaho, Esq., and Major Thomas Murray were by this act appointed Commissioners. It was further provided by the act that "the town so laid off should be known by the name of Gallatin," in honor of Albert Gallatin. Thus Gallatin became the permanent county seat. It was not incorporated until November 7, 1815.

The Tennessee Legislature on October 25, 1797, passed an act establishing a town by the name of "Bledsoeborough on the north bluff of the Cumberland river, known by the name of Sanders' Bluff, between the mouth of Dixon's creek and Dry creek, in Sumner county, on the lands of Will Saunders."

During the year 1787, beginning with the April term, the court met at the house of John Hamilton. In 1788 it met at the house of Elmore Douglass; the January and April terms of 1789 at Simon Kuykendall's, then until July, 1790, at Elmore Douglass'; then in the first court-house, a small log building erected on West Station Camp creek at a place then known as Mrs.

CRAGFONT, FORMER RESIDENCE OF GEN. JAMES WINCHESTER; NOW THE HOME OF CAPT. W. H. C. SATTERWHITE. ERECTED ABOUT 1798.

Clarke's. The courts continued to meet there until January, 1793, when it met at the house of John Dawson. The April term of 1793 met at Pearce Wall's, and after that until January, 1796, at Ezekiel Douglass'. From that date to January, 1800, the sessions were held at the home of William Gillespie. From April, 1800, to July, 1802, they were held at Ca Ira ("Cairo"), the county seat. From October, 1802, to January, 1803, they were held at the house of James Trousdale in Gallatin, and then at the house of James Crier until October, when the first term was held in the first court-house in the permanent capital.

The first court held under the Tennessee State government was in July, 1796 (previous to that date they were held under the jurisdiction of North Carolina), at the home of Ezekiel Douglass. It was composed of the following members, commissioned by Governor John Sevier: William Cage, Stephen Cantrell, James Douglass, Edward Douglass, James Gwyn, Wetheral Lattimore, Thomas Masten, Thomas Donald, James Pearce, David Wilson, James Winchester and Isaac Walton.

The first grand jury was composed of the following named gentlemen: Archibald Martin, foreman; Armond Alton, William Crabtree, Lazarus Cullum, Jeremiah Doney, William Edwards, James Farr, Robert Hamilton, Peter Looney, James Snowden, Edward Williams, Joshua Wilson and Thomas Walton.

The first school in Sumner county was at Bledsoe's Lick. General Hall, in his narrative, mentions it as early as 1787. George Hamilton was the "schoolmaster." One night "the little schoolmaster" was sitting in Anthony Bledsoe's room at his brother's fort singing at the top of his voice. Indians were prowling around, and one of them found a hole in the back of the chimney through which he poked his gun and fired, hitting Hamilton in the mouth. The teacher recovered, but what became of him afterwards history does not record and tradition is silent.

The ground upon which Gallatin was located originally belonged to James Trousdale, father of William Trousdale, afterwards Governor, and grandfather of the late Hon. J. A. Trousdale. The deed called for forty-one (41.80) acres and eighty one-hundredths.

CIVIL GOVERNMENT 31

The fraction, the deed stated, was for a road. One acre was reserved by Mr. Trousdale for himself, which left forty acres for the town site. The acre reserved was on the south side of the public square, and upon this he built the first house to be built in Gallatin. It was afterwards torn down and a part of the material used in a house still standing in the rear of the original site.

Following is a schedule of taxes levied by the first court of Sumner county: One shilling on every poll and four pence on every 100 acres of land to defray the contingent charges of the county, also one shilling on every poll and four pence on every 100 acres of land for the purpose of building the court-house, prison and stocks; and that corn be received in taxes at 2s 6p per bushel, beef at 3p per pound, pork at 4p per pound, 4p per pound for good fat bear meat, if delivered at the place where the troops are stationed, 3p per pound for prime buffalo beef; 1p per pound for good venison, if delivered aforesaid; 9p per pound for bacon; each person to pay in proportion as follows, to wit: One-fourth in corn, one-half in meat, one-eighth in salt and one-eighth in money."

At the October term, 1788, the following rates were fixed: "The court regulates and rates taverns and ordinaries in the following manner, to wit: One-half pint of whiskey, such as will sink tallow, 2s; ditto of taffia, 2s; ditto of West India rum, 2s 6p; ditto Jamaica spirits, 3s; one bowl of toddy made of loaf sugar and whiskey, per quart, 3s 6p; ditto of taffia, 3s 6p; ditto of West Indian rum, 3s 6p; ditto Jamaica spirits, 4s; dinner and grog at dinner, 4s; dinner and toddy, 4s 6p; dinner, 3s; breakfast, 2s; supper, 2s; one horse feed of corn, 3p; lodging, 6p; pasture for horse twenty-four hours, 9p; stableage with fodder, 2s; horse feed of oats, per quart, 3p; one-half pint of brandy, 2s; one quart bowl of punch made with fruit, 19s; one bottle of wine called port, 10s; ditto Madeira, 15s; ditto Burgundy, 15s; ditto champagne, 20s; ditto claret, 8s."

The census of 1830 gave Sumner county a population of 20,606. Gallatin at that time contained a population of 666. It contained a court-house, a jail, a large brick church, Cumberland Presbyterian church, but free for all denominations of Christians, a Masonic hall, a printing office, twelve stores, two taverns, eleven lawyers, four doctors, one cabinet shop, one chair factory, three tailor shops, two shoe-maker's shops, two saddler-shops, one wagon-maker, one tanyard, one tinner, three blacksmith shops, one hatter, one male and two female academies, thirty-five log, thirty-eight frame and twenty-seven brick houses. Of the 666 inhabitants 234 were black. The mail stage between Lexington, Kentucky, and Nashville passed three times a week, and the eastern stage to Carthage arrived and departed semi-weekly.

At that time Cairo contained thirty families, two physicians, an academy and church, one tavern, one cabinet-maker, one machine-maker, one cotton and wool factory, one rope walk, two tailors, two blacksmiths, one gunsmith, and two shoemakers.

Hendersonville at that time contained one store and a stage office.

The first annual conference of the Methodist church held in Middle Tennessee met at Strother's meeting-house, near the head of Big Station Camp creek, in Sumner county, a few miles northwest of Gallatin, Bishop Asbury presiding.

Dr. McFerrin, in his "Methodism in Tennessee," says the Cumberland Presbyterian church had its origin in the great revival held on Desha's creek, near the Cumberland river, in 1800, though the organization was not perfected until 1810.

CIVIL GOVERNMENT 33

THE FIRST LAND OWNERS.

The first settlers in the county located claims, or preempted lands, and as soon as possible thereafter they entered them. In almost every instance the first entries were made by land warrants received for services in the Revolutionary War. In 1786 Isaac Bledsoe, Robert Desha, Jordon Gibson, Henry Loving, William Morrison, John Morgan, John Sawyer, Robert Steele and Jacob Zeigler each entered 640 acres, all on or near Bledsoe's Creek. The next year Colonel Anthony Bledsoe entered 6,280 acres on warrants given him for his services in the Continental line. The same year his brother, Isaac, located 370 acres granted for services as a guard to the Commissioners, who set apart the lands granted to the above named soldiers. In the same year Henry Ramsey located 960 acres for similar service. Later Colonel Isaac Bledsoe located 1,836 acres. About the same time William Hall, Hugh Rogan, David Shelby, George D. Blackmore, James and George Winchester, Robert Peyton, Joseph Wilson, Michael Shafer, James Hayes, Charles Morgan, Gabriel Black, John Carr, and Robert Brigham settled on Bledsoe's creek and tributaries. Charles Campbell, William Crawford, Edward and Elmore Douglass, James Franklin, Richard Hogan, Robert and David Looney, George Mansker, Benjamin Kuykendall, Thomas Spencer, John Peyton, James McCain, Benjamin Porter, John Withers, John Hamilton, John Latham and William Snoddy each entered 640 acres on Station Camp creek and its branches, James Cartwright, James McCann, John and Joseph Byrns, James Trousdale, Benjamin Williams, John Edwards, Samuel Wilson and John Hall were the pioneer settlers of the Gallatin neighborhood. William Montgomery, Thomas Sharp Spencer and Edward Hagan each entered 640 acres on Drake's creek. General Daniel Smith located 3,780 acres and William Frazier 320 acres on the same creek. Benjamin Sheppard entered by land warrants 10,880 acres in the northern part of the county, and Redmond D. Barry in 1800 entered 26,400 acres north of the rim.

After 1800, when the settlers felt no fear of the Indians, "new-comers" came fast, and all the best lands were soon taken up and much of them occupied.

TOPOGRAPHY OF SUMNER COUNTY

The topography of Sumner county is varied, level valleys, gently undulating uplands breaking into hills, some of which are too steep for cultivation. Numerous creeks, each bearing a historic name, murmuring mystic music as their limpid waters now creep, then rush and leap to pour their flood into the beautiful Cumberland. Well-cultivated farms, fields of waving grain, pastures in which well-bred horses and cattle stand knee-deep in bluegrass. Orchards, where all the fruits grown in a temperate climate are produced in abundance. Attractive homes, in which every comfort, convenience and luxury demanded by a refined and cultured people can be found. School-houses and churches surrounded by shady groves in every neighborhood. A climate almost perfect, neither intensely cold in winter nor oppressively warm in summer. What more can be desired to render a people happy and contented? No wonder that Sumner county has produced so many good soldiers and so many great statesmen. And can we wonder that the Indians fought so hard and so long to hold their ancient possessions in such a land? A man, savage or civilized, who would not shed his blood for such a country deserves to be a slave. Patriotism, love of home and of native land is not exclusively a virtue of civilized man. The Bedouin loves the parched desert because it is his home. The Eskimo loves the bleak, ice-bound region of the frozen North for the same reason. And so, too, did the Indian love the hills and valleys of Tennessee because they were his own. For his own he shed his blood and that of the invaders who came to deprive him of the sacred soil.

Driving along the well-kept turnpikes, hedged by stone fences in this "dimple of the universe," one can scarcely realize that only a century and a quarter ago it was an unbroken wilderness, the home of wild beasts and the haunt of wilder men; that countless numbers of buffalo, deer and elk, fed on the succulent grass which grew upon these hills and in these smiling vales; that the bear, the wolf and the catamount roamed undisturbed in the forest. The early explorers of Sumner county beheld an enchanting scene from the tops of these hills. It was a fair land, fresh from the hand of its Maker. The sound of the woodman's ax had never been heard in its forests primeval, and the virgin soil had never been scarred by the white man's plow. Then, as now, sparkling waters bubbled from unknown depths; crystal streams flowed over pebbly beds and dashed against boulders, moss-covered and venerable with age. Doubtless the Creator could have made a fairer land, but He never did. Rich in natural beauty, and no land surpasses it in varied resources. It was a fit place for the home of the highest type of men and women, and such men and women found and occupied it, but at fearful cost in precious blood. Such a land in Japan, where nature is worshipped, would have a shrine at every turn and a temple on every prominence.

To the east can be seen in all their purple beauty the foothills of the far-stretching Cumberland Mountains, and beyond the mist are the "towering crags that meet the bending sky." Lady Mary Wortley Montague said: "The most romantic region of every country is where the mountains unite themselves with the plains and lowlands." Sumner county is one of those regions.

One might travel far without finding a more picturesque stream than Bledsoe's creek, or one with more historic associations. Somewhere among the hills in the northern part of Sumner county it has its source. Probably a big spring bubbles up out of the bowels of the earth and sends its limpid waters dancing and singing on their way toward the sea, the little brook gathering volume, force and strength as it rushes on and on through sun and shadow. Now sleeping in the shade of overhanging trees and vines, now suddenly awaking, it dashes out into the bright sunlight where it mirrors the thickly wooded hills, then gliding on over its mosaic bed it encounters a gray, moss-covered stone, tosses its jewels in the air and hurries on to meet the great river.

If we could understand the never-ceasing voices of the waters of this beautiful stream, what a story they could tell. They could tell us of the days long gone when the only sounds heard along its course were the music of its own purling waters; the soughing of the wind; the rustle of the leaves; the songs of the birds; the bark of the wolf; the growl of the bear; the scream of the catamount; the bleat of the fawn and the bellow of the buffalo. They would tell us of the long years when the red man held undisputed possession; of dusky lovers; of the hopes and the fears and the tragedies of a people who live with nature and with nature's god. They would tell us of the days when the stranger came with guns and powder, and ax and plow. They could tell us of the civilized man's book, his bottle and his craft.

They could tell us of the red man lurking along its shady banks, and how it heard his whispered councils as he planned death and destruction to the encroaching white; how it heard the sharp crack of the rifle and the whiz of the deadly bullet as it sped on its fatal mission. It would tell of the groans of the victim and the shriek of the bereft wife and orphaned children. What tales of horror and blood it could repeat.

When Middle Tennessee was first explored by the whites they found no Indians living here, though occasional hunting parties were encountered. The territory was claimed as a common hunting ground by several tribes. But a long time before, so long that not even a tradition remains, it was the scene of busy life, the home of a people well advanced in the arts of civilization. Who these people were, whence they came and whither they went is a mystery which we have never been able to solve. That they remained long in this region is evidenced by their numerous remains, mounds, earthworks, stone and flint implements and fragments of pottery. It has been estimated that over fifty thousand graves of pre-historic people have been found within a radius of forty miles from Nashville, and that one-half of them have been explored by the antiquarian. We call these people "Mound Builders," and properly so, but that they were a race separate and distinct in blood and origin from the Indians whom the white people found, this writer must dissent. All the Indians found on this continent by the white discovers and explorers were practically of the same type, and had the same origin. In color they were copper-bronze, with coarse, black hair, keen, black eyes, high cheek-bones and arched noses. They had fixed homes, cultivated the soil to a limited extent, but their chief dependence for food was the abundant game in the forest, the fish in the streams and the natural products of the soil.

In all ages and among all people the centres of population have been where there was an abundance of good, pure water. The villages of the American Indians were invariably clustered around large springs where never-failing water could be had, and where fish and game abounded. There they built their huts and erected their altars. Bledsoe's Lick seems to have been one of the centres of population of the pre-historic Indians.

A village called Castalian Springs has grown up around Bledsoe's Lick, which is a spring of white sulphur water, slightly impregnated with salt. It bubbles up in a beautiful valley a few rods south of Bledsoe's creek. The village, surrounded by picturesque hills, is in the midst of a fine farming section, where "the people live at home and board at the same place." About two hundred yards southwest from the Lick,

BLEDSOE'S LICK AS IT NOW APPEARS

embowered in a grove of stately trees, on the slope of the hill, stands the hotel, a large building, erected about three-quarters of a century ago of hewn logs, on a stone foundation. The house is two stories high, with a broad passage between the two main buildings and with a porch extending the full length on the south side.

The Bledsoe Lick property passed from the heirs of Colonel Isaac Bledsoe more than a century ago to General James Winchester, and from him it was inherited by his daughter, the wife of Colonel A. R. Wynne, and from her it passed to her children, the present owners.

TERRITORIAL LAWS

During the administration of William Blount, Governor of the Territory of the United States of America South of the River Ohio, the following ordinances relating to Sumner county, and citizens of the county, were promulgated:

December 15, 1790. Also that tract of country heretofore distinguished and known by the name of Sumner county, in the State of North Carolina, into a county to in future be distinguished and known by the name of Sumner county, in the Territory of the United States of America, South of the River Ohio.

And also laid out the three counties of Davidson, Sumner and Tennessee, being the same that heretofore formed the District of Mero in North Carolina, into a District in the future to be distinguished and known by the name of the District of Mero in the Territory of the United States of America South of the River Ohio.

David Shelby, Clerk for the Court of Pleas and Quarter Sessions for the County of Sumner.

James Wilson, for Stray Master for Sumner County.

And commissioned Bennet Searcy County Attorney and Solicitor for the counties of Sumner and Tennessee.

Appointed Isaac Walton Coroner for the County of Sumner.

Appointed and commissioned for the County of Sumner, Isaac Bledsoe, David Wilson, George Winchester, William Walton, Anthony Sharp, Edward Douglas, Joseph Kuykendall, James Winchester and

Thomas Masten Justices of the Peace for Sumner county, of whom George Winchester, Anthony Sharp, and Edward Douglass, being those present, did take before Judge McNairy in presence of the Governor an oath to support the Constitution of the United States and also an oath of office.

William Cage, Sheriff of Sumner county until the Court of Pleas and Quarter Sessions in July next and to the end thereof, and no longer.

The militia officers for the county of Sumner were as follows: James Winchester, Lieutenant-Colonel, Commandant; Kasper Mansker, Lieutenant-Colonel; Anthony Sharp, First Major; Edward Douglass, Second Major; James McKean, Jr., Zebulon Hubbard, Joseph McClewrath, John Morgan, James Frazier, Captains; Elisha Clary, James Yates, John White, Steven Cantril, and Thomas Patton, Lieutenants; Peter Looney, James Hamilton, William Snoddy, John Rule, and Joseph Morgan, Ensigns.

George Winchester, Register of Sumner county.

George Winchester, Second Major in the Cavalry of Mero District; George Blackmore, Captain, and Reuben Douglass, Lieutenant.

June 2, 1791. William Cage was reappointed Sheriff of Sumner county, until the July term, 1792, and to the end thereof, and no longer.

June 14, 1791. Richard Cavet appointed a Justice of the Peace for Sumner county; George Winchester, First Major of Cavalry, in the place of Edwin Hickman, killed.

July 3, 1792. William Cage was appointed Sheriff of Sumner county until the Court of Pleas and Quarter Sessions in July next, and to the end thereof, and no longer.

July 14, 1792. Appointed and commissioned the following militia officers for Sumner county: Lieutenant Thomas Patton promoted to be a Captain in the place of Captain Wilson, resigned; Richard King, Lieutenant, and James Wilson, Ensign; Peter Looney, a Captain, heretofore a Lieutenant, in the place of Captain McKain, resigned; Ezekiel Norris, Captain; Joseph Morgan, Robert Brigance and John Cummings, Lieutenants; John Butler, an Ensign, and sent to Colonel Winchester five blank commissions to be filled by him, whose names he has not yet reported.

March 16, 1793. John Young, Captain, in the Sumner Regiment of Militia.

June 16, 1793. William Cage, Sheriff of Sumner county to the July term, 1794, and to the end thereof, and no longer.

September 27, 1794. David Wilson appointed Register of Sumner county.

December 26, 1794. Isaac Walton, a Lieutenant, and James Whitson, an Ensign in the Regiment of Infantry of Sumner county.

January 1, 1795. William Hall and Edward Hogan, Ensigns in the Sumner County Regiment of Infantry.

January 16, 1795. Edward Douglass, Lieutenant-Colonel of the Sumner County Infantry; George Dawson Blackmore, Second Major of the Cavalry of Mero District.

January 17, 1795. Reuben Douglass, Captain, and Wilson Cage, Lieutenant of the Cavalry of Mero District; James Frazier, First Major, and Joseph McElurath, Second Major of the Sumner County Regiment of Infantry; William Snoddy and Samson Hansborough, Captains of the same; William Hankins and John Williams, Lieutenants, and —— Latimer, Ensign of the same.

February 2, 1795. William Cage, Sheriff of Sumner county, Collector of the same in Sumner county for the year 1795.

March 2, 1795. The Governor appointed and commissioned Thomas Donald a Justice of the Peace for the County of Sumner.

July 6, 1795. Reuben Cage, Sheriff of Sumner county till the end of the July term, 1796; William

Hall, Cornet of the Sumner county troop of cavalry.

July 27, 1796. Reuben Cage, Collector of Sumner County and Public Taxes, for the year 1796.

SUMNER COUNTY IN WAR

In war, as in peace, Sumner county has ever responded to the calls of duty. The pioneers themselves were for the most part battle-scarred veterans—veterans in experiences, though not in years. Almost every man of them, and not a few of the women, and every boy that was large enough to handle a gun, had taken part in skirmishes with the Indians, and many of the men had fought the British. General Griffith Rutherford, General James Winchester, General Daniel Smith, Colonel Anthony Bledsoe, Major David Wilson, Colonel Edward Douglass, Major William Cage, Major George Winchester, Captain William Bowen, Captain George D. Blackmore and others had held commissions in the war for independence. Isaac Bledsoe, some of the Wilsons, Frank Weathered, James Gwin, Nathan Parker, Hugh Rogan, David Shelby, George Gillespie, John Morgan, James White, some of the Neely's and others had fought in the ranks in the same war.

In the second war with the British, Sumner county furnished a company commanded by Captain Hamilton. This company served under Jackson and was at New Orleans. In the Seminole war, in 1836, a full company went out from Sumner, and the three highest officers of the regiment to which the company was assigned were Colonel William Trousdale, Lieutenant-Colonel Joseph Conn Guild and Major Joseph G. Meadows, all Sumner countians.

When the war with Mexico broke out, Sumner county furnished three companies: the Polk Guards, officered by Captain Robert A. Bennett, Lieutenants J. M. Shaver and Patrick Duffey; the Tenth Legion, commanded by Captain S. R. Anderson, afterwards a Brig-

SUMNER COUNTY IN WAR   43

adier-General in the Confederate service; Lieutenants W. M. Blackmore and P. L. Solomon; and Legion Second, commanded by Captain W. S. Hatton. The names of all of those who lost their lives are all inscribed on a monument erected by the people of the county in the cemetery at Gallatin. There are now living in the county two survivors of these companies: W. F. Clendenning and J. W. Rutherford.

Colonel Trousdale was twice wounded at the battle of Chepultepec and was brevetted Brigadier-General in the regular army for gallantry. William B. Campbell, afterwards Governor, who gave the famous command, "Boys, follow me," and won for his regiment the title of the "Bloody First," was born in Sumner county.

Again, in 1861, when the sound of battle was heard throughout the land, the gallant sons of Sumner rallied around the Southern Cross and gave to the Confederate armies more soldiers than she had voters, and no more gallant men ever wore the gray. In all it furnished more than twenty-seven companies. The first to be formed was mostly raised by William B. Bate, and was commanded by Captain Charlton. Another was commanded by Captain Humphrey Bate, another by Captain D. L. Goodall. These formed a part of the Second Tennessee, of which William B. Bate was the first Colonel. After his promotion, Colonel W. J. Hale, now living in Hartsville, commanded the regiment. The formation of other companies immediately followed, one under Captain James Barber, and another under Captain D. C. Douglass, were mustered into the Seventh Tennessee. Captain Barber died in December, 1861, at Millsboro, Va., and John D. Fry, First Lieutenant, was elected Captain and O. H. Foster First Lieutenant. Captain Fry was seriously wounded at the battle of Seven Pines, and being disabled for further services, resigned. Lieutenant Foster was made Captain, and as such served until the close of the war. When the regiment was reorganized in

April, 1862, James Franklin was elected Captain in place of D. C. Douglass. At the battle of Cedar Run, August 9, 1862, he received a wound which necessitated his retirement from the service, and Robert G. Miller was elected Captain and served to the close of

FORMER HOME OF GOVERNOR WILLIAM TROUSDALE; NOW THE HOME OF THE DAUGHTERS OF THE CONFEDERACY. CONFEDERATE MONUMENT IN FOREGROUND.

the war. Captain W. H. Joyner organized a company which was mustered into the Eighteenth Tennessee in June, 1861. About the same time Captains Frank Duffey and James A. Nimmo raised companies which formed part of the Twentieth Tennessee. Captain Alexander Baskerville raised a company, which was mustered into the Twenty-fourth Tennessee. A little later in the same year, Captains J. L. Carson, William A. Lovell, William T. Sample and John Turner raised companies which became part of the Thirtieth Tennessee. In the latter part of 1861, Captains Joyner and James L. McKoin raised companies, which were mustered into the Forty-fourth Tennessee. Captains C. L. Bennett, H. H. Boude, Mr. Griffin, —— Minnis, J. E. T. Odom and Baxter Smith recruited companies for the cavalry service. The first of the cavalry companies to be raised in the county was in the summer of 1861, when Captain (afterwards Colonel) Baxter Smith raised a company of eighty men. His company was attached to the Seventh Tennessee Cavalry, and he was promoted to Major of the battalion. Afterwards the battalion was consolidated with other troops and formed the Second Tennessee Cavalry. Major Smith was then transferred and made the Colonel of the Fourth Tennessee, and commanded what was called the "Texas Brigade," composed of his own regiment, two Texas regiments and one Arkansas regiment, in the last campaign of the war.

The citizens of Sumner county contributed a fund sufficient to build a handsome monument to the Confederate heroes. It stands on the grounds of the Trousdale home, now the home of the Daughters of the Confederacy. The county has erected a splendid monument to its heroes of the Mexican war, but many of the men who fought in the battles of the Revolution and the men who fell victims to Indian ferocity sleep in unmarked graves.

In 1840, when the pension list was revised, the following named Sumner countians were on the pension rolls, all of them being Revolutionary soldiers:

NAMES.	AGES.
William Bell	82
William Beard	86
William Bruce	87
Elijah Bayless	81

Historic Sumner County, Tenn.

Samuel Cockran, Sr.	84
John Cleburn	82
John Carney, Sr.	106
William Fortune	94
James Gamblin	90
Albert Hendrix	80
Benjamin Haynes	94
Richard Johnson	80
Joseph Jackson	84
John McMurtry	86
John B. Miller	79
William Morris	80
William May	85
Ezekiel Marshall	82
John McAdams	79
John McClung	80
Henry Pitt	75
James Pond	75
Reuben Prewett	80
Thomas Parish	80
John Sloan	82
Bathl. Stovall	80
Hudson Thompson	77

Hal. Malone, and probably others, refused a pension.

From the *Sumner County News*, October 14, 1899:

SUMNER COUNTY IN THE WAR WITH MEXICO.
BY HON. J. W. BLACKMORE.

Sumner county furnished three companies for the war with Mexico, 1846-7. Two of these were in the First Tennessee Regiment Infantry, commanded by W. B. Campbell. These companies were commanded by Captains W. M. Blackmore and Robert A. Bennett, the former being known as the "Tenth Legion," and the latter as the "Polk Guards." The Tenth Legion was composed of volunteers from Gallatin and its vicinity, while the Polk Guards was made up from enlistments at Hartsville and that neighborhood. These companies were enlisted for and served twelve months and there were about one hundred men in each company. S. R. Anderson, the Lieutenant-Colonel of the

Hon. James W. Blackmore

First Tennessee Regiment, was from Sumner county, as was also Major Richard B. Alexander, and was seriously wounded at Monterey. The third company was known as Legion Second, and was a part of the

Third Tennessee Regiment Infantry, commanded by Colonel B. Frank Cheatham. This company was commanded by Captain William Hatton. Major Perrin Solomon, of the Third Tennessee Regiment, was a Sumner countian. Lieutenant Nimrod D. Smith acted as Adjutant of the First Tennessee for a while.

As in the late war with Spain, so it was in the war with Mexico, the inhospitable climate was often more destructive to life than the missiles of the enemy, and many a young life succumbed to the ravages of disease.

The First Tennessee Regiment won distinction and gained the praise of the General commanding the American forces for the valor and dash displayed by it in its charge on the enemy's defenses at Monterey on September 21, 1846. This regiment was brigaded at Monterey with the Mississippi Regiment known as the Mississippi Rifles, and commanded by Colonel Jefferson Davis, and were in Quitman's Brigade.

General Zachary Taylor, commanding the army, in his dispatch to Washington in regard to this battle, said: "The Fourth Infantry and three regiments of volunteers were ordered to march at once upon the heavy battery, which was pouring a continuous fire from five pieces of cannon. The Mississippi and Tennessee troops, preceded by three companies of the Fourth, advanced against the works, while the Ohio Regiment, entered the town to the right. The advance of the Fourth was received by so destructive a charge that one-third of the officers and men were instantly killed or disabled. They were compelled to retire until reinforced. The Tennessee and Mississippi corps, under General Quitman, pushed onward, and with the aid of Captain Backus, whose men occupied the roof of a house in the rear of the redoubt, captured it in gallant style, taking five pieces of ordnance, a large quantity of ammunition and several Mexican officers and men prisoners."

SUMNER COUNTY IN WAR   49

In this charge the First Tennessee suffered heavily in killed and wounded and won for itself the name of the "Bloody First." Many noble Sumner countians gave up their lives in this charge at their country's behest, while others were maimed for life. Here Booker H. Dalton and John F. Ralphfile, of the Polk Guards, and First Corporal Julius C. Elliott, Peter Hinds Martin, Edward Pryor, Benjamin Soper, Isaac Inman Elliott and Thomas Jones of the Tenth Legion were killed, and Lieutenant J. Cam. Allen, of that company, lost a leg. History states that there were one hundred and twenty American soldiers killed at the battle of Monterey. Eight of these were Sumner countains, so out of every fifteen killed in that battle, Sumner county mourned one dead son or six and two-thirds per cent. of the slain in that engagement. Out of these three companies forty-five men died of disease contracted in the service in the war with Mexico.

The Third Tennessee Regiment was formed about the close of the war, after the First Regiment had been mustered out, and this regiment reached Mexico after the fighting had ceased.

The First Tennessee Regiment participated also in the investment and siege of Vera Cruz and in the battle of Cerro Gordo, April 18, 1847, where Samuel W. Lauderdale of the Tenth Legion was killed.

General W. B. Bate was a soldier in the war with Mexico, first as a member of a Louisiana regiment, and afterwards as a Lieutenant in Captain Hatton's Company of the Third Tennessee Regiment, and acted Adjutant of that regiment. Sumner county sent, in the person of General Wm. Trousdale, another distinguished soldier to the war with Mexico. He was Colonel of the Fourteenth Regular Infantry, but commanded a brigade in the operations of the army in the capture of the City of Mexico, and was wounded and brevetted for gallantry in the storming of the heights of Chepultepec, and was given honorable mention in General Scott's report to the Government. Sumner county sustained in the war, as she had in every war before and has in every war since, her title to the name of the "Volunteer County of the Volunteer State."

MONUMENT TO THE MEXICAN SOLDIERS FROM
SUMNER COUNTY

By the liberality of its citizens the county erected, in 1848, a stone monument in the cemetery here to the memory of her sons who died in that war, but time and the elements have so wrought upon it that it is now toppling over, and soon even "Old Mortality," with chisel and hammer, could not preserve from utter defacement the names of those who are inscribed on its roll of honor. To preserve these names and the inscriptions on this monument we present them hereunder:

East Side.

This monument was erected by the citizens of the County of Sumner, to the memory of her patriotic sons who sacrificed their lives in defense of the flag of their country, in the war with Mexico in 1846, 1847 and 1848.

Glory followed their train, and by their death, was increased. Their fame is all that survives them. In their graves, all their remembrances are buried. Virtuous and esteemed in life, they have become glorious and immortal in death.

May our country never feel the want of such heroes.

John F. Ralphfile—Born in Philadelphia, Pennsylvania; received wound in the battle of Monterey on the 21st day of September, 1846, and died on the 24th day of September, 1846; aged 30 years.

Briscoe Hatchett—Born in Sumner county, Tennessee; died in Camargo on the 24th day of September, 1846; aged 21 years.

Joseph Marshall—Born in Sumner county, Tennessee; died in Camargo on the 5th day of September, 1846; aged 21 years.

Richard Latham—Born in Sumner county, Tennessee; died in Jallappa on the 3d day of September, 1847; aged 26 years.

Thomas Young—Born in Macon county, Tennessee; died in Lomita on the 9th day of August, 1846; aged 28 years.

King Carr—Born in Sumner county, Tennessee; died in Camargo on the 10th day of September, 1846; aged 23 years.

Booker H. Dalton—Born in Sumner county, Tennessee; killed in battle at Monterey on the 21st day of September, 1846; aged 30 years.

Thomas E. Harris—Born in Smith county, Tennessee; died in Camargo on the 8th day of November, 1846; aged 27 years.

George Barker—Born in Sumner county, Tennessee; died at his father's in Sumner county, Tennessee, on the 12th day of December, 1848, of disease contracted in service of United States Army; aged 21 years.

William Gambell—Belonged to Captain Hatton's company. Born in Sumner county, Tennessee; died at his uncle's in Sumner county, Tennessee, about the 16th day of November, 1846, of disease contracted in service of United States Army; aged 21 years.

West Side—Tenth Legion.

Captain William M. Blackmore's Company—First Regiment of Tennessee Volunteers.

First Corporal Julius C. Elliott—Born in Sumner county, Tennessee; died at Monterey on the 3d day of November, 1846, of wounds received in battle on the 21st day of September, 1846; aged 21 years.

Peter Hynds Martin—Born in Sumner county, killed in battle at Monterey on the 21st day of September, 1846; aged 22 years.

Edward Pryor—Born in Sumner county, Tennessee; was killed in battle at Monterey on the 21st day of September, 1846; aged 23 years.

Benjamin Soper—Born in Sumner county, Tennessee; was killed in battle at Monterey on the 21st day of September, 1846; aged 21 years.

Isaac I. Elliott—Born in Sumner county, Tennessee; was killed in battle at Monterey on the 21st day of September, 1846; aged 22 years.

Samuel W. Lauderdale—Born in Sumner county, Tennessee; killed in battle at Cerro Gordo on the 18th day of April, 1847; aged 21 years.

John D. Watson—Born in Sumner county, Tennessee; died at Matamoras on the 18th day of August, 1846; aged 22 years.

William L. Cantrell—Born in Sumner county, died at his father's home in Sumner county on the 20th day of October, 1846, of disease incurred in service of United States Army; aged 21 years.

William Bradley—Born in Sumner county; died in Camargo on the 11th day of September, 1846; aged 24 years.

Zaccheus D. Wilson—Born in Sumner county; died in Camargo on the 31st day of August, 1846; aged 23 years.

Thomas Jones—Born in England; killed at Monterey on the 2d day of October, 1846; aged 43 years.

South Side—Legion Second.

Captain William S. Hatton's Company, Third Regiment of Tennessee Volunteers.

Pleasant V. Bell—Born in Sumner county; died in City of Mexico on the 10th day of January, 1848; aged 28 years.

Powhattan Childress—Born in Sumner county; died in the City of Mexico on the 31st day of December, 1847; aged 19 years.

Joseph Henry—Born in Sumner county; died in the City of Mexico on the 1st day of January, 1848; aged 19 years.

Henry W. Perry—Born in Pennsylvania; died in City of Mexico on the 5th day of January, 1848; aged 22 years.

Patrick Saunders—Born in Sumner county; died at Vera Cruz on the 19th day of December, 1847; aged 18 years.

Joseph S. Tennison—Born in Sumner county; died the City of Mexico on the 13th day of January, 1848; aged 19 years.

Marley Young—Born in Sumner county; died at Molino del Rey on the 5th day of May, 1848; aged 22 years.

John G. Kirby—Born in Sumner county; died at Penal, Mexico, on the 10th day of April, 1848; aged 26 years.

Joseph Rhodes—Born in Sumner county; died in hospital at New Orleans on the 18th day of June, 1848; aged 22 years.

Joseph Taylor—Born in Sumner county; died at Pueblo, Mexico, on the 5th day of June, 1848; aged 21 years.

Joseph Blair—Born in Sumner county; died here at his father's house on the 6th day of August, 1848, of disease incurred in service of U. S. Army; aged 23 years.

William Curry—Born in Sumner county; died here at his father's house on the 5th day of August, 1848, of disease incurred in service of United States Army; aged 19 years.

Alexander R. Schell—Born in Sumner county; died at Jalappa on the 17th day of December, 1847; aged 18 years; buried here.

Albert King—Born in Sumner county; died at Jallappa on the 14th day of May, 1848; aged 33 years.

Richard C. Ainsworth—Born in Sumner county, died in City of Mexico on the 29th day of June, 1848; aged 26 years.

Josephus Zarecor—Born in Sumner county, died on the Gulf of Mexico on the 29th day of June, 1848; aged 22 years.

Aser Lemons—Born in Sumner county, died on the Mississippi river on the 10th day of July, 1848; aged 21 years.

Stephen Goarley—Born in Sumner county, died at Memphis on the 19th day of July, 1849; aged 18 years.

James T. Leddy—Born in Sumner county, died at Memphis on the 21st day of July, 1848, of disease incurred in service of United States Army; aged 20 years.

William Turner—Born in Sumner county, died at Memphis on the 21st day of July, 1848, of disease incurred in service of the United States Army; aged 22 years.

James K. Frazier—Born in Sumner county, died at his father's in Sumner county on the 16th day of November, 1848, of disease incured in service of United States Army; aged 25 years.

Eli Robertson—Born in Sumner county, died at his father's in Sumner county on the 5th day of August, 1848, of disease incurred in the service of the United States Army; aged 22 years.

James H. Hogan—Born in Sumner county, died at his father's in Sumner county on the 23d day of August, 1848, of disease incurred in the service of the United States Army; aged 21 years.

William Henry—Born in Sumner county, died at his father's in Sumner county on the 20th day of December, 1848, of disease incurred in service of United States Army; aged 21 years.

COLONEL ANTHONY BLEDSOE

The origin of the Bledsoe family is lost in obscurity. There is a tradition that it came originally from the northern part of Italy during the time of the Crusades, and settled in Kent, England; but of this we can find no proof. It is believed that the name was originally Bletsoe, and that the family belonged to the old nobility of England. But this is not claimed as a fact. John Beauchamp, Lord of Bletsoe, died in the early part of the fifteenth century, leaving no issue. His estate, in County Northumberland, passed to his sister, Margaret, who married Sir Oliver St. John, who, by this marriage, acquired the Lordship of Bletsoe during the reign of Henry VI. Sir Oliver died in 1437, and sometime thereafter Margaret married John Beaufort, Duke of Somerset, by whom she had a daughter, Margaret, who married Edward Tudor, Earl of Richmond, and by him was the mother of Henry VII. From the elder son of Sir Oliver St. John and Margaret, descended the Lords of St. John of Bletsoe.

When the Bledsoes came to the American colonies we do not know, but they evidently came at a very early date, and were people of consequence, owning a large estate in Northumberland County, Virginia, where we find the will of George Bledsoe recorded on July 23, 1704. He mentions in the will, his daughter, Elizabeth, and his sons, John, William, Abraham and Thomas. Later these sons, or some of them, moved to Spottsylvania county, and some to Culpeper county. Abraham, son of George Bledsoe, settled in Spottsylvania. There is a record of a suit, in 1722, John Richardson vs. Abraham Bledsoe. In the same county, in August 1727, Elizabeth, wife of William Bledsoe, and formerly widow of Charles Stevens, executed a bond. William Bledsoe was Sheriff of Spottsylvania in 1723. There was recorded a deed from William Bledsoe, in 1759, to his sons, Moses and Joseph. It is probable that this was the same William Bledsoe whose will was probated in Culpeper County on April 19, 1770. He names his wife, Elizabeth, his sons George and Aaron, daughter, Hannah Cave (she was the wife of Benjamine Cave, Burgess for Orange County, 1756, and ancestor of Vice-President Richard M. Johnson), the children of his deceased son, Moses, Mills Wetherell (wife of George Wetherell) and Mumford. Joseph, who was not named in the will, was probably Rev. Joseph Bledsoe, father of Jesse Bledsoe, United States Senator, from Kentucky.

Abraham Bledsoe, son of the George Bledsoe, mentioned above, was the father of Colonels Anthony and Isaac, and of Abraham Bledsoe, who played important parts in the early history of Southwestern Virginia and the Cumberland country in Tennessee.

The will of Abraham Bledsoe was dated March 15, 1753, in Granville County, and was probated on May 29 of the same year. He names his wife, Sarah, his sons Isaac, Abraham, Thomas, Jacob, Moses and Aaron, and refers to "the rest of my children." The executors were his wife, Sarah, and his son-in-law, Henry Thornton.

Aaron Bledsoe was given a Captain's commission in Spottsylvania county in 1756.

Anthony Bledsoe, who was not named in the above-mentioned will, was commissioned a Captain in the colonial troops about 1774.

Isaac Bledsoe served as a private in Dunmores War, and in the subsequent Indian wars.

Abraham Bledsoe was an Ensign in Captain David Long's company in 1774.

Isaac and Abraham Bledsoe were famous as hunters and explorers in Kentucky and what is now Tennessee.

Of the other brothers we can find no trace. But doubtless each of them preformed his part well. Of the sisters we can find no account.

Abraham, Anthony, William and George Bledsoe, noted Indian fighters, who removed from Augusta to Washington county, Virginia, at an early date, were probably cousins of Anthony, Isaac and Abraham Bledsoe, who settled in Tennessee. One of the four brothers, Abraham, had sons, Thomas, Loven, Anthony, William and Isaac. The last named, Isaac, has a son, Austin Bledsoe, now living at Blackwater, Virginia.

Hon. Jesse Bledsoe, United States Senator from Kentucky, was born in Culpeper county, Virginia, on the 6th of April, 1776. His father, Joseph Bledsoe, was a Baptist preacher. His mother's maiden name was Elizabeth Miller. He received a classical education in Transylvania University, then studied law, and soon won fame at the bar. He was repeatedly elected to the Legislature of Kentucky, serving in both houses. He was Secretary of State under Gov. Scott, and during the second war with Great Britain, was elected to Congress as a Senator. In 1822 he was appointed by Governor Adair, a Circuit Judge. Later he was appointed professor of law in Transylvania University. In 1833 he removed to Mississippi, and in 1835 to Texas, and commenced gathering materials for a history of that young republic. In 1836 he died at Nacodoches.

In early life he married a daughter of Colonel Nathaniel Gist, who survived him.

Judge Bledsoe was a cousin of Colonel Anthony Bledsoe.

Probably the most distinguished man of the Bledsoe name was Albert Taylor Bledsoe, editor, author, preacher and lecturer. He was born in Frankfort, Kentucky, in 1809, and died in 1877. He was a Colonel in the Confederate Army, and was for a time chief of the War Bureau and Acting Assistant Secretary of War. He was professor of mathematics in the Universities of Mississippi and Virginia; later editor of the *Southern Review*. He was the author of "Examination of Edwards on the Will," "Theodley," "Liberty and Slavery," "Was Jeff Davis a Traitor?" and "Philosophy of Mathematics." He was eminent as a Methodist preacher.

One of the most noted of the Bledsoes in the Civil War was Captain Hiram M. Bledsoe, who was a member of the Missouri branch of the family. He was born in Kentucky, and left there when he was 17 years of age and went West; crossed the plains with General Donovan's brigade and went to the Mexican War, then returned and tried to lead a settled life in Missouri, but was attracted by the Kansas trouble in 1856. For four years he fought in the Border war, and when the Civil war commenced he entered the service of the

Colonel Anthony Bledsoe 59

Confederacy as Captain of a Missouri battery. He was a favorite with Generals Price and Joe Shelby, and, in fact, with all the officers and men. No braver man ever followed the "Bonny Blue Flag" than Captain Hiram Bledsoe. He crossed the river with his battery with Price in 1862, and was in all the battles at Corinth and Shiloh, and between Chickamauga and Jonesboro. After the war he returned to his home in Missouri, where he continued to reside until a few years ago, when he passed to his reward.

The only monument erected by the Confederates at Chickamauga was the Missouri monument. The Legislature of his State, recognizing the splendid record made by Bledsoe's battery, complimented Captain Bledsoe by putting his name on the monument.

Captain Bledsoe had a brother, Joseph, who commanded a battery under gallant Joe Shelby, in Missouri. He died at his home in Texas, in October, 1898.

Colonel Anthony Bledsoe was born in that part of Orange county which is now embraced in Culpeper county, Virginia, in 1733. He received a liberal education for the time, and became a surveyor. In early life he removed to the frontier, and settled in Augusta county, in that section which was afterwards embraced in Botetourt county, the new county being formed in 1770. Col. Bledsoe had his home at Fincastle, the seat of justice of the new county, where he was a merchant, trader and surveyor. He was one of the justices of the peace for the new county and held that position for several years. In 1772 a number of the citizens of Botetourt county petitioned the Legislature to divide the county, and out of the western half, form a new county, to be called Fincastle, which was accordingly done. In May 1770, Anthony Bledsoe was appointed to take "the tithables from Stalnackers to the lowest inhabitants," on the South Fork of Holston. The settlers on the Holston, below Bledsoe's Fort, at that time, believed that they were in Virginia, but in 1771 Anthony Bledsoe made a survey, which showed that they were in the territory of North Carolina.

On May 5, 1773, Anthony Bledsoe was appointed to "take the list of the tithables from Captain Campbells down to the county line, on north, south and middle fork of the Holston river." On May 4, 1774, he was directed by the County Court to take a list of the tithables in Captain Looney's, Captain Shelby's and Captain Cocke's companies.

As early as 1774 Anthony Bledsoe was a Captain in the colonial troops. Among the papers borrowed by Dr. Draper from the Tennessee Historical Society, and which he later gave to the Wisconsin Historical Society, were a number of letters written by Captain Bledsoe, and others referring to him. In Haywood's "Civil and Political History of Tennessee," and in Ramsey's "Annals of Tennessee," we find published an affidavit of Jarrett Williams on the conduct of the Indians, made before him on July 8, 1776. Gilmore says of Anthony Bledsoe: "He was one of those who rushed to the rescue of Watauga in 1776." In that year he served in the expedition commanded by Colonel William Christain, against the Indians. In September of that year that portion of the troops under Colonel William Russell began their march to the Great Island of the Holston, at which time Bledsoe entered two wagons in the public service, to convey the baggage and provisions of the troops. This was the first time that a wagon was taken as low down as Long Island. The expedition was out three months, and but a single white man was killed; his name was Duncan, who left a widow and five small children, to whom, the Legislature of Virginia, in June, 1777, "allowed the sum of £20 for their present relief, and the further sum of £5 per annum for a period of five years," with directions to Anthony Bledsoe and William Cocke to "lay out and expend the same for the support of Mrs. Duncan and her children."

Upon the return of the army to Long Island, Colonel Christain reorganized the same, and for the protection of the frontiers left 600 men at the island under command of Major Anthony Bledsoe, who continued in command until April 1777, when Colonel Christain returned and resumed the command.

About this date the General Assembly of Virginia passed an act dividing the County of Fincastle and forming Washington county. At an election held in the spring of 1777 to elect members of the Legislature from Washington county, Arthur Campbell and William Edmiston were opposed by Anthony Bledsoe and William Cocke. The election was hotly contested, and resulted as follows: Bledsoe received 297 votes. Cocke received 294 votes. Campbell and Edmiston received, respectively, 211 and 144 votes.

The defeated candidates contested the election on the grounds that citizens of North Carolina had voted for their opponents, and that Bledsoe held a military command, and was, therefore, incapable of sitting as a member of the Legislature. Bledsoe and Cocke were declared elected, whereupon Major Bledsoe resigned his Major's commission in the militia.

At the next election, in the spring of 1778, Major Bledsoe and Arthur Campbell were elected members of the Legislature. On August 19, 1779, Anthony Bledsoe, Daniel Smith, Joseph Black and John Blackamore were appointed examiners of the bills of credit of the State of Virginia and other states, to guard against counterfeiting. While a member of the Legislature Major Bledsoe presented a bill for the extension of the line between Virginia and North Carolina, which was passed. In this year he was in the "Battle of the Flats."

In 1760 Anthony Bledsoe married Mary Ramsey, of Augusta county, and soon afterwards removed to his new home on the frontier. The exact location of his settlement is in doubt. He located 700 acres of land on the waters of the Holston river, where he built his fort, about thirty miles east from Long Island, on the Fort Chiswell road, near the line of Virginia. During the pioneer period all the settlers located contiguous to the larger water courses, and it is probable that Anthony Bledsoe was not an exception to that rule. In 1776, when the Legislature of Virginia passed a law with reference to the distribution of salt among the settlements of the southwestern frontier, commissioners were appointed to take a list of the tithables. Among others we find William Edmiston was appointed to do this work from Stalnacker's to Black's Fort, which was located where Abingdon now is, on the south fork of Wolf Creek. James Montgomery was appointed to the work from Black's Fort to Major Bledsoe's. John Anderson's duties extended from Major Bledsoe's as low down as there were settlers. It is not probable that the duties of any of these assessors required them to cross the mountain ridges, but, instead, that they followed the courses of the streams where the settlements were. Thus Edmiston's territory extended from Abingdon down Wolf Creek to Black's Fort, probably the place where that stream empties its waters into South Fork of Holston. From there James Montgomery was assigned to do the work down the Holston to Major Bledsoes, which was on the Virginia line, about the mouth of Spring creek, some ten miles east from the present town of Bristol. Haywood says that Colonel Bledsoe extended the line of the State as far west as Beaver Creek, (at Bristol).

In the fall of 1781 Colonel Anthony Bledsoe removed with his family to what is now Sumner county, Tennessee, and there, two miles north from Bledsoe's Lick, located 6,280 acres of land, giving to the place the name "Greenfield." The tract has been divided into a number of splendid farms, owned for the most

Colonel Anthony Bledsoe   63

part by members of the Chenault family. Not one acre of it belongs to any member of the family of the original owner.

Next to James Robertson, Colonel Bledsoe was the most valuable member of the Cumberland settlement. He was a man of education, of cool courage, sound judgment and of wide experience in public affairs, having held various civil and military positions in the older settlements. His relations with John Sevier, Governor Caswell and other prominent men, were of an intimate character. For many years he was the bosom friend and trusted counselor of James Robertson, who after Bledsoe's arrival in the Cumberland country, acted in no affair of importance without his advice and coöperation. In the event of Robertson's death, he was probably the only man who could have brought the settlements safely out of the ordeal through which they were passing.

On October 6, 1783, the County Court of Davidson county, was instituted. Anthony Bledsoe, Daniel Smith, James Robertson, Isaac Bledsoe, Samuel Barton, Thomas Mulloy, Francis Prince and Isaac Lindsey constituted the court. Anthony Bledsoe was elected Colonel of the Davidson County Militia. In 1782 Anthony Bledsoe, Isaac Shelby and Absalom Tatum were appointed commissioners to select and lay off a tract or tracts of land sufficient to meet the grants which North Carolina had made to the officers and soldiers of the Revolutionary War. Early in 1783 these commissioners met at Nashborough, and entered upon their duties. The line which they ran was styled the "Commissioners' line." It began at a point near where Elk river crosses the southern boundary, and which has since been called "Latitude Hill." The commission laid off, near Columbia, a tract of 25,000 acres for General Nathaniel Greene, which had been granted by North Carolina, as a mark of the high sense of his extraordinary services in the war of the revolution.

The commission was accompanied by a guard of one hundred men, each of whom received grants of land for his services.

Colonel Bledsoe was one of the first trustees of Davidson Academy, 1785, now the University of Nashville. In the same year he was elected a member of the General Assembly of North Carolina, and served in that capacity until his death, three years later.

Colonel Putnam, in his "History of Middle Tennessee," says: "In the severe winter of 1781-82, there was much dissatisfaction in the Cumberland settlements. The weaker began to loose heart, and there was much talk of abandoning the settlements and returning to a safer country. Bledsoe, the stout-hearted surveyor, the shadow of whose destiny was already lengthening towards him, pointed to the future: 'If we perish here, others will be sure to come, either to avenge our deaths, or to accomplish what we have begun. If they find not our graves, or our scattered bones, they may revere our memories and publish to the ages to come that we deserved a better fate.'"

Col. Bledsoe opposed the formation of the State of Franklin, and wrote to Governor Caswell, of North Carolina, advising moderation, and suggesting that the Governor address a letter to the disaffected people, advising them to return to their duty to the mother State. In compliance with this suggestion, Governor Caswell wrote a conciliatory letter to the people of Franklin, which letter had the effect of allaying the intense feeling which prevailed against the parent State. On June 1, 1787, Colonel Bledsoe addressed a letter to Governor Caswell, asking permission to carry an expedition against the Chickamaugas. On the 12th of the same month he and Colonel James Robertson addressed the Governor jointly, advising him of the deplorable state of affairs on the Cumberland. On August 5, Colonel Bledsoe wrote the following letter:

"Dear Sir: When I last had the pleasure of seeing Your Excellency, I think you was kind enough to propose that in case the perfidious Chickamaugas should infest this country, to notify Your Excellency, and you would send a campaign against them without delay. The period has arrived that they, as I have good reason to believe, in combination with the Creeks, have done this count v very great spoil by murdering numbers of our pea :eful inhabitants, stealing our horses, killing our cattle and hogs, and burning our buildings through wanton less, cutting down our corn, etc.

"I am well assured that the distress of the Chickamauga tribe is the only way this defenseless country will have quiet. The militia being very few, and the whole, as it were, a frontier, its inhabitants all shut up in stations, and they, in general, so weakly manned that in case of invasion, one is scarcely able to aid the other, and the enemy daily in our country committing ravages of one kind or another, and that of the most savage kind. Poor Major Hall and his eldest son fell a sacrifice to this savage cruelty, a few days ago, near Bledsoe's Lick. They have killed about twenty-four persons in this county in a few months, besides numbers of others in the settlements near to it. Our dependence is much that Your Excellency will revenge the blood thus wantonly shed.

"ANTHONY BLEDSOE.

"To John Sevier, Governor of the State of Franklin, to be forwarded to Governor Caswell, of North Carolina."

Had this appeal been complied with it would have saved many valuable lives, among them, possibly, that of the writer of the letter.

Early in the year 1788, Colonels Robertson and Bledsoe addressed a joint letter to McGillevray, the Indian chief, with reference to the repeated attacks of the Indians. To this communication the chief replied from Little Tallassee, promising that he would use his best endeavors to put a stop to the depredations. But soon afterwards hostilities were again renewed, and Colonel Bledsoe was one of the first victims.

In 1788, for greater security, Colonel Bledsoe moved his family to the fort of his brother, Isaac, at Bledsoe's Lick, where on the night of July 20, he was killed by the Indians. At the time of his death he was the first Colonel of militia, a Justice of the Peace and a member of the Legislature.

Following is an account of the killing of Colonel Anthony Bledsoe, given by General William Hall, who was present with his mother, brothers and sisters in the fort:

"Of those killed at Bledsoe's Fort and in the neighborhood, about this time, an account may be interesting. The fort was an oblong square, and built all around in a regular stockade except at one place, where stood a large double cabin. This was occupied by the two brothers, Colonel Anthony and Colonel Isaac Bledsoe. This cabin stood in the front line of the fort, the whole being built, it will be understood, around an open square. Excepting the open passage between the two cabins, the whole was completely enclosed. Here Colonel Anthony Bledsoe was killed, with a servant of his, by the Indians. The circumstances were these:

"A lane came down at right angles to the fort thus described, the mouth of it being about thirty yards distant, whilst the Nashville road ran along in front. The Indians, it appears, had been reconnoitering the place in their prowlings through the day, and the night being a bright, moonlight one, the savages posted themselves in the fence corners fronting the passage referred to as between the two cabins. Then they got a party to mount on horseback and gallop past, in order to attract persons into the passage through which the moonlight poured in full splendor. The plot succeeded. At the sound of the horses' feet, Colonel Anthony Bledsoe and Campbell, the servant, both jumped up and stepped into the passage, when the Indians shot them both down. The Colonel died next morning, the servant the morning afterwards. I was in the fort at the time. The occurrence took place about midnight. This was on the 20th of July, 1788."

Gilmore, in his "Advance Guard of Civilization," says: "Bledsoe was taken up, carried into the house and laid upon a bed, while Hall, Rogan and Clendenning maned the port holes in expectation of an attack from the savages. No attack followed, but it was soon discovered that Colonel Bledsoe was mortally wounded and could live but a few hours. Then occurred one of those instances of heroism which were so common among the settlers. Bledsoe had two sons and seven daughters, and by the North Carolina law of that period only male heirs inherited the real estate of an intestate. He desired to make a will to protect his daughters, but it was discovered that there was no fire nor any means of striking a light on the premises. Then Hugh Rogan volunteered to go for a light to a neighboring station. This he did, and returned safely with a burning brand in his hand, though he had to run the gauntlet of not less than fifty savages."

The suggestion that a will be made came from the wife of Colonel Bledsoe's brother, Isaac. (Gilmore is in error as to the number of children.)

WILL OF COLONEL ANTHONY BLEDSOE.

"In the name of God. Amen.

"Being near to death, I make my will as follows: I desire my lands at Kentucky to be sold; likewise my lands on Holston, at the discretion of my executors; my children to be educated in the best manner my estate will permit; my estate to be equally divided between my children; to each of my daughters a small tract of land; my wife to keep possession of the four oldest negroes for the maintenance of the family; my lands and slaves to be equally divided between my children. I appoint my brother, Isaac Bledsoe, and Colonel Daniel Smith executors, with my wife, Mary Bledsoe, executrix. At the decease of my wife, the four above negroes to be equally divided among my children. ANTHONY BLEDSOE (Seal).

"Signed, sealed and delivered in presence of us, this 20th day of July, 1788.
"JAMES CLENDENNING,
"THOMAS MURRAY,
"HUGH ROGAN."

Colonel Putnam, in his "History of Middle Tennessee," in speaking of the death of Colonel Bledsoe, says: "The heart of Colonel Robertson had been pierced again and again. This death was an almost crushing blow to him. With the Bledsoes he had long been intimate; they had taken counsel together; they had toiled and traveled together; they were steadfast friends, and by their offices as Representatives to the Legislature (of North Carolina), and in the recent measure to discover, and if possible, abate or remove the cause of enmity on the part of the Creeks, they fervently hoped to render lasting service.

"But now this earliest of pioneers, this upright man, reliable friend and valuable citizen, is suddenly cut down, savagely murdered in his own house, and in the presence of his own family. There were lamentations throughout the settlements, and had there been any intermission to the duty of watchfulness and defense, public demonstrations of sad respect would have attended his funeral. Armed men came to bury him; hardy woodsmen were there; every man came and marched in the solemn procession with his rifle upon his shoulder and deep grief within his heart; and there they buried him."

Any descendant of Colonel Anthony Bledsoe desiring to become a member of the Sons or Daughters of the American Revolution can do so by tracing their descent in the genealogy, and referring to the follow-

ing authorities for his services in the war for independence:
Virginia Magazine of History, July, 1899, pages 2 and 11.
Same, October, 1899, page 123.

D. SHELBY WILLIAMS

"Ramsey's Annals of Tennessee," pages 170 and 190.
"Phelan's History of Tennessee," pages 32, 130, 134, 140, 144 and 157.
"Dunmore's War," by Thwait and Kellogg, page 106.

"Sumner's History of Southwest Virginia," pages 221, 242, 245, 263, 264, 270, 287, 292, 625 and 748.
"Ellett's "Pioneer Women of the West," page 19.

MARY RAMSEY BLEDSOE

Mary Ramsey was born in Augusta county, Virginia, in 1734. She was a daughter of Thomas Ramsey, who removed from the eastern section of the State at an early date and settled on the extreme frontier, where he became prominent. Several members of her family are mentioned in the early annals of Virginia, and during the Revolutionary war. In 1760 Mary Ramsey married Anthony Bledsoe, and became the mother of his five sons and six daughters,* one of whom was born four months after the death of her husband. The first chapter of "Pioneer Women of the West" is devoted to Mrs. Bledsoe, but it gives only small space to her personal history. It says: "She was a woman of remarkable energy, and was noted for her independence of thought and action. She never hesitated to expose herself to danger whenever she thought it her duty to brave it; she was foremost in urging her husband and friends to go forth and meet the foe, instead of striving to detain them for the protection of her own household. Mary Bledsoe was almost the only instructor of her children, the family being left to her sole charge while her husband was engaged in his toilsome duties, or harassed with the cares incident to an uninterrupted border warfare.

"In person she was attractive, being neither large nor tall until advanced in life. Her hair was brown, her eyes gray, and her complexion fair. Her useful life was closed in the autumn of 1808. The record of her worth, and what she did and suffered may win little attention from the careless many, who regard not the memory of our pilgrim mothers; but the recollection of her gentle virtues has not yet faded from the

*See Eleventh Howard, U. S. Reports.

hearts of her descendants; and those to whom they tell the story of her life will acknowledge her the worthy companion of those noble men to whom belongs the praise of having originated a new colony and built up a goodly state in the bosom of the forest."

Mrs. Bledsoe's brother, Josiah Ramsey, was captured by the Indians when a child, being returned to the settlements after Boquet's treaty in 1764. He was in the battle of Point Pleasant. He was a scout in the Cherokee campaign of 1776; and in 1780 removed to Kentucky, the next year coming to the Cumberland settlement, where he was a major of militia. He died at an advanced age, at the home of his son in Missouri. Other brothers of Mrs. Bledsoe, who came to Sumner county, were Henry Ramsey, the bravest of the brave, and William, both of whom were killed by Indians.

Mrs. Bledsoe was fifty-four years of age when her husband was killed. Five years thereafter, when she was in her sixtieth year, she married Nathan Parker, an old man, a pioneer, and the father of several children, some of whose descendants are prominent citizens of this and other states. Among them are ex-Mayor James M. Head, of Nashville, and Hon. John H. DeWitt, a Nashville lawyer.

From the *Nashville Banner,* October 21, 1908:

MONUMENT TO BLEDSOE'S AT BLEDSOE'S LICK
IN SUMNER

BY A. V. GOODPASTURE

The attention of the public cannot be too often drawn to the fact that the landmarks which connect us with our pioneer ancestors—their noted buildings, the scenes of their heroic deeds, the graves that contain their sacred ashes—are fast disappearing; many of them are already difficult to identify and some of them are lost forever. In 1889 the Legislature removed the remains of Governor John Sevier from an unmarked grave in Alabama to his old home in Knoxville, and erected a handsome monument over them. Recently the active and patriotic Historical Society of. Maury county has identified the grave of General Richard Winn, and caused it to be suitably marked. But General Griffith Rutherford, famous for his campaign against the Cherokee Indians; President of the Legislative Council of the Southwest Territory; for whom both North Carolina and Tennessee have named counties, still sleeps in an unknown grave. Judge John Haywood, the father of Tennessee history, sleeps in the quiet garden of his old home, but at a place that can no longer be determined. The individual or society that hunts out and marks such sacred spots does a patriotic service, and deserves the thanks of the public; for there is no stronger tie that binds the affections of a people to their country than the graves of their honored ancestors.

IN UNMARKED GRAVES.

For almost a century and a quarter two brothers, Colonels Anthony and Isaac Bledsoe, have slept in unmarked and neglected graves near Bledsoe's Lick, in Sumner county, where they were killed by the Indians in the first settlement of the county. Their descendants have long wished to· see a monument erected to their memory, but until recently they have taken no definite action in the matter. A few years ago Judge D. D. Shelby, of Huntsville, Ala., and Judge Eli Shelby Hammond, of Memphis, Tenn., and later Colonel Oscar F. Bledsoe, of Grenada, Mississippi, visited their graves for the purpose of devising some means of having them properly marked. While these several visits did much to stimulate sentiment favorable to the movement, nothing further resulted from them for want of an active and intelligent agent who was willing to take the burden of the work on his shoulders and make himself personally responsible for its success.

In the month of June, 1906, Major J. G. Cisco, of

Nashville, whose deceased wife was a great great granddaughter of Colonel Anthony Bledsoe, visited the Bledsoe graves for the first time, and seeing their neglected condition determined to have a monument erected over them. He took up the work actively, in-

GRAVES OF COLONELS ANTHONY AND ISAAC BLEDSOE BEFORE THE MONUMENT WAS BUILT

telligently and disinterestedly. During the next year he wrote letters to many of the descendants of the Bledsoes, and saw others in person, urging the organization of a monument association. Being unable to get a sufficient number of them together to effect such an organization, after consulting with Colonel O. F.

Bledsoe, Judge D. D. Shelby, and some others who took an active interest in the matter, he requested the following gentlemen to act as officers and committeemen for the Bledsoe Monument Association, namely: Colonel O. F. Bledsoe, Grenada, Mississippi, President; Mr. C. B. Rogan, Gallatin, Tennessee, Vice-President; D. Shelby Williams, Nashville, Tennessee, Treasurer; J. G. Cisco, Nashville, Tennessee, Secretary. Monument Committee: Judge David D. Shelby, Huntsville, Alabama; R. C. K. Martin, Nashville, Tennessee; Colonel O. F. Bledsoe, Grenada, Mississippi; D. Shelby Williams, Nashville, Tennessee; Mr. C. B. Rogan, Gallatin, Tennessee; Mrs. W. H. B. Satterwhite, Castalian Springs, Tennessee; J. G. Cisco, Nashville, Tennessee.

NAMES OF BLEDSOE DESCENDENTS

Having now effected an organization in which he occupied the modest, but all-important position of Secretary, he undertook to ascertain the names and addresses of the descendants of the Bledsoes. This involved an extensive correspondence, and still his list was necessarily incomplete. To each of those found he mailed a circular letter, offering them an opportunity to contribute to the Bledsoe monument fund, and naming a day at which the subscription books would be closed. The circular letter was as follows:

"THE BLEDSOE MONUMENT ASSOCIATION,
"NASHVILLE, TENNESSEE.
"Nashville, Tenn., April 10, 1908.

"Mr _____

"Dear _____. Our common ancestors, Colonels Anthony and Isaac Bledsoe, have slept side by side, in unmarked graves, near where they were killed by Indians, in Sumner county, Tennessee, during pioneer days, for near a century and a quarter. This Association, composed of descendants of these heroic men, has

Names of Bledsoe Descendants 75

been formed for the purpose of erecting a monument over their graves near the site of Bledsoe's Fort at Bledsoe's Lick in Sumner county, Tennessee.

"The kind of monument to be erected will depend entirely upon the sum total of money contributed by their descendants, each of whom, we believe, will gladly give according to his or her means. It is not expected, nor desired, that a large or showy memorial will be erected, but a plain, substantial one, suitable to the character of the two heroic brothers.

"As it is desired that this work shall be speedily accomplished, a copy of this letter will be sent to each of the descendants whose names may be known to the Secretary, and should be considered an invitation to assist in this laudable work.

"All contributions must be sent to the Treasurer, Mr. D. Shelby Williams (Vice-President of the First National Bank of Nashville, Tennessee, and President of the Nashville Gas Company), Nashville, Tennessee, not later than July 15, 1908. This will, it is hoped, enable the committee to lay the corner stone of the monument during the 'Tennessee Home-Coming Week' in September, 1908.

"You can facilitate this enterprise by notifying the Secretary of your intention to contribute to the fund, and the amount you propose to contribute, at your earliest convenience. You are also requested to send to the Secretary the names and addresses of other descendants whom you may know.

"All moneys received will be deposited in the First National Bank at Nashville, of which the Treasurer is a director, and Vice-President, and there remain until the monument is completed and ready to be paid for. There will be no salaries nor fees paid to any one. All the money contributed will be used in building the monument, excepting the small amount necessary for printing and postage.

"It is earnestly hoped that each descendant of either of the two Colonels Bledsoe shall contribute, be the amount ever so small, that all may have an interest in the memorial. Fraternally,

"J. G. Cisco, *Secretary,*
"*Vanderbilt Law Building, Nashville, Tennessee.*"

The responses were generous. On the day named he closed the subscription books, having in the hands of the Treasurer the handsome sum of $753.

The names of the contributors are as follows:

CONTRIBUTORS TO THE BLEDSOE MONUMENT FUND.

Colonel Oscar F. Bledsoe, Grenada, Mississippi, great grandson of Colonel Anthony Bledsoe	$500 00
Mrs. O. H. P. Belmont, New York, great great granddaughter of Colonel Anthony Bledsoe	100 00
Mr. D. Shelby Williams, Nashville, Tennessee, great great great grandson of Colonel Anthony Bledsoe	25 00
Judge David D. Shelby, Huntsville, Alabama, great great grandson of Colonel Anthony Bledsoe	15 00
Mrs. E. M. Satterwhite, Castalian Springs, Tennessee, great great granddaughter of Colonel Isaac Bledsoe	10 00
Miss Nellie Satterwhite, Castalian Springs, Tenn., great great great granddaughter of Colonel Isaac Bledsoe	5 00
Miss Eleanor Desha Pickett, Chicago, Illinois, great great granddaughter of Colonel Isaac Bledsoe	10 00
James A. Satterwhite, Castalian Springs, Tennessee, great great great grandson of Colonel Isaac Bledsoe	5 00
Hon. J. G. H. Buck, Palestine, Texas, great great grandson of Colonel Anthony Bledsoe	5 00

Names of Bledsoe Descendants

Mr. J. A. Massengill, Diboll, Texas, great great grandson of Colonel Anthony Bledsoe	5 00
Mrs. L. S. Converse, Washington, D. C., great great granddaughter of Colonel Anthony Bledsoe	5 00
Mrs. M. M. Walsh, New York, great great granddaughter of Colonel Anthony Bledsoe	5 00
Hon. J. Minnick Williams, Olustee, Oklahoma, great great great grandson of Colonel Anthony Bledsoe	5 00
Hon. James W. Blackmore, Gallatin, Tennessee	5 00
Mrs. Elizabeth Desha Davis, New York, great great granddaughter of Colonel Anthony Bledsoe	2 50
Mrs. Martha Rogan Morrison, Gallatin, Tennessee, great great granddaughter of Colonel Isaac Bledsoe	2 50
Mrs. Augusta Rogan Brown, Gallatin, Tennessee, great great granddaughter of Colonel Isaac Bledsoe	2 50
Captain C. B. Rogan, Rogana, Tennessee, great great grandson of Colonel Isaac Bledsoe	2 50
Mr. William R. Rogan, Rogana, Tennessee, great grandson of Colonel Isaac Bledsoe	2 50
Mr. R. D. Bledsoe, Humboldt, Tennessee	2 50
Mrs. Fredrika L. Cisco Jones, Chattanooga, Tennessee, great great great granddaughter of Colonel Anthony Bledsoe	2 00
Master Robert Cannon Jones, Chattanooga, Tennessee, great great great great grandson of Colonel Anthony Bledsoe	1 00
Master Guy Ozment Jones, Chattanooga, Tennessee, great great great great grandson of Colonel Anthony Bledsoe	1 00
Miss Fredrika Elizabeth Jones, Chattanooga, Tennessee, great great great great granddaughter of Colonel Anthony Bledsoe	1 00

Jay Guy Cisco, Nashville, Tennessee, in memory of his wife, Mildred Georgie Cisco, great great granddaughter of Colonel Anthony Bledsoe _____ 5 00
Miss Bertie Cisco, Nashville, Tennessee, great great great granddaughter of Colonel Anthony Bledsoe _____ 2 00
Miss Mozelle Cisco, Nashville, Tennessee, great great great granddaughter of Colonel Anthony Bledsoe _____ 2 00
Ruperto Francoise Cisco, Nashville, Tennessee, great great great grandson of Colonel Anthony Bledsoe _____ 2 00
Rudolf Wezinski Cisco, Nashville, Tennessee, great great great grandson of Colonel Anthony Bledsoe _____ 2 00
Walter Jay Cisco, New Orleans, Louisiana, great great great grandson of Colonel Anthony Bledsoe _____ 1 00
Walter Jay Cisco, infant, New Orleans, Louisiana, great great great great grandson of Colonel Anthony Bledsoe _____ 1 00
Victor W. Cisco, New Orleans, Louisiana, great great great grandson of Colonel Anthony Bledsoe _____ 1 00
George Guy Cisco, New York, great great great grandson of Colonel Anthony Bledsoe 1 00
Mrs. Priscilla Hammond Scruggs, Holly Springs, Mississippi, great great granddaughter of Colonel Anthony Bledsoe____ 1 00
Mrs. J. Hancock Robinson, Washington, D. C., great great great granddaughter of Colonel Anthony Bledsoe, for self and daughter____ 2 00
Mr. J. M. Scruggs, Memphis, Tennessee, great great great grandson of Colonel Anthony Bledsoe _____ 1 00
Miss Nettie Shelby Watkins, Jackson, Mississippi, great great great granddaughter of Colonel Anthony Bledsoe_____ 2 00

Names of Bledsoe Descendants

Mrs. Fannie Boyd Finch, Batesville, Arkansas   1 00
Hon. Robert L. Burch, Nashville, Tennessee__   1 00
Mrs. Kate Shoffner Caldwell, Memphis, Tennessee, great great great granddaughter of Colonel Anthony Bledsoe _____   1 00
Mrs. Addie Laura Pursley Shoffner, Memphis, Tennessee, great great granddaughter of Colonel Anthony Bledsoe _____   1 00
Mrs. Inez Shoffner White, Memphis, Tennessee, great great great granddaughter of Colonel Anthony Bledsoe _____   1 00
Major B. B. Buck, 13th U. S. Infantry, great great grandson of Colonel Anthony Bledsoe   5 00

Total_____$758 00

The necessary funds being in the treasury, Major Cisco contracted for a monument to be erected over the graves of the Bledsoes (the title to the lot having been secured to the Bledsoe Monument Association), after a design suggested by himself. It is to be of gray granite, will stand sixteen feet high, and will bear the following inscriptions:

West Side.
Sacred to the memory
of
Colonel Anthony Bledsoe.
Mary Ramsey Bledsoe.

Colonel Isaac Bledsoe.
Katherine Montgomery Bledsoe.

Inseparable in life; united in death.
East Side.
Erected in 1908 by
Descendants of the two brothers.
Five-sevenths of its cost was contributed by Colonel Oscar F. Bledsoe, of Grenada, Mississippi, great grandson of Colonel Anthony Bledsoe.

North Side.

Colonel Anthony Bledsoe was born in Culpepper county, Virginia, in 1733; married Mary Ramsey in 1760. He was a justice of the peace in Botetourt, Fincastle, and Washington counties, Virginia; was a Captain in the Colonial Army; Major of Virginia Militia in the Revolutionary War; was in the "Battle of the Flats;" Commander of the troops at Long Island from December, 1776, to April, 1777; first Representative from Washington county in the Virginia Legislature. Removed to Sumner county, Tennessee, in 1781. One of the first justices of the peace for Davidson county; first Colonel of the Davidson County Militia; one of the three Commissioners appointed to run the "Commissioners' Line;" one of the first Trustees of Davidson Academy; first Representative in the North Carolina Legislature from Sumner county. Killed by Indians about 200 yards west from this spot, on July 20, 1788. Left five sons and six daughters.

South Side.

Colonel Isaac Bledsoe was born in Culpeper county, Virginia about 1735; married Katherine Montgomery about 1771. Was one of the "Long Hunters;" one of the first explorers of the Cumberland Country. Discovered Bledsoe's Lick, which was so named for him. Removed to Sumner county, Tennessee in 1780. Was one of the justices of the peace for Davidson and Sumner counties; first major of Davidson County Militia. Was killed by Indians about 300 yards west from this spot on April 9, 1793. Left three sons and five daughters. The Indians gave him the name "Tullatoska."

Mrs. T. H. Clarke in the *Nashville Tennessean,* December 19, 1908:

GRANITE SHAFT HONORS MEMORY OF THE BLEDSOES.

The substantial monument of gray granite that has been erected to the memory of those sturdy pioneer heroes, Anthony and Isaac Bledsoe, by their descendants, near the spot where they were killed by the Indians over a century ago, was dedicated with appropriate and interesting ceremonies yesterday at Bledsoe's Lick, near Gallatin, in Sumner county, Tennessee.

The monument surmounts a proud eminence, overlooking an area every inch of whose soil is sacred in the heart and hallowed in the memory of every loyal American.

Nature chose a most beautiful and fitting setting for the enactment of one of the most thrilling and tragic stories of early American civilization, and no wonder that the surrounding hills and the rich valleys intervening have been enriched by the association of some of the bravest, the truest and knightliest of men, who have blazed the way and upheld the standard of southwestern civilization.

It has been said by some loyal and enthusiastic son of Sumner that the county is the fourth grand division of the State of Tennessee, and that the State is divided into East Tennessee, West Tennessee, Middle Tennessee and Sumner county. Standing on the brow of that stately hill, looking over the graceful hills and fertile valleys and hearing the stories of Bate, Hall, Winchester, the Bledsoes and Edward Carmack, the visitor is not disposed to dispute the propriety of this division.

APPROPRIATE MONUMENT.

The monument is of gray granite, and the design is plain, unpretentious, rugged and substantial, as is suggested by the character of those splendid men whose memory it perpetuates.

Across gently undulating meadows, fertile and beautiful, and scarcely a stone's throw to the right, lies the old farm upon which the beloved Edward Ward Carmack first saw the light, and over whose fields, rich in harvest yield, he played in boyish glee; about an equal distance in the other direction the sky line is fringed with the tops of the trees that adorn the former home of General William B. Bate, of sacred memory; in the nearer distance, untouched by the hand of time, and the plowshare of progress, a dozen marble slabs, dimmed by time, marked the resting places of the contemporaries of the Bledsoes, who shared with them the hardships and the dangers of those early days; while the monument itself marks the graves of Colonels Anthony and Isaac Bledsoe.

CREDIT TO COLONEL CISCO.

That this beautiful monument has been erected to perpetuate the memory and tell to future generations the thrilling life story and the tragic ending of these heroes, is due to the patriotic heart of Colonel J. G. Cisco, of Nashville, whose wife was a lineal descendant of Colonel Anthony Bledsoe.

Colonel Cisco, in the warmth of a patriotic spirit, and the appreciation of the worth of his ancestors, conceived the idea of the erection of this monument some two years ago, and to his patriotism and his loyalty are due the credit. The final consummation of his wishes not only marks the graves of heroes, but stands a tribute to his own patriotism and devotion.

Although the day was cold and dreary, those who gathered on that sacred spot yesterday to witness the interesting ceremonies attendant upon the dedication of the monument, composed a company of men and women who are worthy representatives of their heroic ancestors.

It was not for them, with a dauntless spirit inherited from a line of heroes, to be deterred by wind or cold or rain, and they delighted to honor with their presence so significant an occasion.

Not only did the Sumner County descendants of the Bledsoes attend, but quite a number from Nashville went up on the morning train, including Colonel Cisco and his daughters, Misses Bertie and Mozlle, Major George B. Guild, D. Shelby Williams, Mrs. Williams, her son, Mr. Frazier, and wife, and Mr. Martin. Mr. S. A. Cunningham, editor of the Confederate Veteran, and Henry Bledsoe and Miss Pearl Bledsoe, also attended the dedication.

STRONG STATE-WIDE SENTIMENT.

The meeting was presided over by Mr. Donoho, principal of the Bledsoe Academy, on whose grounds the monument stands. When Colonel Cisco had located the graves and found they were on the academy grounds he requested space for the monument, and a plot thirty feet square was cheerfully given. The exercises were held inside the school building, owing to the inclemency of the weather. After "America" was sung in ringing tones by the audience, Dr. John A. McFerrin, a venerable and greatly beloved resident of Sumner county, led in a fervent and eloquent prayer.

Mr. Donoho then introduced Colonel James Malone, also a resident of Sumner county since his birth, and who is connected with the Bledsoe family. Colonel Malone said that the first word he learned to lisp was that of the Bledsoe's, and that he loved and revered it. He said that while he was not expecting to be called upon, he deemed it an honor and a privilege to speak a few words.

SENATOR CARMACK.

Colonel Malone paid a beautiful tribute to Senator Carmack, who was expected to have made the opening oration of the day, and when he said that he hoped the principles for which Carmack stood in life would be perpetuated in his death, the audience broke into enthusiastic and spontaneous applause. Colonel Malone introduced Col. Oscar Bledsoe, of Grenada, Miss., a great grandson of Colonel Anthony Bledsoe, who had contributed more than two-thirds of the cost of the monument. Colonel Bledsoe is the oldest living descendant bearing the Bledsoe name.

COLONEL BLEDSOE SPEAKS.

Colonel Oscar F. Bledsoe, great grandson of Colonel Anthony Bledsoe, and a resident of Grenada, Miss., spoke as follows:

"Ladies and Gentlemen, Friends and Countrymen: It is with the greatest satisfaction that I am, on this occasion, permitted to view and help dedicate this beauiful monument to two of Tennessee's pioneer heroes. And I will acknowledge right here that this monument is due in the highest and main degree for its inauguration, design and completion to the patient perseverance and high sentiment of Colonel J. G. Cisco, of Nashville. The thought took possession of my mind a few years ago on a visit I was making to Bledsoe's Lick, that these two brother heroes ought to have a monument to forever mark their graves and record their deeds to posterity I have always had an extreme veneration for the memory of my father, whose entire name I bear, though I was less than 14 years old when he died, and I thought that a little of the money derived from the start he gave me by his self-sacrifice could not be employed more agreeably to the behests of his invisible spirit than to help erect a monument in this beautiful and heaven-blessed section of his native State to the memory of our ancestral heroes. The object accomplished is incomparably more valuable than the pecuniary outlay. For money perishes—its continued possession is always uncertain, but monuments like this are eternal and imperishable in their record. They are not like books that grow musty and need new editions and frequent perusal.

COLONEL OSCAR F. BLEDSOE, SECOND

"This monument will always be an open book to future generations—to the mind, the eye, the heart, involuntarily and without an effort on the part of the beholder—and will not only invoke high sentiment and patriotism, but will keep imperishable on earth the names of these early heroes and martyrs to civilization.

A land without monuments is a land without great memories and high ideals, and what grander memories could be perpetuated than those who fell in advancing the civilization we now enjoy?

"We will now notice a few facts concerning these two brothers who were so closely united in life and so little divided in death, and which entitle them to have their memories preserved by such a monument as this.

COLONEL ANTHONY BLEDSOE.

"Colonel Anthony Bledsoe was the eldest of the two brothers, having been born in Virginia about 1733. His ancestors came from England to Virginia as early or earlier than the reign of Queen Anne. Born in Culpeper county, in early manhood, he moved into southwest Virginia when it was a wilderness, and was a prominent citizen in Fincastle county, a member of the Virginia House of Burgesses from that county and a Justice of the Peace. In the beginning of the war of the Revolution, he bore a commission from his native State, and with a strong force rescued Fort Watauga from the Indians, who were besieging it. The two brothers settled on the Holston river. Being a man of education, and well versed in public affairs, his worth was immediately acknowledged by Governor Caswell, of North Carolina. He, at that time, held a commission as Major in the Virginia militia. Governor Caswell appointed him Colonel of militia of the western region. Isaac Shelby, a younger brother, and closely associated with the Bledsoes and a constant companion in their emigration movements, was appointed Lieutenant-Colonel under him, and it took all of their united skill and vigilance to protect the western settlements from the Indians, who were constantly on the warpath, being instigated and armed by the British and Tories against the struggling colonists.

"But just here a great opportunity presented itself to these brave men to serve their country with their efficient and well-organized mountain men eastward of the mountains. The early part of the year 1780 was shrouded in gloom for the patriots of the South in the struggle for independence. The British had been almost uniformly successful. Charleston and Savannah were in their hands. Gates had been completely routed at Camden in August, in 1780. The only resistance was a desultory partisan warfare kept up by Generals Marion, Sumter, Pickens and Colonel Harry Lee. Cornwallis had been ordered by Clinton, who had been present, but had returned to New York, to complete the subjugation of the Carolinas and Georgia by vigorous movements. He accordingly directed Ferguson to proceed westward with a body of British regulars to protect and assist the Tories and destroy their opponents.

"In this crisis a great effort was called for to avert the threatening desolation. Every available band of armed patriots was called upon to unite for resistance to Ferguson. Colonel McDowell, of the Continental Line, called on Colonel Anthony Bledsoe and Colonel John Sevier to send help from west of the mountains. To this appeal they promptly responded. After consultation it was deemed best that Colonel Bledsoe should retain a part of the force to hold back the Indians from a slaughter of the settlers, their women and children—the massacre in Wyoming Valley and the murder and scalping of Miss McRea were ever before their minds—and that his younger subordinate, Lieutenant Colonel Isaac Shelby, should lead all the forces that could be spared to help their struggling brothers in the East.

BATTLE OF KING'S MOUNTAIN.

"The result was the battle and victory of King's Mountain, one of the most important in its consequence of the minor engagements of the Revolutionary War. Complete darkness seemed to have settled on the patriot cause in the South. The paralyzing defeat of

Gates, at Camden, had caused even Marion, Sumter and Pickens to disband their forces or retire to the swamps. The defeat of Ferguson was the first rift in the dark cloud. Ferguson, under orders from Cornwallis, went too far beyond Ninety-Six towards Augusta, and as the patriot bands drew together, commenced a hasty retreat to join Cornwallis at Charlotte, North Carolina.

"Colonels Campbell, Cleveland, Williams, Sevier, Shelby and Major Winston hastily concentrated their mounted riflemen and with a select detachment of 900 men pursued Ferguson by night and day through a heavy rain, until they overtook him on October 17, 1780, in a defensive position near the line of North Carolina, on King's Mountain, an elevation of 500 or 600 yards long and 60 or 70 yards wide. The battle commenced immediately—Colonel Campbell commanded the whole, and with Lieutenant-Colonel Shelby directed the center of attack. Colonel John Sevier and Major Winston commanded the right, and Colonels Williams and Cleveland the left. Ferguson charged repeatedly with bayonets, but was met without flinching by the stern and determined patriots, though he threw the center and right together in confusion at one time, but in his last charge the left turned on him successfully. Ferguson met instant death, and his whole force, with all their stores, were immediately surrendered.

"The consequences were signal and immediate. The patriots resumed the offensive throughout the Southern colonies. Tarleton was defeated soon after by Morgan at the Cowpens. The great Nathaniel Greene, having superseded Gates, held his own against Cornwallis—gained the brilliant victory of Eutaw Springs —only Savannah and Charleston remained in British hands by the fall of 1781. Cornwallis was compelled to retreat, and the final culmination was Yorktown, and victory and independence—for, when Lord North, the British Prime Minister, heard of the surrender of Cornwallis, he exclaimed: 'Oh, God! it is all over now,' and immediately commenced negotiations to acknowledge the independence of America—and the first bright beginning of this fortunate series of events, which brought us independence by a final victory on Southern soil was the brilliant and heroic affair at King's Mountain.

COLONEL BLEDSOE'S PART.

"The idea that I am trying to impress is that Colonel Anthony Bledsoe, being the superior officer of the force under Lieutenant Colonel Isaac Shelby, which performed such important service in the center of this battle, and having been efficient in organizing, arming and preparing this force, and having sent it forth so promptly at his country's call, deserves, without any disparagement whatever to the gallant Isaac Shelby, more historic recognition than he has ever received, for he was permitted to enter, as reward for his patriotic services, over 6,000 acres of land over yonder at Greenfield, about two miles from here, and in 1807 the Legislature of Tennessee created a new county and named it in his honor. It was in 1781 that Colonel Anthony Bledsoe moved from Holston to Greenfield, following his brother Isaac, who had moved the year before. This removal was an arduous undertaking. The distance, the route they had to take, was more than 400 miles. No wagons or vehicles could be used on the narrow trails through the wilderness. Only pack horses were used to carry the possessions of the immigrants. We can understand from this the privations of our ancestors. But the spirit of true neighborhood prevailed fully. The Bledsoes and Shelbys and Alexanders and Neelys and others always moved together and supported each other. This mutual support was half the victory in those pioneer days.

HONEYMOON TRIP.

"The removal of Colonel Anthony Bledsoe's family to the West was marked by an unusual event—a honeymoon trip. His eldest daughter, Sarah, who lies buried there, had just reached womanhood, and had married David Shelby. I will relate an incident connected with this marriage. Lieutenant-Colonel Isaac Shelby, on his return from King's Mountain, found that a young lady, Miss Susan Hart, to whom he had been showing the greatest devotion, had moved, with her family, to Kentucky, without leaving even a word behind for him to come to see her. He, thereupon, inveighed against the fickleness of the sex, and vowed that he would not go to see her under the circumstances, but, in a teasing, half-earnest way, said that he would wait for Miss Sarah Bledsoe. She replied in the same way, that he had better be true to his Kentucky love instead of waiting for Miss Bledsoe. He afterwards relented, went to Kentucky, and was happily married to Miss Susan Hart, who made him a most excellent wife. Miss Bledsoe was already, in heart, engaged to young David Shelby, a private soldier under him in the battle of King's Mountain. They married in 1781, and made their honeymoon trip from the Holston to Cumberland Valley on horseback —quite a contrast to the grand honeymoon journeys of the present day in palatial cars and steamers. But were they less happy? Did not their privations draw their hearts closer together? She was a model wife— David Shelby was a model husband. The old times, with their simplicity and purity, were best, and well may we exclaim against modern domestic infelicity and discord and say, 'O tempora, O mores.'

"Before leaving the name of Sarah Bledsoe Shelby, who rests there, I will say that her first child, Dr. John Shelby, of Nashville, was the first white child born in Middle Tennessee. Her husband, David Shelby, was a most exemplary and influential man. He died in

1822, after having been Clerk of the County Court of Sumner County for twenty years. His wife survived him thirty years, having lived until 1852. To her death she preserved, and would read with glistening eyes, the dispatch from Lieutenant-Colonel Isaac Shelby to her father giving an account of the battle of King's Mountain. She said on her death-bed at Nashville that she desired her remains should be buried by the side of her 'honest old father,' and there she lies, with the record behind her of having been a perfect woman, wife and mother.

FIRST REPRESENTATIVE.

"On the organization of Sumner county, so named in honor of General Jethro Sumner, a hero of the Revolution, in 1785, as a part of North Carolina, Colonel Anthony Bledsoe was elected the first representative to the North Carolina Legislature, and continued such until his death in 1788. In 1787, when the Indians renewed, with increased ferocity, their attacks and massacres, the settlers on the Cumberland seriously debated the question of removal back to the Holston. A consultation was held on the subject, and Colonel Bledsoe opposed the movement in about these words: 'If we perish here others will be sure to follow to avenge our deaths and complete the work which we have begun. If they find not our graves nor our scattered bones, they will at least revere and lament our memories as having deserved a better fate.' His ideas prevailed, and we are here today in this beautiful region and on this historic spot to reverence and, I am thankful to say, preserve his memory. His fate was tragic. In the summer of 1788 the Indians were seemingly bent on exterminating the Cumberland intruders on their hunting grounds. The forts were the only protection. Colonel Anthony Bledsoe moved from his fort at Greenfield to his brother Isaac's fort, about 200 yards west from this spot. On July the 20th the Indians, after prowling about all day, stationed themselves, about midnight, in fence corners opposite an open passage between two elevated log cabins on the line of the stockade fort in which Colonel Anthony and Colonel Isaac Bledsoe resided. The Indians caused an apparent stampede of stock by rapid riding along the lane in front, and Colonel Anthony Bledsoe and young Campbell, though warned by his sister-in-law, Mrs. Isaac Bledsoe, that the noise was caused by Indians, imprudently stepped into the open passage into the bright moonlight, and both were shot.

"When it was found that he must die, and no means being at hand to make a light in order that he might make a will, the gallant Hugh Rogan volunteered to go to a nearby settlement and procure a light, risking being waylaid by the Indians, and successfully accomplished his mission, so that Colonel Anthony Bledsoe, in his dying hour, made his will so that his daughters, as well as his sons, shared in his property, a necessary provision at that time under the law of North Carolina.

"Colonel Bledsoe left five sons and five daughters, and another daughter was born a few months after his death. There are many of his descendants now scattered throughout the land. Two of his sons, Anthony and Thomas, were killed by the Indians. One son, Abraham, the eldest, was a Captain under Jackson, in the Indian wars and at New Orleans. His son, Henry Ramsey, also served at New Orleans, and his youngest son, Isaac, my grandfather, was, no doubt, a private soldier under Jackson in his campaigns against the British and Indians. Colonel Anthony's grandson, my father, was Captain of the Sumner Volunteers in the Seminole War in 1836. I kept, for a long time, until destroyed by a household fire, a beautiful silk flag with the inscription in large letters, 'Sumner Volunteers' on its folds. I suppose it was presented to the company by the ladies of Sumner county in 1836, when the command went off to the war in Florida. Thus you see the Bledsoes, no doubt, got full revenge for the injuries done their kindred and neighbors in the race war between the whites and the Indians.

COLONEL ISAAC BLEDSOE.

"I will now give an epitome of the life of Colonel Isaac Bledsoe, younger by a few years than his brother Anthony. They were inseparable in heart and in life. Every fact, the interchange of names of their children show this. Colonel Isaac was one of the long-hunters —he was the pathfinder. In his explorations he discovered the lick and the creek which bear his name, and near which he entered several thousand acres of land. He was made a Major when Davidson county was formed, and was a member of its first court. He was with his brother in all his military operations for the defense of the country. He it was who, in 1878, in order to save the settlement, volunteered to go through the wilderness and Indians up to the Ohio river to get powder and lead, and, with a single negro slave as his companion, executed his task completely, and returned with the powder and lead, and the settlers felt safe. Just to the west of us, in sight, was the field where Thomas Sharp Spencer planted the first corn ever raised in Sumner county. Colonel Isaac Bledsoe was enlarging this field, in April, 1793, by additional clearing, and went out on a bright morning with his hands to mend his log heaps. The Indians were lurking in that ravine yonder just south of the public highway. Colonel Isaac Bledsoe, being in front, was shot down and mortally wounded. He told his hands, perhaps his sons with them, to rush to the fort— that he could not live, and that they could do nothing for him. The Indians scalped him, while dying, and made off with their ghastly trophy.

"Colonel Isaac Bledsoe's son, Anthony, and his nephew, Anthony, were both killed shortly afterwards, in this neighborhood, while going to school, and were scalped by the Indians.

"General Robertson, who was a warm personal friend of the Bledsoes, and felt their loss deeply, was aroused by these tragedies, and led an expedition to the Tennessee river and destroyed, utterly, the Indian villages at Nickojack, and killed all the Indians they could find. Then, and not till then, did Sumner county have rest. But till the great Tennessean, Andrew Jackson, gave the final blow with Sumner and other troops, at Tohopeka, or Horseshoe Bend, on the Tallapoosa, was the race question between the Caucasian and Indian finally settled.

"No wonder when we consider these tragedies so frequently enacted by the rifle and tomahawk and scalping knife, that the common saying among the settlers was 'There's no good Injun but a dead Injun.' Even the African slaves of the settlers were eager to fight the Indians, and I have heard my father relate, with zest, how a faithful negro slave killed an old Indian chief, somewhere in this neighborhood, as the chief was climbing over a rail fence.

WERE SLAVE OWNERS.

"These men, whose memory we perpetuate today, and who fell in the most implacable of all war—a race war—were the owners of African slaves, and may the race contest which the freedom of the blacks has inaugurated never reach the acute stage as that between the white race and the Indians or red race.

"Now let me notice some of the companions of the Bledsoes. There was Hugh Rogan, the gallant Irishman, the companion of Grattan, who fled to America in order to breathe the air of freedom. He was always ready for service, always ready to fight the Indians and help protect his neighbors. He was with the Halls when, in the summer of 1788, they moved from their place, about a mile from here, to Colonel

Isaac Bledsoe's fort, in order to escape the Indians, who, by ambush, killed and scalped the father, Major Hall, and two of his sons, and would have killed young William Hall, a boy of 13, and afterwards Governor of Tennessee, but the boy, having barely escaped the tomahawk that killed his father, did some running through the cane and over the open ground in order to escape the Indians, such as no Olympic runners ever excelled. The mother saved her life by catching the mane of the swift and powerful horse she was riding and bolting right through the file of Indians till she got to the fort, escaping both tomahawk and bullet.

"The names Shelby, Neely, Alexander, Deshas, Wilsons, Peyton, Winchester, Smith, Blackmore, Douglass, Cage, Donoho, and many others, were sooner or later associated with the Bledsoes, and as a result of their united sacrifices and labors you have now this unsurpassed, well-developed country, whose prospects for the future are as bright as the sacrifices of the past have been great. May this monument serve only to arouse and preserve noble memories and sacrifices, and may the silent influences which proceed from it tend to elevate patriotism and every high sentiment of humanity and progress."

HON. JAMES W. BLACKMORE SPEAKS

The address of Hon. James Blackmore, of Gallatin, was one of peculiar force and eloquence, and before beginning the historic sketch of the Bledsoe brothers he spoke in eloquent and inspiring words of Senator Carmack, avowing that his death would mean the triumph of the cause for which he lived, and again the audience applauded enthusiastically.

Adding to the impressiveness of the program was the singing of "The Hills of Tennessee" by a chorus of young ladies and the opening song "America" and the closing song "Sweet Bye and Bye" were also very much enjoyed.

The closing prayer was offered by the Rev. Willie Wilkes, whose beautiful prayer at the funeral of General Bate was widely copied and commented upon. Mr. Wilkes, it will be remembered, baptized General Bate a few years before his death in the clear waters of Bledsoe's Creek, which flows peacefully through the ravines near where the monument was dedicated yesterday.

HON. BLACKMORE'S ADDRESS.

Hon. James Blackmore, one of the best known lawyers at the Gallatin bar, spoke in part, as follows:

"This is an unusual occurrence, remarkable in the fact that today the descendants of two pioneer heroes, Anthony Bledsoe and Isaac Bledsoe, brothers, with the descendants of relatives and friends of these pioneers, and their friends and acquaintances, have assembled for the purpose of unveiling a monument and to do honor to the memory of these worthy patriarchs, 115 years in the one case and 120 years in the other, after they had, respectively, laid down their lives for the advancement of civilization and for the purpose of giving to their contemporaries and to those who should come after them this beautiful and fertile section of country, wherein peace, progress and prosperity now reign.

"Like Abram of old, each of these pioneers heard and recognized a call to go out into a strange land to subdue it, and make it fit for an inheritance of future generations. Each was peculiarly fitted for subjugating the wilderness and laying the foundations of social order and civil government, and each became, in the language of a fellow pioneer, 'a file leader among the people,' and each was a tower of moral strength to those who with them had plunged into the wilderness and braved the hardships and dangers of border life and Indian warfare to establish settlements and to act as the advance guard of western civilization.

"They were 'notables, or general arbitrators, as the judiciary of the Cumberland country was called, but they seem to have been more than judges; they were legislators, too, who prescribed the rules and regulations for civil conduct of the settlers during the time the parent state, being engrossed with the affairs of the Revolutionary War raging within its borders, left these far away subjects or settlers on her territory to be a law unto themselves.' And after the parent state turned its attention to these struggling and neglected subjects and extended the ægis of her laws and courts over this territory and its inhabitants and accorded to them the right of representation in its law-making bodies, these brothers were selected to participate and aid in enacting laws and dispensing justice through the organized courts.

"Anthony Bledsoe was a practical surveyor, in whom much confidence was reposed, and in 1771 he examined the boundary line between Virginia and North Carolina (then), but now between Kentucky and Tennessee. He was a captain from Virginia in the Continental army.

"In 1783 he was a commissioner of the State of North Carolina to lay off lands granted to officers in the Revolutionary war.

"In 1787 he was a member of the legislature of North Carolina. In 1788, July 20, he was killed by the Indians in an attack, at night, on Bledsoe fort, built by his brother Isaac, which stood on, or near, the spot where we are now assembled. He had two sons, Thomas and Anthony, killed by the Indians.

LEADING MAN.

"Next to Robertson, Colonel Anthony Bledsoe was the most valuable member of the Cumberland community. He was an educated man of cool courage, sound judgment and wide experience in public affairs, having held various civil and military positions of importance in older settlements. His relations with Sevier, Governor Caswell and other prominent men were of an intimate character; but, for many years he had been the bosom friend and trusted counselor of Robertson, who, since Bledsoe's arrival on the Cumberland, had acted in no affair of importance without his advice and co-operation. In the event of Robertson's death he was probably the only man in the settlement who could have brought it safely out of the fiery ordeal through which it was passing.

"Isaac Bledsoe, in 1771, came to this section of the country with Kasper Mansker and others, known as the 'Long Hunters,' on a hunting and prospecting expedition, 'to spy out the land,' and, like Caleb of old, he took back with him to the older settlements such a good impression of the country and gave such glowing accounts of the abundance of game and the fertility of the soil, that he determined himself and he induced others to 'go up and possess it.' When he returned to the Cumberland country is not definitely stated, but presumably as early as 1779.

"In 1784 he built 'Bledsoe's Fort,' on, or near, the ground on which we are assembled today. In 1786 Sumner county was laid off and established by the Legislature of North Carolina, and he was one of the first magistrates of this county. April 9, 1793, he was killed by Indians while working in his field, which is adjoining the site of this monument, dedicated today. His son, Anthony Bledsoe, Jr., had met his death at the hands of these foes prior to this date.

"Each of the Bledsoes had sons in school as early as 1784, and it was while on their way to school they were killed by Indians. This is the first historical record of any school in this section. The laws or regulations prescribed by the 'notables,' who were the lawmakers for the settlers on the Cumberland river, were based on temperance and good morals.

Spring From Which the Inmates of Colonel Isaac Bledsoe's Fort Procured Water

BLEDSOE MONUMENT

TEMPERANCE SENTIMENT.

"At that early day we find that they promulgated prohibitive laws against the manufacture and sale of intoxicating liquor. In the year 1785 an ordinance was passed that there shall be no distillation of liquors in Davidson county, and Colonel James Robertson, the father of the Cumberland settlement, declared that 'the conversion of crops of grain into spiritous liquors is an unwarranted perversion, unserviceable to white men and devilish for Indians,' and expressed the hope 'that there may never be any waste of grain by distillation or waste of estates and ruin of soul by drinking liquor.'

"This county and State have held in grateful remembrance the distinguished services and high character of these brother pioneers. The State has honored them with the name of a county, the county has perpetuated their name in the name of a noble stream and in institutions of learning, and the county seat by one of its chief avenues. The streams are made to proclaim their fame as they rush with swollen tide to the sea as well as when appropriated as the motive power of mills and manufactories: the schoolhouses, like beacon lights, lend lustre to their names; the atmosphere here is made vibrant with the praise of the Bledsoe's, and the example which they have set by their courageous devotion to duty, wisdom displayed in the discharge of public trust and the sacrifices they made for others encouraged their contemporaries and have borne good fruit in the generations which have followed them.

"Their descendants in this and other States have proven that they were worthy sons of illustrious sires, and the story of their lives has inspired the men of this and other sections to deeds of valor and endurance in times of war and to lofty ambition and high ideals of statesmanship and public service in times of peace.

"Let us rejoice then today that we can, with sentiments of gratitude and with reverence for their memories, participate in these exercises of unveiling this monument to mark the hallowed ground where these worthy patriarchs have slept for these more than one hundred years. They were careless, perhaps, of monuments by their graves when they lived and wrought, but they have built one themselves in the world—a monument by which men are taught to remember not where they died, but where they lived."

Professor H. H. Donaho, who acted as master of ceremonies at the dedication exercises, is a great grandson of Billie Donaho, a pioneer to Sumner county, and a friend and companion of the Bledsoes. On one occasion he had his hat knocked off by an Indian tomahawk, near Bledsoe's Lick, but escaped being hurt. On another occasion when the Indians attacked the fort, he had the presence of mind to extinguish the fire, which, by its light, favored the attacking party.

Professor Donaho has for the past several years been principal of Bledsoe Academy on the grounds of which the monument was built.

GENEALOGY OF THE BLEDSOE FAMILY

FIRST GENERATION.

No. 1.

George Bledsoe was the first of the family of which we can find any trace in America. He lived in Northumberland county, Virginia. His will was probated in that county July 23, 1704. Doubtless had other children, but the only one we can find was—

2   Abraham Bledsoe.

SECOND GENERATION.

No. 2.

Abraham Bledsoe was probably born in Northumberland county, Virginia, but after his marriage settled in that part of Orange county which

GENEALOGY OF THE BLEDSOE FAMILY 103

was afterwards embraced in Culpeper county. Among his children were—

3   Anthony Bledsoe.
4   Isaac Bledsoe.
5   Abraham Bledsoe, Jr.

THIRD GENERATION.
No. 3.

Col. Anthony Bledsoe, son of Abraham Bledsoe, was born in what is now Culpeper county, Virginia, then Orange county, in 1733. About 1760 he married Mary Ramsey, of Augusta county. He was killed by Indians at Bledsoe's Lick, Summer county, Tennessee, on July 20, 1788. Mary Ramsey was born in Augusta county, Virginia in 1734, and died in Sumner county, Tennessee, in 1808. They had eleven children—five sons and six daughters, one of which was born four months after the death of Colonel Bledsoe. Their children were—

6   Abraham Bledsoe, born in Virginia about 1762.
7   Thomas Bledsoe.
8   Sarah Bledsoe, born in Virginia in 1763.
9   Anthony Bledsoe, Jr.
10 Isaac Bledsoe.
11 Henry Ramsey Bledsoe.
12 Rachael Bledsoe.
13 Polly Bledsoe, born in Virginia in 1780.
14 Betsy Bledsoe.
15 Prudence Bledsoe.
16 Susan Bledsoe.

FOURTH GENERATION.
No. 6.

Abraham Bledsoe, son of Colonel Anthony and Mary (Ramsey) Bledsoe, was born in what is now Fincastle county, Virginia, about 1762; came to Sumner county, Tennessee, with his parents in 1781. He served as captain of a company in the Tennessee Regulars under Jackson in the Creek War. He was in the battle of the Horseshoe, and the several battles at New Orleans in December, 1814, and January, 1815. He married Amelia Weathered, daughter of Frank Weathered, a soldier of the Revolutionary War. Her mother was a sister of General Sumter of South Carolina. Died on his farm in Sumner county, and was buried at Hopewell church. They had children—

17   David Bledsoe; died young.
18   A daughter, who married Alfred Shoulders and moved to West Tennessee. No other information.

No. 7.

Thomas Bledsoe, son of Colonel Anthony and Mary (Ramsey) Bledsoe, was born in Virginia about 1774. Was killed by Indians near Greenfield, Sumner county, Tennessee, on October 2, 1794. Unmarried.

No. 8.

Sarah Bledsoe, daughter of Colonel Anthony and Mary (Ramsey) Bledsoe, was born in Virginia in 1763. Came to Sumner county, Tenn., in 1781. Married David Shelby. Died March 11, 1852, aged 89 years. David Shelby was a son of Captain John Shelby, of Washington county, Virginia. He was born in Virginia about 1763. Of his early life but little is known. He was a soldier in the regiment which Isaac Shelby commanded in the battle of King's Mountain. He married Sarah, the oldest daughter of Colonel Anthony Bledsoe, in 1781, and the same year came with the Bledsoe family to Sumner county. When the county was organized he was chosen Clerk of the court, and held that position until his death in 1822. Had children—

19   John Shelby, born May 24, 1785.
20   Anthony Bledsoe Shelby, born January 15, 1789.

GENEALOGY OF THE BLEDSOE FAMILY 105

21 Philip Davies Shelby, born March 7, 1791, died May 27, 1799.
22 Priscilla Shelby, born March 8, 1793.
23 Lucinda Shelby, born March 24, 1795.
24 James Shelby, born July 13, 1797, died August 28, 1797.

MRS. SARAH BLEDSOE SHELBY

25 Nellie Shelby, born January 14, 1799.
26 David Davies Shelby, born July 15, 1801, died August 2, 1805.
27 Orville Shelby, born January 21, 1803.
28 Sarah Bledsoe Shelby, born January 21, 1806.
29 Albert Shelby, born May 25, 1808.

No. 9.

Anthony Bledsoe, Jr., son of Colonel Anthony and Mary (Ramsey) Bledsoe, was born in Virginia; was killed by Indians near Rock Castle, the residence of General Daniel Smith, where he was boarding and attending school, on April 21, 1794. Unmarried.

No. 10.

Isaac Bledsoe, son of Colonel Anthony and Mary (Ramsey) Bledsoe, was born in Washington county, Virginia; came to Sumner county, Tennessee, with his parents in 1781. Married Margaret Neely. Had children—

30   William Bledsoe. No information.
31   Abraham Bledsoe. No information.
32   Zurithy Bledsoe. Never married. Died in California.
33   Oscar F. Bledsoe.
34   Anthony C. Bledsoe.
35   Amanda Bledsoe.
36   Gertrude Bledsoe.

No. 11.

Henry Ramsey Bledsoe, son of Colonel Anthony and Mary (Ramsey) Bledsoe, was born in Washington county, Virginia. Came to Sumner county, Tennessee with his parents in 1781. He served as a private in brother Abraham's company in the Creek War and at New Orleans. Died at Natchez, Mississippi, with yellow fever about 1738, while on a trading expedition. His companion on the journey was attacked by the disease, and Mr. Bledsoe remained and nursed him until he had recovered, when he himself was stricken. His comrade whom he had so generously cared for deserted him to die among strangers. He married Nancy Gillespie. Had children—

37   Isaac Newton Bledsoe.

GENEALOGY OF THE BLEDSOE FAMILY 107

38 Thomas Jefferson Bledsoe.
39 George Washington Bledsoe.
40 Richard Bledsoe.
41 Henry Ramsey Bledsoe, Jr.
42 Polly Bledsoe.
43 Ophelia Bledsoe.
44 James Bledsoe.

No. 12.

Rachel Bledsoe, daughter of Colonel Anthony and Mary (Ramsey) Bledsoe, was born in Washington county, Virginia. Came to Sumner county, Tennessee, with her parents in 1781. Married William Neely, a brother of Margaret Neely, who had married her brother, Isaac. Had children—

45 Anthony Neely.
46 Joseph Neely.
47 Polly Neely.
48 Caroline Neely.

No. 13.

Polly Bledsoe, daughter of Colonel Anthony and Mary (Ramsey) Bledsoe, was born in Washington county, Virginia, about 1780. Came to Sumner county, Tennessee, with her parents in 1781. In 1799 she married James Weatherred, son of Frank Weatherred, a Revolutionary soldier, and who was under General La Fayette at the seige of Yorktown. After the close of the Revolutionary War he married a sister of General Sumter, of South Carolina. James Weatherred was for many years a justice of the peace in Sumner county. In 1826 he removed to Mississippi, where he remained several years, then returned to Sumner county. Had children—

49 Emma Weatherred.
50 Richard Weatherred.
51 Mildred Weatherred.
52 Mary Weatherred.
53 Sarah Shelby Weatherred.

54 Charlotte Weatherred.
55 Bledsoe Weatherred. No information.
56 Marcus Weatherred. No information.
57 Abraham Weatherred. No information.

No. 14.

Betsy Bledsoe, daughter of Colonel Anthony and Mary (Ramsey) Bledsoe, married James Clendening, who wrote the will of her father after he had received his mortal wound from an Indian rifle. Had children—

58 Thomas Clendening. Was killed. Never married.
59 Anthony Clendening.
60 Richard Clendening.
61 Patsey Clendening.
62 Elizabeth Clendening.
63 Rachael Clendening.

No. 15.

Prudence Bledsoe, daughter of Colonel Anthony and Mary (Ramsey) Bledsoe, married Captain Joseph Sewell. No information.

No. 16.

Susan Bledsoe, daughter of Colonel Anthony and Mary (Ramsey) Bledsoe, married William Penny. No information.

FIFTH GENERATION.

No. 19.

John Shelby, son of David and Sarah (Bledsoe) Shelby, was the first white child to be born in what is now Sumner county, Tennessee, on May 24, 1785. He received a liberal education, then went to Philadelphia, where he studied medicine, and where he married Anna Maria Minnick. After his return to Tennessee, he located on a large tract of land on the east side of the Cumberland river, where East Nashville now is. He

Genealogy of the Bledsoe Family

was for many years one of the most useful and enterprising citizens of Davidson county. He was the founder of Shelby Medical College, afterwards merged into the medical department of the University of Nashville. He was the prime mover in the company which built the first suspension bridge at Nashville. He was one of the founders of St. Ann's Episcopal church. It was for him that Shelby avenue was so named. He was a warm personal friend of Sam Houston and other men of prominence of his day. His residence stood near the centre of Woodland street, directly in front of the present residence of Hor. A. V. Goodpasture. Had children —

64 Anna Shelby.
65 Priscilla Shelby.

No. 20.

Anthony Bledsoe Shelby, son of David and Sarah (Bledsoe) Shelby, was born in Sumner county on January 15, 1789. Married Marian Winchester, daughter of Stephen Winchester. He studied law, and after practicing at Gallatin for some time removed to Texas and assisted in gaining independence for that State. He was one of the Justices of the Supreme Court of the Republic of Texas, and was prominent in other ways. Later he removed to Mississippi and settled at Brandon, where he died about 1855. Had children—

66 Sallie Shelby, born in Sumner county, May 10, 1812.
67 David Shelby, born in Sumner county, May 7, 1814.
68 Marian Jane Shelby, born July 31, 1816; died September 6, 1817.
69 Priscilla Kate Shelby, born July 15, 1818.
70 Annie W. Shelby, born July 10, 1820; died August 27, 1821.
71 Julia Winchester Shelby, born July 15, 1822.

110 HISTORIC SUMNER COUNTY, TENN.

72 Stephen Winchester Shelby, born July 22, 1824; died July 15, 1828.
73 Winchester Bledsoe Shelby, born January 18, 1827.

JUDGE ANTHONY BLEDSOE SHELBY

74 Lucinda Henderson Shelby, born December 31, 1829.
75 Marian P. Shelby, born November 10, 1831.
76 Bennett Henderson Shelby, born March 24, 1834.
77 Antonette Marian Shelby, born November 16, 1834; died in 1837.
78 Nelson Shelby, died in 1838.

GENEALOGY OF THE BLEDSOE FAMILY 111

No. 22.

Priscilla Shelby, daughter of David and Sarah (Bledsoe) Shelby, was born in Sumner county. Married Henry L. Douglass, a native of Sumner county. He was a merchant in Vicksburg, Mississippi, where he died in 1854. Had children—

79   Priscilla Douglass.

After the death of his wife, Priscilla Shelby, Henry L. Douglass married Miss Alcorn, sister of the late Governor Alcorn, of Mississippi. After her death he married Mrs. Jane Crabb, mother of Henry Crabb, of Sonora fame. Colonel Douglass was one of the largest merchants in Vicksburg, and was owner of the first cotton compress in Mississippi.

No. 23.

Lucinda Shelby, daughter of David and Sarah (Bledsoe) Shelby, was born in Sumner county, March 24,1795. No information.

No. 25.

Nellie Shelby, daughter of David and Sarah (Bledsoe) Shelby, was born in Sumner county, at Spencer's Choice, January 14, 1799. Married General Robert Desha, son of Robert Desha. General Desha's mother was, before her marriage, Eleanor Wheeler, who was a daughter of Joseph Wheeler, a Captain in the Revolutionary War. He served as a Captain and a Brigade-Major in the war of 1812. Was a representative in Congress from Tennessee from 1827 to 1831. He was for some time a merchant in Gallatin and later removed to Mobile, Alabama, where he conducted a flourishing business until his death, February 8, 1849. Had children—

80   Caroline Desha.
81   Phoebe Ann Desha.
82   Julia Desha. No information.

No. 27.

Orville Shelby, son of David and Sarah (Bledsoe) Shelby, was born in Sumner county on January 21, 1803. Married Caroline Winchester, daughter of General James Winchester, and soon

DOCTOR THOMAS FEARN

thereafter removed to Lexington Kentucky. Had children—

83 Joseph Orville Shelby.
84 Carrie Shelby.
85 Isaac Shelby.

GENEALOGY OF THE BLEDSOE FAMILY 113

No. 28.

Sarah Bledsoe Shelby, Daughter of David and Sarah (Bledsoe) Shelby, was born in Sumner county, January 21, 1806. Married Dr. Thomas Fearn on February 26, 1822. Died May 22, 1842. Dr. Fearn was a son of Thomas Fearn, and was

MRS. MARIA ELIZA FEARN GARTH

born in Pittsylvania County, Virginia, November 15, 1789; died January 16, 1863. Had children—

86   Mary Fearn.
87   Sarah Fearn.
88   Kate Fearn.

89 Ada Fearn.
90 Maria Fearn.
91 Bernice Fearn. Never married.
92 Lucy Lee Fearn.

No. 29.

Albert Shelby, son of David and Sarah (Bledsoe) Shelby, was born in Sumner county, May 25, 1808. No information.

No. 33.

Oscar F. Bledsoe, son of Isaac and Margaret (Neely) Bledsoe, was born in Sumner county. He served as a commissioned officer in the Florida War. Studied law and removed to Columbus Mississippi, where he became prominent in his profession, and where he accumulated a large fortune. He married Mary Hardwick. Had children—

93 Randall Bledsoe. Died young.
94 Gertrude Bledsoe.
95 Isaac Bledsoe. Died in 1857, while at school in Lebanon, Tennessee.
96 Oscar F. Bledsoe, second.

No. 34.

Anthony Clinton Bledsoe, son of Isaac and Margaret (Neely) Bledsoe, was born in Sumner county. Married Elizabeth Green and removed to California. Had children—

97   Margaret Bledsoe. No information.
98   Linn Bledsoe. No information.
99   Jefferson Davis Bledsoe. No information.
100 William Oscar Bledsoe. No information.
101 Carson Bledsoe.

No. 35.

Amanda Bledsoe, daughter of Isaac and Margaret (Neely) Bledsoe, married Lucellius Winchester. No issue.

No. 36.

Gertrude Bledsoe, daughter of Isaac and Margaret (Neely) Bledsoe, was born in Sumner county. Married a Mr. Straughton and removed to California. No information.

No. 37.

Isaac Newton Bledsoe, son of Henry Ramsey and Nancy (Gillespie) Bledsoe, was born in Sumner county. Married and removed to Lafayette county, Missouri. Had children—

102   Elizabeth Bledsoe. No information.
103   Amanda Bledsoe. No information.
104   Ophelia Bledsoe. No information.
105   Francis Bledsoe. No information.
106   Cordelia Bledsoe. No information.
107   Sarah Bledsoe. No information.
108   Clara Bledsoe. No information.
109   Callie Bledsoe. No information
110   Graham Bledsoe. Killed in the Civil War.
111   Dick Bledsoe. Killed in the Civil War.

No. 38.

Thomas Jefferson Bledsoe, son of Henry Ramsey and Nancy (Gillespie) Bledsoe, was born in Sumner county. Married a Miss White and removed to Missouri. Had children—

112   William Bledsoe. No information.
113   Abraham Bledsoe. No information.
114   Isaac Bledsoe. No information.
115   Rina Bledsoe. No information.
116   A daughter, name unknown. No information.

No. 39.

George Washington Bledsoe, son of Henry Ramsey and Nancy (Gillespi) Bledsoe, was born in Sumner county. Married Martha Lauderdale and removed to Missouri. Had children—

117   John Bledsoe. Died in LaFayette county, Missouri.

118 James Bledsoe. Killed in the Civil War.
119 Joseph Bledsoe. Removed to Texas.
120 Bettie Bledsoe. No information.
121 Laura Bledsoe. No information.
122 Richard Bledsoe. No information.

No. 40.

Richard Bledsoe, son of Henry Ramsey and Nancy (Gillespie) Bledsoe. No information.

No. 41.

Henry Ramsey Bledsoe, Jr., son of Henry Ramsey and Nancy (Gillespie) Bledsoe, was born in Sumner county. Married Nancy Byrns and removed to Missouri. He was murdered in Texas before the Civil War. Had children—

123 Abraham Bledsoe. No information.
124 Plunk Bledsoe. Killed in the Lawrence raid.
125 Isaac Bledsoe. Murdered by Federal soldiers in 1862.
126 Henry Ramsey Bledsoe, third. Murdered by Federal soldiers after he had been wounded and surrendered.

No. 42.

Polly Bledsoe, daughter of Henry Ramsey and Nancy (Gillespie) Bledsoe. Married, first, Charles Bealer; second, Alexander Baskerville. No information.

No. 43.

Ophelia Bledsoe, daughter of Henry Ramsey and Nancy (Gillespie) Bledsoe. Was a famous beauty. Married Rev. George Gillespie. No information.

No. 44.

James Bledsoe, son of Henry Ramsey and Nancy (Gillespie) Bledsoe, was born in Sumner county. Married Harriet Armstrong, of the same county. Had children:

Genealogy of the Bledsoe Family

127 Thomas Jefferson Bledsoe.
128 William Henry Bledsoe.
129 Lydia Melvina Bledsoe. Died in Nashville at the age of 10 years.
130 James Bledsoe, Jr. Died in Nashville at the age of 12 years.
131 Eliza Ann Bledsoe.

No. 45.

Anthony Neely, son of William and Rachael (Bledsoe) Neely. Married Margaret Read. No information.

No. 46.

Joseph Neely, son of William and Rachael (Bledsoe) Neely. Married Miss Deloach. Had children—

132 Julia Neely. No information.

No. 47.

Polly Neely, daughter of William and Rachael (Bledsoe) Neely. Married Charles Blakemore. No information.

No. 48.

Caroline Neely, daughter of William and Rachael (Bledsoe) Neely. Married a Mr. Greer, of Memphis. Had children—

133 J. Neely Greer. No information.

No. 49.

Emma Weatherred, daughter of James and Polly (Bledsoe) Weatherred, was born in Sumner county. Married, first, Mr. Frainham; second, Mr. McLeod; third, Mr. Pratt. This branch of the family lived in Mississippi. No other information.

No. 50.

Richard Weatherred, son of James and Polly (Bledsoe) Weatherred, was born in Sumner county. Married a Miss King, of Alabama. No information.

No. 51.

Mildred Weatherred, daughter of James and Polly (Bledsoe) Weatherred. Married a Mr. Buck of Mississippi. No information. Has numerous descendants, among them Mr. J. G. H. Buck, of Texas, and his two sons, Major Buck and Lieutenant Buck of the United States Army.

No. 52.

Mary Weatherred, daughter of James and Polly (Bledsoe) Weatherred, was born in Sumner county. Married, first, Mr. Briggs; second, Mr. Kelly, third, James Blair, a native of New York, who was postmaster at Tuskaloosa, Alabama, in the early seventies. She died at Tuskaloosa in 1874. Had children by Kelly—

134   A daughter, who married a Mr. Skelton, Sheriff of Tuskaloosa county.
135   Alice Kelly. Married Judge Ford. No issue.

No. 53.

Sarah Shelby Weatherred, daughter of James and Polly (Bledsoe) Weatherred, was born in Sumner county. Married William L. Malone, son of Hal. Malone, a Revolutionary soldier, who came to Tennessee from Petersburg, Virginia, about 1798. Had children—

136   Harriet Malone.
137   Bettie Malone.
138   Mildred Malone.
139   Susan Malone.
140   Mary Catherine Malone.
141   Thomas Malone. Never married.
142   McMurray Malone. Never married.
143   John Wesley Malone.

No. 54.

Charlotte Weatherred, daughter of James and Polly (Bledsoe) Weatherred. Married Mr. Massengill, of Mississippi. Has descendants living

GENEALOGY OF THE BLEDSOE FAMILY 119

in Texas, among them Mr. J. A. Massengill, of Diboll. No information.

No. 59.

Anthony Clendening, son of James and Betsey (Bledsoe) Clendening. Married Miss Patterson and removed to Arkansas. Had a son—

144   Fulton Clendening, who lived at Helena. No information.

No. 60.

Richard Clendening, son of James and Betsey (Bledsoe) Clendening. Married a Miss Patterson and removed to Giles county. Had children—

145   John C. Clendening. No information.
146   James Clendening. No information.
147   Violet Clendening. No information.
148   David Clendening. No information.

No. 62.

Elizabeth Clendening, daughter of James and Betsey (Bledsoe) Clendening. Married John Patterson. No information.

No. 63.

Rachel Clendening, daughter of James and Betsey (Bledsoe) Clendening. Married William Patterson and settled in Giles county. Had children—

149   John Clendening Patterson.
150   Maria Henderson Patterson.
151   William Bledsoe Patterson. Never married.
152   David Shelby Patterson.
153   James Henderson Patterson. Never married.
154   Martha Eliza Patterson.
155   Logan Madison Patterson.
156   Margaretta Violet Patterson. Never married.

SIXTH GENERATION.

No. 64.

Ann Shelby, daughter of Dr. John and Anna Maria (Minnick) Shelby. Married Washington Barrow, who was born in Davidson county, Tennessee, October 5, 1817. He was a lawyer by profession, and a man of affairs. He was the first President of the Nashville Gas Company. He was Minister to Portugal from 1841 to 1844, and a Representative in Congress from 1847 to 1849. Was for a time editor of the Nashville Banner. Was State Senator in 1860 and 1861. Was identified with the Confederacy during the Civil War. Was arrested by order of Andrew Johnson, but soon afterwards was released by order of the President. Died in St. Louis October 19, 1866. Had children—

157 John Shelby Barrow.
158 A daughter, who died young.

No. 65.

Priscilla Shelby, daughter of Dr. John and Anna Maria (Minnick) Shelby. Married David Williams, of West Tennessee. Had children—

159 John Shelby Williams.
160 Joseph Minnick Williams.
161 Anna Minnick Williams.

No. 66.

Sallie Shelby, daughter of Judge Anthony Bledsoe and Marian (Winchester) Shelby, was born in Sumner county, May 10, 1812. Married Dr. Miles Selden Watkins, of Mississippi. Had children—

162 Selden Watkins.
163 Leigh Watkins.
164 Marian Shelby Watkins.
165 Erskine Watkins.

GENEALOGY OF THE BLEDSOE FAMILY   121

166 Nettie Shelby Watkins.
167 Fearn Watkins. No information

No. 67.

David Shelby, son of Judge Anthony Bledsoe and Marian (Winchester) Shelby, was born at Gallatin, May 7, 1814. Married Mary T. Bouldin, January 14, 1837. Had children—

168 Anthony Bouldin Shelby. Born October 10, 1845.
169 David D. Shelby, born October 24, 1847.
170 Maria Bledsoe Shelby.
171 Marian Winchester Shelby. No information.
172 Yancy Howard Shelby. No information.

No. 69.

Priscilla Kate Shelby, daughter of Judge Anthony Bledsoe and Marian (Winchester) Shelby, was born in Sumner county, July 15, 1818. Married J. C. P. Hammond, of Mississippi. Had children—

173 Eli Shelby Hammond.
174 F. McLaren Hammond.
175 Priscilla Hammond.

No. 71.

Julia Winchester Shelby, daughter of Judge Anthony Bledsoe and Marian (Winchester) Shelby, was born at Gallatin, July 15, 1822. Married Mr. Ware, a lawyer, of Jackson, Mississippi. Had children—

176 Winchester Bledsoe Ware. Died young.

No. 73.

Winchester Bledsoe Shelby, son of Judge Anthony Bledsoe and Marian (Winchester) Shelby, was born at Dixon Springs, Tennessee, January 18, 1827. He served in the Confederate Army,

with the rank of Colonel. Married Margaret Alexander. Had children—
177 Bledsoe Alexander Shelby.
178 William H. Shelby.
179 Edwin Shelby.
180 David Shelby.
Had daughters, but have no information,

No. 79.

Priscilla Douglass, daughter of Henry L. and Priscilla (Shelby) Douglass, married Dr. Robert C. K. Martin, who was born in Nashville, August 9, 1808. After receiving a classical education he graduated from Franklin Medical College, Philadelphia, with distinguished honors, then successfully practiced medicine for approximately forty years, winning eminence in his profession, and was noted for his philanthropy. His life and character can best be described by the following epitaph on his monument, which was erected to his memory by his female patients:

"An accomplished physician, he gave his life
To the afflicted. Honored by his bretheren,
And beloved by the public.
Of men the most genial and gentle,
Of physicians the most generous and laborious."

He died in Nashville, February 9, 1872. Had children—

181 Bettie Martin.
182 Mary Shelby Martin. Never married.
183 Alice Martin.
184 Henry Douglass Martin.
185 Player Martin. Never married.
186 Robert C. K. Martin, Jr.
187 Maria Martin.
188 Shelby Martin. Never married.

GENEALOGY OF THE BLEDSOE FAMILY   123

No. 80.

Caroline Desha, daughter of General Robert and Nellie (Shelby) Desha. Married, first, Robert Barney; second, Lloyd Abbott. No information.

No. 81.

Phoebe Ann Desha, daughter of General Robert and Nellie (Shelby) Desha, married Dr. Murray Forbes Smith, of Mobile, Alabama. Had children—

189   Armide Smith. No information.
190   Desha Smith. No information.
191   Alva Erskine Smith.
192   Mary Virginia Smith.
193   Florence Smith.

No. 83.

General Joseph Orville Shelby, son of Orville and Caroline (Winchester) Shelby, was born at Lexington, Kentucky, in 1831. Received a liberal education and engaged in mercantile pursuits. Removed to Waverly, Missouri, in 1850, and commenced the manufacture of baled rope. Soon afterwards the Kansas trouble broke out, and he returned to Kentucky, where he organized a company for territorial service. When quiet had been restored he returned to his rope factory. At the breaking out of the Civil War he raised a company of cavalry and entered the Confederate service with the rank of Captain. In 1862 he recruited a regiment, of which he was chosen Colonel, and was given command of a brigade, of which his regiment formed a part. In March, 1864, he was commissioned a Brigadier General, and later a Major General. "Shelby's Brigade was one of the most famous commands in the Confederate service. General Shelby was a born leader of men. Brave, daring, chivalrous, and knew not the meaning of the word fear. He was the idol of his men, and was feared and dreaded by his country's foes. He was to the Trans-Mississippi department what Forrest was to the East. No braver man than 'Old Joe Shelby,' ever drew a sword." In 1893 he was appointed United States Marshall by President Cleveland, and held that office until his death, February 13, 1897, at his home in Adrian, Missouri.

No information as to his marriage and descendants.

No. 84.

Carrie Shelby, daughter of Orville and Caroline (Winchester) Shelby. Married Henry Blood. Had children—

194	Henry Blood.	Dead.
195	Lawton Blood.	No information.
196	May Blood.	
197	Laura Blood.	
198	Olga Blood.	No information.
199	Maude Blood.	

No. 85.

Isaac Shelby, son of Orville and Caroline (Winchester) Shelby, a younger brother of General Joe O. Shelby, was born in Lexington, Kentucky. Removed to Missouri. He served in the Confederate Army as color-bearer in Gordon's Brigade, in the Trans-Mississippi department, and was distinguished for his daring. No other information.

No. 86.

Mary Fearn, daughter of Dr. Thomas and Sarah Bledsoe (Shelby) Fearn. Married Gustavus L. Mastin. Had children—

200	Arabella Mastin.	Never married.
201	Thomas Mastin.	
202	Frank Mastin.	Never married.

GENEALOGY OF THE BLEDSOE FAMILY 125

203 James Mastin.. No information.
204 Sallie Shelby Mastin.
205 Gustavus L. Mastin, Jr.

No. 87.

Sarah Fearn, daughter of Dr. Thomas and Sarah Bledsoe (Shelby) Fearn. Married Colonel William F. Barry. Had children—

206 William Shelby Barry.

No. 88.

Kate Fearn, daughter of Dr. Thomas and Sarah Bledsoe (Shelby) Fearn. Married Colonel Matthew Steele. Had children—

207 Thomas Steele.
208 Sallie Steele.
209 Eliza Steele. Never married.
210 George Steele. Never married.
211 Robert Steele.
212 Bernice Steele.
213 Matthew Steele, Jr.
214 Tracy Steele.
215 Katy Willie Steele. Never married.

No. 89.

Ada Fearn, daughter of Dr. Thomas and Sarah Bledsoe (Shelby) Fearn. Married Dr. George Steele. Had children—

216 Anna Steele.
217 Fearn Steele.

No. 90.

Maria Fearn, daughter of Dr. Thomas and Sarah Bledsoe (Shelby) Fearn. Married Colonel William W. Garth, of Huntsville, Alabama, who served on the staff of General Longstreet during the Civil War. He was born in Morgan County, Alabama; pursued classical studies at Lagrange and at Emory and Henry colleges, then studied law at the University of Virginia. Com-

menced practice at Huntsville. Elected a Representative in Congress in 1877, and served one term as a Democrat. Had children—
218   Winston F. Garth.

Hon. WILLIAM WILLIS GARTH

No. 92.

Lucy Lee Fearn, daughter of Dr. Thomas and Sarah Bledsoe (Shelby) Fearn, married George Mills. No issue.

No. 94.

Gertrude Bledsoe, daughter of Oscar F. and Mary (Hardwick) Bledsoe, married George B.

Schlater, of Plaquemine, Louisiana. Had children—
219   Rissa Desha Schlater. Unmarried.
220   Nannie Schlater.

OSCAR F. BLEDSOE, THIRD

No. 96.

Oscar F. Bledsoe, second, son of Oscar F. and Mary (Hardwick) Bledsoe, was born in Columbus, Mississippi, in 1840. Graduated with the first honors from the literary department of the University of Mississippi, and then from the law department. At the commencement of the Civil War he entered the Confederate service as a private in Blyth's battalion. Afterwards was appointed a member of the staff of General John Adams, who was killed at the battle of Franklin. After the close of the war he became a planter, and is now one of the largest cotton planters and one of the wealthiest men in his State. He resides in Grenada. He was the President of the Bledsoe Monument Association, which was organized in 1908, for the purpose of erecting a monument over the graves of Colonels Anthony and Isaac Bledsoe, at Bledsoe's Lick, Tennessee, and contributed for that purpose $500, double the sum given by all the other descendants of the two distinguished brothers. At the time this is written he is a candidate for Congress. He married, first, Florence Pegues, a member of an old Huguenot family, of South Carolina. Eleven months after their marriage his wife died, leaving a daughter—

221   Florence Bledsoe.

He then married Sallie Cannon, of Columbus, Mississippi, a member of the same family as Gov. Newton Cannon, of Tennessee. Had children—

222   Oscar F. Bledsoe, third.
223   Cannon Bledsoe. Died young.
224   Mary Lou Bledsoe.

No. 100.

William Oscar Bledsoe, son of Anthony C. and Margaret (Neely) Bledsoe, married and is living at Healdsburg, California. Has children—

225   Howard Bledsoe. No information.
226   Clifton Bledsoe. No information.
227   Alva Bledsoe. No information.

No. 101.

Carson Bledsoe, son of Anthony C. Bledsoe, is married and living at Healdsburg, California. Has a daughter—

228   Name unknown.

No. 112.

William Bledsoe, son of Thomas Jefferson and (White) Bledsoe, lived in Missouri. Unable to get information.

CLIFTON BLEDSOE
Healdsburg, California

No. 113.

Abraham Bledsoe, son of Thomas Jefferson and (White) Bledsoe, married Miss Lauderdale. No information.

No. 120.

Bettie Bledsoe, daughter of George Washington and Martha (Lauderdale) Bledsoe, married Thomas White, of Odessa, Missouri. Had one son—

229 Eugene White. No information.

No replies have been received from the Missouri branch of the Bledsoe family, and the little information received from various sources is not entirely reliable. But it is a well known fact that the Confederacy had no more gallant defenders in the Trans-Mississippi department than the Bledsoes. Captain Hiram Bledsoe's battery, which formed a part of Shelby's brigade, will not be forgotten as long as any of the Federal soldiers who served in the West are living. Captain Josiah Bledsoe was equally famous in the Missouri and Arkansas campaigns.

No. 127.

Thomas Jefferson Bledsoe, son of James and Harriet (Armstrong) Bledsoe, married Zettira Reed, and died March 2, 1908; buried at Atlanta, Georgia. Had children—

230 Eliza Ann Bledsoe.
231 Mollie Craig Bledsoe.
232 William Duncan Bledsoe.
233 Henry Perry Bledsoe.
234 Hattie Belle Bledsoe. Died at the age of eight months.
235 Thomas Mallory Bledsoe.
236 Pearl Hines Bledsoe, resides with her mother in Nashville.
237 Stella Brent Bledsoe.

No. 128.

William Henry Bledsoe, son of James and Harriet (Armstrong) Bledsoe, was a Captain in the Confederate Army, and was killed at Port Hudson, Louisiana, in 1864.

No. 131.

Eliza Ann Bledsoe, daughter of James and Harriet (Armstrong) Bledsoe, married John F. Locken. Died January 12, 1908. No issue.

No. 136.

Harriot Malone, daughter of William L. and Sarah Shelby (Weatherred) Malone, married Charles Goodall. No information.

No. 137.

Bettie Malone, daughter of William L. and Sarah Shelby (Weatherred) Malone, married George Wray, of Tipton county. No information.

No. 138.

Mildred Malone, daughter of William L. and Sarah Shelby (Weatherred) Malone, married Charles E. Smith, of Tipton county. Had children—

238 Fannie G. Smith, born in Tipton county, October 15, 1854. Unmarried.
239 John W. Smith, born May 24, 1857.
240 Charles E. Smith, Jr., born February 8, 1862. Never married.
241 Catherine Smith, born July 22, 1867.
242 Bettie Sue Smith, born September 11, 1869.
243 Blanch Smith, born May 9, 1872. Died March 12, 1879.

No. 139.

Susan Malone, daughter of William L. and Sarah Shelby (Weatherred) Malone, was born in Sumner county, March 4, 1840. Married Thomas W. Winn, of Tipton county, September 16, 1856. Died in Tipton county. Had children—

244 Sarah Winn.
245 Willie P. Winn.
246 Mary A. Winn.

132   HISTORIC SUMNER COUNTY, TENN.

No. 140.

Mary Catherine Malone, daughter of William L. and Sarah Shelby (Weatherred) Malone, was born in Sumner county, April 2, 1824. Married May 16, 1839, Halem L. Pursley, who was born January 2, 1814, and died at his farm near Union City, Tennessee, July 19, 1866. In 1871 Mary Catherine married Colonel Bert Stovall, who was Speaker of the Tennessee State Senate in 1861. She died at Union City, August 7, 1886. Had children—

247 Pattie J. Pursley, born October 1, 1840. Died in young womanhood.
248 Bettie E. Pursley, born September 3, 1842. Died young.
249 Brice W. Pursley, born June 6, 1844. Died when a young man.
250 Jennie S. Pursley, born February 25, 1846.
251 Laura Addie Pursley, born February 14, 1848.
252 Mildred Georgie Pursley, born August 2, 1851.

No. 143.

John Wesley Malone, son of William L. and Sarah Shelby (Weatherred) Malone, married Bettie Yost, of Kentucky. No information.

No. 149.

John Clendening Patterson, son of William and Rachael (Clendening) Patterson, married Eleanor Benson. Had children:

253 William Early Patterson. Never married.
254 Hugh Lawson Patterson.
255 Pressley Foster Patterson.
256 Mary Jane Patterson.
257 Eleanor Obedience Patterson.
258 Sue Patterson.
259 Benjamin Bledsoe Patterson.
260 Maria Patterson.

GENEALOGY OF THE BLEDSOE FAMILY 133

261 Mattie Bell Patterson.
262 Violet Rachael Patterson.
263 Francis Ann Patterson. Never married.
264 Joseph Thomas Patterson.

No. 150.

Maria Henderson Patterson, daughter of William and Rachael (Clendening) Patterson, married A. A. Sherrell. Had children—

265 William Sherrell. Never married.
266 Belle Sherrell.
267 After the death of A. A. Sherrell she married Drew M. Perkins. Had children—
269 Elizabeth Perkins.
270 Francis Perkins.
271 Vance Perkins.

No. 152.

David Shelby Patterson, son of William and Rachael (Clendening) Patterson, married Elizabeth Cheatham. Had children—

272 Maria Susan Patterson.
273 James Solomon Patterson. Never married.
274 Francis Elizabeth Patterson. Never married
275 Dr. William B. Patterson. Never married.
276 David Henderson Patterson.
277 Violet Patterson. Unmarried.
278 Cornelia Rebecca Patterson.
279 Virginia Belle Patterson.
280 Emma Josephine Patterson.

No. 154.

Martha Eliza Patterson, daughter of William and Rachael (Clendening) Patterson, married Dr. J. L. Sherrell. Had children—

281 D. C. Patterson Sherrell.
282 Violet Ann Sherrell.
283 Jennie Sherrell.
284 E. Matt Sherrell.
285 Benjamin Sherrell.

No. 155.

Logan Madison Patterson, son of William and Rachael (Clendening) Patterson, married Priscilla Leatherwood. He was shot at the battle of Shiloh, while commanding his company, and died two days later, April 8, 1862. Had children—

286   James Lawson Patterson.
287   William Shelby Patterson.
288   Logan Madison Patterson, Jr.

SEVENTH GENERATION.

No. 157.

John Shelby Barrow, son of Washington and Ann (Shelby) Barrow, married Miss Armstrong. Had children—

289   A daughter, who died young.
290   John Shelby Barrow, Jr.

No. 159.

John Shelby Williams, son of David and Priscilla (Shelby) Williams, married Mattie Sevier, daughter of Hon. Ambrose H. Sevier, formerly a Senator in Congress from Arkansas. Had children—

291   David Shelby Williams.
292   Juliette Sevier Williams; died young.
293   Maude Johnson Williams.
294   Anna Fassman Williams.
295   Ambrose Sevier Williams.

No. 160.

Joseph Minnick Williams, son of David and Priscilla (Shelby) Williams, married Emily Polk, daughter of General Lucius Polk, of Maury county. Had children—

297   Emily Williams. Died young.
298   Henry Yeateman Williams.
299   Joseph Minnick Williams, Jr.

GENEALOGY OF THE BLEDSOE FAMILY 135

300 Anna Maria Williams. Died young.
301 Eliza Williams. Died young.
302 Lucius Williams. Unmarried.
303 Priscilla Shelby Williams.

No. 161.

Anna Minnick Williams, daughter of David and Priscilla (Shelby) Williams, married Frank Fassman, of New Orleans. Had children—

304 Maria Shelby Fassman.
305 Anna Minnick Fassman.

No. 162.

Seldon Watkins, son of Dr. Miles Selden and Sallie (Shelby) Watkins.

No. 163.

Leigh Watkins, son of Dr. Miles Selden and Sallie (Shelby) Watkins, married Willie Kearney, of Madison county, Mississippi. Had children—

306 Mary Leigh Watkins.
307 Leigh Watkins.

No. 164.

Marian Shelby Watkins, daughter of Dr. Miles Seldon and Sally (Shelby) Watkins, married William Ewing Ross, of Madison county, Mississippi. Had children—

308 Willie B. Ross.
309 Marian Shelby Ross.
310 Sally Shelby Ross.
311 Watkins Ross.
312 James B. Ross.

No. 165.

Erskine Watkins, son of Dr. Miles Selden and Sally (Shelby) Watkins, married Alice Petrie, of Jackson, Mississippi, where they now reside. Had children—

313 Rosa Farrar Watkins.
314 Marian Shelby Watkins.

315 Erskine Watkins, Jr.
316 Herbert Petrie Watkins.
317 Alice Petrie Watkins.
An infant who died unnamed.

No. 166.

Nettie Shelby Watkins, daughter of Dr. Miles Seldon and Sally (Shelby) Watkins. Unmarried. Resides in Jackson, Mississippi.

No. 168.

Anthony Bouldin Shelby, son of David and Mary T. (Bouldin) Shelby was born December 10, 1845. No information.

No. 169.

David D. Shelby son of David and Mary T. (Bouldin) Shelby, was born October 24, 1847; married August 8, 1872, Annie Eason Davis. In 1882-86 he served in the Alabama Senate, was appointed Judge of the United States Court, Fifth Circuit, 1899. Resides in Huntsville, Alabama. No children.

No. 170.

Maria Bledsoe Shelby, daughter of David and Mary T. (Bouldin) Shelby, married May 14, 1871, Samuel Pleasants. Had children—

318 Nellie S. Pleasants, born May 2, 1872.
319 Marian Shelby Pleasants, born in March, 1874.

No. 173.

Eli Shelby Hammond, son of J. C. P. and Priscilla Kate (Shelby) Hammond, was born at Brandon, Mississippi, April 21, 1838. Served in the Confederate army, then studied law and practiced until 1878, when he was appointed United States District Judge for West Tennessee, and served to his death, December 17, 1904. He married January 13, 1864, Fannie Davis. Had children—

320 Patty Hammond.
321 Orlando D. Hammond.

Genealogy of the Bledsoe Family 137

No. 174.

F. McLaren Hammond, son of J. C. P. and Priscilla Kate (Shelby) Hammond, married Mary Mayes. Had children—

322 Cora Hammond.
323 Ferdinand McLaren Hammond.
324 Mary Hammond.
325 Harry Hammond.

No. 175.

Priscilla Shelby Hammond, daughter of J. C. P. and Priscilla Kate (Shelby) Hammond, married J. M. Scruggs, at Byhalia, Mississippi, October 19, 1864. Had children—

326 Francis Lynn Scruggs.
327 James Merriwether Scruggs.

No. 177.

Bledsoe Alexander Shelby, son of Winchester Bledsoe and Marian (Winchester) Shelby, was a merchant in St. Louis. No other information.

No. 178.

William H. Shelby, son of Winchester Bledsoe and Marian (Winchester) Shelby, was a merchant in St. Louis. No other information.

No. 179.

Edwin Shelby, son of Winchester Bledsoe and Marian (Winchester) Shelby, is an insurance agent in New Orleans. No other information.

No. 180.

David Shelby, son of Winchester Bledsoe and Marian (Winchester) Shelby, is a lawyer in Oklahoma. No other information.

No. 181.

Bettie Martin, daughter of Robert C. K. and Priscilla (Douglass) Martin, married W. C. Butterfield. Had children—

328 William Butterfield. Unmarried.

329   Robert M. Butterfield.
330   Nellie Butterfield. Unmarried. Resides at Little Rock, Arkansas.

No. 183.

Alice Martin, daughter of Dr. Robert C. K. and Priscilla (Douglass) Martin, married W. H. Hart. No issue. After the death of Mr. Hart, she married John Lannahan, Auditor of the American Telephone Company of New York. Died in 1907. No issue.

No. 184.

Henry Douglass Martin, son of Dr. Robert C. K. and Priscilla (Douglass) Martin, married Lizzie Nichols. No issue.

No. 186.

Robert C. K. Martin, son of Dr. Robert C. K. and Priscilla (Douglass) Martin, married Sarah Shelby Anderson. Resides in Nashville. Have one child—

331   Bettie Martin. Unmarried.

No. 187.

Maria Martin, daughter of Dr. Robert C. K. and Priscilla (Douglass) Martin, married W. C. Butterfield, who had previously married her sister, Bettie. Had children—

332   Bettie Butterfield. Unmarried.
333   Duncan Butterfield. Unmarried. Resides in Nashville.

No. 191.

Alva Erskine Smith, daughter of Dr. Murray Forbes and Phoebe (Desha) Smith, was born in Mobile, Alabama. Married, first, William K. Vanderbilt, of New York; second, Oliver H. P. Belmont, who was born in New York, November 12, 1858, son of Augustus Belmont; educated at the U. S. Naval Academy, and served two years in the navy; then resigned. Was for some time a member of the banking firm of August Belmont & Co. Elected to the Fifty-seventh Congress as a Democrat. Died in New York, June 8, 1908. Had children—

334 Consuela Vanderbilt, born in New York, March 2, 1877.
335 William Kissam Vanderbilt, born in New York, October 26, 1878.
336 Harold Stirling Vanderbilt, born in New York, July 6, 1884.

No. 192.

Mary Virginia Smith, daughter of Dr. Murray Forbes and Phoebe (Desha) Smith, married, first, Fernando Yznaga; second, W. G. Tiffany, of New York.

No. 193.

Florence Smith, daughter of Dr. Murray Forbes and Phoebe (Desha) Smith, married Gaston De Fontenilliat. Had children—
337 Renee Fontenilliat.

No. 196.

May Blood, daughter of Henry and Carrie (Shelby) Blood, married a Mr. Walsh. Resides in New York. No information.

No. 197.

Laura Blood, daughter of Henry and Carrie (Shelby) Blood, married Albert Converse, Admiral in the U. S. Navy.

No. 199.

Maude Blood, daughter of Henry and Carrie (Shelby) Blood, married Harold Sanderson, manager of the White Star line of steamships of Liverpool. He was lost at sea.

No. 201.

Thomas Mastin, son of Gustavus L. and Mary (Fearn) Mastin, married Mary Irby Bate, daughter of the late Senator William B. Bate, of Tennessee. Resides in Grand View, Texas. Have children—

338 Bate Maston.
339 Mary Eleanor Masten.
340 Julien Masten.

No. 203.

James Mastin, son of Gustavus L. and Mary (Fearn) Mastin, married Mattie Tutwiler of Alabama. No issue.

No. 204.

Sallie Shelby Mastin, daughter of Gustavus L. and Mary (Fearn) Mastin, married Eugene Bucknor. No issue.

No. 205.

Gustavus L. Mastin, Jr., son of Gustavus L. and Mary (Fearn) Mastin, married Lucy Matthews. Had children—

341 John Mastin.
342 Sallie Shelby Mastin.
343 Clara Mastin.
344 Lucy Mastin.
345 Frank Mastin.

No. 206.

William Shelby Barry, son of Colonel William F. and Sarah (Fearn) Barry, married, first, Bernice Steele, a first cousin. Had one child:

346 William Shelby Barry, Jr.

Second marriage, Josephine Holliquest. Had one child:

347 Josephine Barry.

GENEALOGY OF THE BLEDSOE FAMILY 141

No. 207.

Thomas Steele, son of Colonel Mathew and Kate (Fearn) Steele, married Lovie Strode. Had children—

348 Shelby Steele.
349 Kate Steele.
350 May Steele.
351 Sallie Steele.
352 Stella Steele.
353 Bernice Steele.
354 Mathew Steele, Jr.
355 Annie Steele.

No. 208.

Sallie Steele, daughter of Colonel Mathew and Kate (Fearn) Steele, married John Newman. Had one child—

356 Robert E. Newman.

No. 211.

Robert Steele, son of Colonel Mathew and Kate (Fearn) Steele, married Tillie Weaver. No issue.

No. 212.

Bernice Steele, daughter of Colonel Mathew and Kate (Fearn) Steele, married William Shelby Barry, her first cousin (No. 206). Had one child—

357 William Shelby Barry, Jr.

No. 213.

Mathew Steele, Jr., son of Colonel Mathew and Kate (Fearn) Steele, is a Captain in the U. S. Army, Sixth Regiment of Cavalry. Married Stella Folsom. No issue.

No. 214.

Tracy Steele, son of Colonel Mathew and Kate (Fearn) Steele, married Courtney Crutchfield. Have children—

358 Tracy Steele, Jr.
359 William Steele.

No. 216.

Anna Steele, daughter of Dr. George and Ada (Fearn) Steele, married Mr. Eager. Had children—

360 Annie D. Eager.
361 Fearn Eager. Died young.

No. 217.

Fearn Steele, son of Dr. George and Ada (Fearn) Steele, married Sadie ——. Had one child—

362 George Steele.

No. 218.

Winston Fearn Garth, son of Colonel William Willis and Maria Eliza (Fearn) Garth, married Lena Garth, a cousin. Had children—

363 William Willis Garth, Jr.
364 Alice Dashiell Garth. Unmarried. Resides in Huntsville, Alabama.
365 Maria Fearn Garth.
366 Horace Everett Garth.

No. 220.

Nannie Schlater, daughter of G. B. and Gertrude (Bledsoe) Schlater, married Mr. Randolph. One son—

367 Schlater Randolph.

No. 221.

Florence Pegues Bledsoe, married Mr. Crofford. She is a writer of wide reputation. They reside in New Mexico. Have children—

368 William Crofford.
369 Roy Crofford.
370 Sallie Crofford.
371 Oscar Crofford.

No. 222.

Oscar F. Bledsoe, third, son of Colonel Oscar F. and Sallie (Cannon) Bledsoe, is a planter in Mississippi. Married Lulu Aldridge, granddaughter of the late U. S. Senator, J. Z. George, of Mississippi. Have children—

OSCAR FITZALAN BLEDSOE, FOURTH

372   Lulu Bledsoe.
373   Oscar F. Bledsoe, fourth.

No. 224.

Mary Lou Bledsoe, daughter of Colonel Oscar F. and Sallie (Cannon) Bledsoe, married Dr. D. M. McGehee. No issue. Died 1904.

No. 230.

Eliza Ann Bledsoe, daughter of Thomas Jefferson and Zettira (Reed) Bledsoe, married Abraham Leonard Laird. Had children—

374 Leonard Laird.
375 John Hampton Laird.
376 Thomas Hines Laird.

LULU ALDRICH BLEDSOE

No. 231.

Mollie Craig Bledsoe, daughter of Thomas Jefferson and Zettira (Reed) Bledsoe, married William W Powell. Had one child—

377 Charles Leslie Powell.

GENEALOGY OF THE BLEDSOE FAMILY 145

No. 232.

William Duncan Bledsoe, son of Thomas Jefferson and Zettira (Reed) Bledsoe, married Lula Lee. Had children—
378 William Edward Bledsoe.
379 Henry Lee Bledsoe.

No. 235.

Thomas Mallory Bledsoe, son of Thomas Jefferson and Zettira (Reed) Bledsoe, married Wincie Elizabeth Carey. Have one child—
380 Frances Estes Bledsoe.

No. 237.

Stella Brent Bledsoe, daughter of Thomas Jefferson and Zettira (Reed) Bledsoe, married Malvern Hill Wells. Have children—
381 Agnes Wells.
382 Pearl Sears Wells.

No. 239.

John W. Smith, son of Charles E. and Mildred (Malone) Smith, was born in Tipton county, Tennessee, May 24, 1857. Married Pearl Kensey. Resides in Yarbro, Arkansas. Have children—
383 Mabel C. Smith.
384 Bulah V. Smith.
385 Ralph R. Smith.

No. 241.

Catherine Smith, daughter of Charles E. and Mildred (Malone) Smith, was born July 22, 1867. Married O. W. Williams, of Memphis, Tennessee. Died in July, 1906. Had children—
386 Lillian Lilly Williams.
387 Charles Williams.
388 Blanch Williams.

No. 242.

Bettie Sue Smith, daughter of Charles E. and Mildred (Malone) Smith, was born September 11, 1869. Died in 1906. Married W. P. Bradford, of Memphis. Have children—

389 William Bradford.
390 Hunt Bradford.

No. 244.

Sarah Winn, daughter of Thomas W. and Susan (Malone) Winn, was born in Tipton county. Married, first, Edward M. Jones, of Hartford, Connecticut. Had children—

391 Mabel W. Jones.
392 Annie B. Jones.
393 Thomas Winn Jones. Unmarried.

After the death of Mr. Jones, Sarah married James Clark, of Connecticut. Had one child—

394 Katie Sue Clark.

After the death of Mr. Clark, Sarah married John Paine, a native of England. They now reside in Memphis. No issue.

No. 245.

Willie P. Winn, daughter of Thomas W. and Susan (Malone) Winn, was born in Tipton county. Married William H. Paine. Have their home in Covington, Tennessee. Have children:

395 Susan M. Paine.
396 William P. Paine.
397 John H. Paine.
398 Ebenezer Paine.
399 Frank Troy Paine.
400 Mary Elizabeth Paine.

No. 246.

Mary A. Winn, daughter of Thomas W. and Susan (Malone) Winn, was born in Tipton county. Married Edwin Paine, one of three brothers,

Genealogy of the Bledsoe Family

two of whom had married her elder sisters. They reside in Covington, Have children—
401 Tom Pete Paine.
402 Edwin Milton Paine.
403 Mary Agness Paine.
404 Richard Haynes Paine.

No. 250.

Jennie S. Pursley, daughter of Halem L. and Mary Catherine (Malone) Pursley, was born in Sumner county, Tennessee, February 25, 1846. Married John B. Jones in 1866. Died in 1871, and was buried in the family graveyard near Union City, Tennessee. Had children—
405 John B. Jones, Jr.
406 Stephen M. Jones. Died in Nashville in 1897.

No. 251.

Laura Addie Pursley, daughter of Halem L. and Mary Catherine (Malone) Pursley, was born in Sumner county, February 14, 1848. Married in June, 1869, M. R. Shoffner, a native of Bedford county. Had children—
407 Inez Moss Shoffner.
408 Maurice Shoffner. Died in infancy.
409 Kate Malone Shoffner.
410 Robert Shoffner. Died in young manhood.

No. 252.

Mildred George Pursley, daughter of Halem L. and Mary Catherine (Malone) Pursley, was born in Sumner county, August 2, 1851. Died at Jackson, Tennessee, April 1, 1894, and was buried in Riverside cemetery. On January 30, 1870, she was married to Jay Guy Cisco, who was born in New Orleans, April 25, 1844. Grandson of the Marquis De Seso de Touchaire; descended, 13th generation, from Don Carlos De Seso, who was burned at the stake for heresy, at Valladolid, Spain, on October 29, 1559. Mr. Cis-

FIVE GENERATIONS—DESCENDANTS—COL. ANTHONY BLEDSOE

co's mother was a daughter of Baron Wezinski. He served in the Confederate army throughout the war; then engaged in newspaper work for some time; then visited his mother and brother in Europe, and after spending a year in travel on the Continent, and visiting Egypt, returned to America. In 1875 he established "Cisco's Bookstore," at Jackson, Tennessee. Also edited the *Forked Deer Blade.* In 1888 he received from President Cleveland the appointment of U. S. Consul in Mexico. In February, 1898, he was appointed Assistant Industrial and Immigration Agent for Tennessee, for the Louisville & Nashville railroad, which position he still holds. In 1879 he was elected a member of the American Association for the Advancement of Science. In 1904 he published a series of papers, "Counties and County Seats of Tennessee, Their Origin, and Sketches of the Persons for Whom They Were Named." Has in manuscript a biographical dictionary of Tennessee, and one of Tennessee authors. Is interested in lepidoptera and American archæology. Has children—

411 Fredrika Lillian Cisco, born November 28, 1870, in Tennessee.

412 George Guy Cisco, born November 29, 1872, in Tuscaloosa, Alabama. Now resides in New York. Unmarried.

413 Bertie Cisco, born January 1, 1875, in Tuscaloosa, Alabama. Resides with her father in Nashville. Unmarried.

414 Walter Jay Cisco, born July 24, 1877, at Jackson, Tennessee.

415 Victor W. Cisco, born December 28, 1879, at Jackson, Tennessee. Resides in New Orleans. Unmarried.

416 Mozelle Cisco, born September 30, 1882, at Jackson, Tennessee. Resides with her father in Nashville. Unmarried.

150   HISTORIC SUMNER COUNTY, TENN.

417   Rudolf Wezinski Cisco, born July 20, 1885, at Jackson, Tennessee.
418   Ruperto Francoise Cisco, born September 12, 1888, at Jackson, Tennessee. Now principal of a school at Bon Ami, Louisiana. Unmarried.

No. 254.

Dr. Hugh Lawson Patterson, son of John Clendening and Eleanor (Benson) Patterson, married Maria Sue Patterson. Had children—

419   Lilla Edith Patterson. Never married.
420   Leona Pearl Patterson. Unmarried.
421   James Henderson Patterson.
422   Elizabeth Benson Patterson. Unmarried.
423   Sue Belle Patterson. Unmarried.

No. 255.

Presley Foster Patterson, son of John Clendening and Eleanor (Benson) Patterson, married Sallie Rowe. Have children—

424   John Clendening Patterson. Unmarried.
425   Sallie Foster Patterson. Unmarried.

No. 256.

Mary Jane Patterson, daughter of John Clendening and Eleanor (Benson) Patterson, married J. L. Sheppard. No issue.

No. 257.

Eleanor Obedience Patterson, daughter of John Clendening and Eleanor (Benson) Patterson, married Dr. G. W. McGuire. Had children—

426   James Calvin McGuire.
427   Sue McGuire.

No. 258.

Sue Patterson, daughter of John Clendening and Eleanor (Benson) Patterson, married J. McCullum. No children.

Genealogy of the Bledsoe Family 151

No. 259.

Benjamin Bledsoe Patterson, son of John Clendening and Eleanor (Benson) Patterson, married Bettie Dillon. Had children—

428 John James Patterson.
429 Allie Foster Patterson.
430 Eleanor Benson Patterson.
431 Jimmie D. Patterson. Unmarried.

No. 260.

Maria Patterson, daughter of John Clendening and Eleanor (Benson) Patterson, married John M. King. Children died in infancy.

No. 261.

Mattie Belle Patterson, daughter of John Clendening and Eleanor (Benson) Patterson, married P. W. Nave. Had children—

432 Lovie Belle Nave.
433 Presley Ward Nave. Unmarried.
434 Hugh Benson Nave.

No. 262.

Violet Rachael Patterson, daughter of John Clendening and Eleanor (Benson) Patterson, married Dr. J. J. Upshaw. Had children—

435 Lovie Belle Upshaw.
436 Minnie Lee Upshaw. Unmarried.
437 Tazewell Upshaw. Unmarried.

No. 264.

Joseph Thomas Patterson, son of John Clendening and Eleanor (Benson) Patterson, married Mollie Copeland. Had children—

438 John Thomas Patterson.
439 Juniaetta Patterson. Unmarried.
440 Mary Eleanor Patterson. Unmarried.

No. 266.

Belle Sherrell, daughter of A. A. and Maria H. (Patterson) Sherrell, married M. C. Atkinson. Had children—

441 William Sherrell Atkinson.
442 Ola Maria Sherrell Atkinson. Unmarried.
443 Alexus Sherrell Atkinson. Unmarried.

No. 269.

Elizabeth Perkins, daughter of Drew M. and Maria H. (Patterson-Sherrell) Perkins, married. No information.

No. 270.

Francis Perkins, daughter of Drew M. and Maria H. (Patterson-Sherrell) Perkins, married F. P. Carpenter. No issue.

No. 271.

Dr. Vance Perkins, son of Drew M. and Maria H. (Patterson-Sherrell) Perkins, married Mollie Fisher. Had children—

444 M. V. Perkins.
445 D. W. Perkins.
446 Francis Perkins.
447 Belle Perkins.

No. 272.

Maria Susan Patterson, daughter of David Shelby and Elizabeth (Cheatham) Patterson, married Dr. Hugh Lawson Patterson. Had children—

448 Lillian Edith Patterson. Never married.
449 Leona Pearl Patterson.
450 James Henderson Patterson.
451 Elizabeth Benson Patterson.
452 Susie Belle Patterson.

No. 276.

David Henderson Patterson, son of David Shelby and Elizabeth (Cheatham) Patterson, married Belle Sheffield. No information.

GENEALOGY OF THE BLEDSOE FAMILY 153

No. 278.

Cornelia Rebecka Patterson, daughter of David Shelby and Elizabeth (Cheatham) Patterson, married W. B. Stevens. Had children —

453 Jerentha Rentha Stevens.
454 Zana Stevens.
455 Anna Henderson Stevens.
456 Pearl Stevens. Never married.
457 Coleman Myles Stevens.

No. 279.

Virginia Belle Patterson, daughter of David Shelby and Elizabeth (Cheatham) Patterson, married, first, W. S. Patterson. Had children—

458 Alma Virginia Patterson.
459 Ethel Patterson. Died in infancy.
460 Annie Sue Patterson. Died in infancy.
461 Mamie Patterson. Died in infancy.

After the death of her first husband, Virginia Belle Patterson married J. W. Young. Had children—

462 Robert Henderson Young.
463 David Whitfield Young.

No. 281.

D. C. Patterson Sherrell, son of Dr. J. L. and Martha Eliza (Patterson) Sherrell, married Mary McCoy. Had children—

464 Horace Everett Sherrell.
465 Aleene Sherrell.
466 Howard Sherrell.

No. 282.

Violette Ann Sherrell, daughter of Dr. J. L. and Martha Eliza (Patterson) Sherrell, married Dr. B. A. Stone. Had children—

467 Emmett Roy Stone.
468 Mary V. Stone.
469 Joe L. Stone.
470 A. Alexus Stone.
471 Floyd Stone.

No. 283.

Jennie Sherrell, daughter of Dr. J. L. and Martha Eliza (Patterson) Sherrell, married J. H. Stevenson. Had children—

472 Sherrell Stone Stevenson.
473 Lucile Stevenson.

No. 284.

E. Matt Sherrell, son cf Dr. J. L. and Martha Eliza (Patterson) Sherrell, married, first, Sallie Ezell. One child—

474 Daisy Mai Sherrell.

After the death of his first wife, E. Matt Sherrell married Sallie Moore. No issue.

No. 285.

Benjamin Sherrell, son of Dr. J. L. and Martha Eliza (Patterson) Sherrell, married Annie Smith. Had children—

475 John Lawson Sherrell.
476 Lulu Sherrell.

No. 286.

James Lawson Patterson, son of Logan Madison and Priscilla (Leatherwood) Patterson, married Lillie Hill. Had children—

477 Selwynne Patterson.
478 W. Clendening Patterson.
479 Kate Patterson. Unmarried.
480 Lon Lee Patterson. Unmarried.
481 Myrtle Patterson. Unmarried.
482 James S. Patterson. Unmarried.
483 Will Lamb Patterson. Unmarried.
484 Carter Patterson.

No. 287.

William Shelby Patterson, son of Logan Madison and Priscilla (Leatherwood) Patterson, married Belle Patterson. Had one child—

485 Alma V. Patterson.

GENEALOGY OF THE BLEDSOE FAMILY 155

No. 288.

Logan Madison Patterson, son of Captain Logan Madison and Priscilla (Leatherwood) Patterson, married Maggie Myers. Had children—

486 Edna Patterson.
487 Lillie Belle Patterson.
488 Logan Patterson.
489 Sam M. Patterson.
490 Grady Patterson.

EIGHTH GENERATION.

No. 290.

John Shelby Barrow, Jr., son of John Shelby and Margaret (Armstrong) Barrow, married a daughter of Colonel Hal Claiborne, of Nashville. They reside in New York Mr. Barrow died December 20, 1908. Have children—

491 John Shelby Barrow, third.
492 Washington Barrow.
492a Ann Barrow.
493 Clayton Barrow.

No. 291.

David Shelby Williams, son of John Shelby and Mattie (Sevier) Williams, married, first, May Lawson McGhee, of Knoxville, daughter of Colonel Charles McGhee. No issue. Second, Mrs. James Frazer, *nee* Washington, of Nashville. No issue. They reside at Glenn Cliff, near Nashville. Mr. Williams is Vice-President of the First National Bank, and President of the Nashville Gas Company.

No. 294.

Anna Fassman Williams, daughter of John Shelby and Mattie (Sevier) Williams, married Wentworth P. Johnson, of Norfolk, Virginia. Have children—

494 Wentworth P. Johnson, Jr.
495 Shelby Williams Johnson (a daughter).
  Three children died in infancy.

No. 296.

Maude Williams, daughter of John Shelby and Mattie (Sevier) Williams, married Robert P. Bonnie, of Louisville, Kentucky. Have children—

496 Shelby Williams Bonnie.
497 Mattie Sevier Bonnie.
498 Robert P. Bonnie, Jr.
499 Hundley Sevier Bonnie.

No. 298.

Henry Yeateman Williams, son of Joseph Minnick and Emily (Polk) Williams, married Miss Pitcher. No issue. Reside in Galveston, Texas.

No. 299.

Joseph Minnick Williams, Jr., son of Joseph Minnick and Emily (Polk) Williams, is a practicing lawyer; resides in Olustee, Oklahoma. Unmarried.

303.

Priscilla Shelby Williams, daughter of Joseph Minnick and Emily (Polk) Williams, married a Mr. Briggs, of Norfolk, Virginia. Have one child—

500 ———

304.

Maria Shelby Fassman, daughter of Frank and Anna Minnick (Williams) Fassman, married a Mr. Brook. Have one child—

501 ———

305.

Anna Minnick Fassman, daughter of Frank and Anna Minnick (Williams) Fassman, married Rev. J. G. Shackelford. Have one child—

502 ———————

No. 306.

Mary Leigh Watkins, daughter of Leigh and Willie (Kearney) Watkins, married William H. McCulloch, of Ferguson, Missouri. Have children—

503 Erskin Watkins McCulloch.
504 Elizabeth Zane McCulloch.
505 William H. McCulloch, Jr.

No. 308.

Willie B. Ross, son of William Ewing and Marian (Watkins) Ross, married Lillie Peatros, of Jackson Mississippi. Have one child—

507 Willie B. Ross.

No. 313.

Rose Farrar Watkins, daughter of Erskine and Alice (Petrie) Watkins, married Calvin Wells, Jr., a lawyer, of Jackson, Mississippi. Have one child—

508 Alice Petrie Wells.

No. 319.

Marian Shelby Pleasants, daughter of Samuel and Maria Bledsoe (Shelby) Pleasants, was born in March, 1874. Married Rev. Oscar Haywood, August, 1896. Died in 1898.

No. 320.

Pattie Hammond, daughter of Judge Eli Shelby and Fannie (Davis) Hammond, was born in Ripley, Mississippi, June 6, 1868. Married Dr.

George W. Jarman, son of Professor George W. Jarman, who was for many years President of the S. W. B. University at Jackson, Tennesee. Residence, No. 54, W. 76th Street, New York. Have children—

509   George Wallace Jarman.
510   Shelby Hammond Jarman.
511   Martha Shelby Jarman.

No. 321.

Orlando Davis Hammond, son of Judge Eli Shelby and Fannie (Davis) Hammond, was born in Memphis, Tennessee, November 6, 1871. Lawyer by profession. Resides in New York. Married at Rosemont, Pennsylvania, February 16, 1901, Lillian Kirk McDowell, of Holly Springs, Mississippi. Have one child—

512   Martha Bonner Hammond, born August 1, 1903.

No. 322.

Cora Hammond, daughter of McLaren and Mary (Mayes) Hammond, married Wesley Owen. Resides in Texas. Has children. No information.

No. 323.

Ferdinand McLaren Hammond, son of McLaren and Mary (Mayes) Hammond, married, and has children. No information.

No. 324.

Mary Hammond, daughter of McLaren and Mary (Mayes) Hammond, married and has children. No information.

No. 325.

Harry Hammond, son of McLaren and Mary (Mayes) Hammond, married and has children. No information.

GENEALOGY OF THE BLEDSOE FAMILY

No. 326.

Francis Lynn Scruggs, daughter of J. M. and Priscilla Shelby (Hammond) Scruggs, was born at Jackson, Tennessee, July 25, 1865. Married J. Hancock Robinson, in Holly Springs, Mississippi, August 24, 1886. They reside in Washington, D. C., Have one child—

513 Shelby Goldsborough Robinson, daughter, born July 8, 1888.

No. 327.

James Merriwether Scruggs, son of J. M. and Priscilla Shelby (Hammond) Scruggs, married Lilly Whitney, of Memphis, where they have their home. Have children:

514 Whitney Scruggs, daughter.
515 James Merriwether Scruggs, Jr.
516 Nolan Fontaine Scruggs.

No. 329.

Robert M. Butterfield, son of W. C. and Bettie (Martin) Butterfield, married Miss Phones, of Little Rock, Arkansas, where they reside. Have children—

517 Joseph Phones Butterfield.
518 Bettie Martin Butterfield.

No. 334.

Consuelo Vanderbilt, daughter of William K. and Alva Erskine (Smith) Vanderbilt, was born in New York, March 2, 1877. Married November 6, 1895, Charles Richard John Spencer Churchill, Duke of Marlborough. Have children—

519 John William Churchill, Marquis of Blandford.
520 Ivor Churchill, (Lord.)

No. 335.

William Kissam Vanderbilt, Jr., son of William K. and Alva Erskine (Smith) Vanderbilt,

was born in New York, October 26, 1878. Married April, 1900, Virginia Fair. Have children—
521   Muriel Vanderbilt.
522   Consuelo Vanderbilt.
523   William Kissam Vanderbilt, third.

JOHN WILLIAM CHURCHILL, MARQUIS OF BLANDFORD

No. 339.

Mary Eleanor Mastin, daughter of Thomas and Mary Irby (Bate) Mastin, married John Stevens Douglass.

GENEALOGY OF THE BLEDSOE FAMILY 161

No. 363.

William Willis Garth, Jr., son of Winston Fearn and Lena Garth, married Louisa Dodsworth. Have one child—

524 Lena Garth.

No. 386.

Lillian Lilly Williams, daughter of O. W. and Catherine (Smith) Williams, married Mr. Quinn, of Memphis.

No. 391.

Mabel W. Jones, daughter of Edward M. and Sarah (Winn) Jones, married Charles Taylor, of Hartford, Connecticut. Now live in Memphis. Have four children.

525 ———————
526 ———————
527 ———————
528 ———————

No. 392.

Annie B. Jones, daughter of Edward M. and Sarah (Winn) Jones, married Samuel Fitch, of Hartford, Connecticut.

No. 405.

John B. Jones, son of John B and Jennie S. (Pursley) Jones, married Mary Gallagher. Resides in Nashville. Have children—

529 Mary Pursley Jones.
530 Addie Magdalene Jones.
531 Edna Julia Jones.
532 Margaret Louise Jones.
533 Jennie Elizabeth Jones.

No. 407.

Inez Moss Shoffner, daughter of M. R. and Laura Addie (Pursley) Shoffner, married Thomas W. White, of Oxford, Mississippi, and who died in 1907. Have children—

534 Shoffner Thompson White, born April 13, 1897.
535 Louise Thornton White, born May 3, 1899.
536 Mary Francis White, born August 6, 1901; died June 27, 1903.
537 Thomas Coleman White, born February 8, 1904.

No. 409.

Kate Malone Shoffner, daughter of M. R. and Laura Addie (Pursley) Shoffner, was born at Union City, Tennessee. Married Will Dave Caldwell, son of ex-Congressman W. P. Caldwell, of Gardner. Resides in Memphis. Have children—

538 Ralph Morrison Caldwell, born May 28, 1899, at Union City.
539 Addie Byron Caldwell, born December 10, 1900, at Union City.

No. 411.

Fredrika Lillian Cisco, daughter of Jay Guy and Mildred Georgie (Purseley) Cisco, was born near Union City Tennessee, November 28, 1870. Graduated from the Memphis Conference Female Institute at Jackson in 1888. Married March 6, 1892, Robert Cannon Jones, a native of Mississippi. They reside in Chattanooga. Have children—

540 Robert Cannon Jones, Jr., born March 1895, at Chattanooga.
541 Guy Ozment Jones, born July 3, 1899, at Chattanooga.
542 Fredrika Elizabeth Jones, born July 3, 1899, at Chattanooga.

No. 414.

Walter Jay Cisco, son of Jay Guy and Mildred Georgie (Pursley) Cisco, was born at Jackson, Tennessee, July 24, 1877. Married at New Orleans, December 27, 1905, to Bettie Pearson, who

GENEALOGY OF THE BLEDSOE FAMILY

was born in Guttenburg, Sweeden, September 27, 1888. They reside in New Orleans. Have one child—

543   Walter Jay Cisco, Jr., born February 19, 1907.

No. 417.

Rudolf Wezinski Cisco, son of Jay Guy and Mildred Georgie (Pursley) Cisco, was born in Jackson, Tennessee, July 20, 1885. Graduated from the Nashville High School, June 14, 1906. Valedictorian and winner of the Elliott Medal. Married June 12, 1907, Annie Mary Davis, daughter of G. A. and Mamie (Lipscomb) Davis, of Nashville. They reside in Nashville. Have one child—

544   Mildred Cisco, born November 1, 1908.

No. 421.

James Henderson Patterson, son of Dr. Hugh Lawson and Maria Sue Patterson, married Virgie Lloyd. Have children—

245   Hugh Loyd Patterson.
546   Mardre Sue Patterson.
547   David Henderson Patterson.

No. 428.

John James Patterson, son of John Clendening and Eelanor (Benson) Patterson, married Mattie Jones. Had children—

548   Mildred Patterson. Never married.

After the death of his first wife, John James Patterson married Mary Espey. Had children—

549   Robert Clendening Patterson.
550   John James Patterson, Jr.
551   Mary Espey Patterson.
552   Hazel Benson Patterson.

No. 429.

Allie Foster Patterson, daughter of Benjamin Bledsoe and Eleanor (Benson) Patterson, married W. M. Pegrim. Had one child—

553   Vernon Patterson.

No. 430.

Eleanor Benson Patterson, daughter of Benjamin Bledsoe and Eleanor (Benson) Patterson, married J. T. Johnson.

No. 432.

Violet Nave, daughter of P. W. and Mattie Belle (Patterson) Nave, married J. W. Crenshaw. Had one child—

554   Thelma Lee Crenshaw.

No. 434.

Hugh Benson Nave, daughter of P. W. and Mattie Belle (Patterson) Nave, married J. B. Byrn. Have one child—

555   Paul Nave Byrn.

No. 438.

John Thomas Patterson, son of Joseph Thomas and Mollie (Copeland) Patterson, married Nuna George. Have one child—

566   Joe Holland Patterson.

No. 441.

William Sherrell Atkinson, son of M. C. and Belle (Sherrell) Atkinson, married Stella Deacon Vaughn. Have children—

557   Issabella Sherrell Atkinson.
558   Currin Atkinson.

No. 455.

Anna Henderson Stevens, daughter of W. B. and Cornelia Rebecka (Patterson) Stevens, married James Whitaker. Have children—

559   Knox Whitaker.
560   Edwin Whitaker.

No. 458.

Alma Virgie Patterson, daughter of W. S. and Virgie Belle (Patterson) Patterson, married T. D. Sugg. Have children—
561 Virginia Sue Sugg.
562 William Conrad Sugg.

No. 468.

Mary V. Stone, daughter of Dr. B. A. and Violet Anne (Sherrell) Stone, married C. G. Welsh. Have children—
563 Stanley Welsh.
564 Louise Welsh.

No. 474.

Daisey Mai Sherrell, daughter of E. Matt and Sallie (Ezell) Sherrell, married Newton Kelsoe. Have one child—
565 Virginia Kelsoe.

No. 477.

Selwynne Patterson, son of J. L. and Lillie (Hill) Patterson, married Kate Leatherwood.

No. 478.

W. Clendening Patterson, son of J. L. and Lillie (Hill) Patterson, married Eva Calhoun. Have one child—
566 Walter Calhoun Patterson.

COLONEL ISAAC BLEDSOE

Isaac Bledsoe was a man of and for the times in which he lived. Strong in mind and strong in body, brave, daring and fond of adventure; a big heart and a generous soul, he was a fit companion of such men as Sevier, the Shelbys, Robertson, and the scores of others who established a new State in the trackless wilderness. Like his elder brother, Anthony, and his younger brother, Abraham, he was born in Culpeper county, Virginia. The date of his birth is supposed to be about 1735. In early manhood, together with his brothers above named, and other adventurous souls, he sought a new home in the then extreme West, and settled on the Holston river at a point near the present line between Virginia and Tennessee, a few miles east from where Bristol now is. There he continued to make his home until in 1780, when he removed to the Cumberland country. After locating on the Holston, he spent most of his time in hunting, exploring and fighting the Indians. He was in Dunmore's war, and in the subsequent wars with the Indians, and was always conspicuous for his bravery and his readiness to face dangers. He was a member of that party of adventurers known to history as "the Long Hunters," some of whom remained in the wilderness for many months. He was one of the witnesses of the treaty with the Indians at Fort Patrick Henry, July 20, 1777. He was a member of the party of hunters and explorers which penetrated to the Cumberland country in 1771. It was on this expedition that he discovered the spring in what is now Sumner county, known as Bledsoe's Lick, to which he gave his name, and near which he afterwards located his home, and where he was killed in 1793.

On a tree in Logan county, Kentucky, on March 11, 1780, Isaac Bledsoe cut his name and the date. The tree, with its precious record, like the heroic man who cut his name thereon, has long since mingled with the soil.

Isaac Bledsoe was one of the first settlers in Middle Tennessee, and upon the organization of a local government he was made one of the justices of the peace of Davidson county, and later one of the first justices of Sumner county. In November, 1781, he set out with his friend, James Robertson, for Kentucky, to secure much-needed ammunition for the Cumberland settlers. With the party were Robertson's son and a faithful negro servant. It was a trip of two months through a trackless forest, infested by savage foes, and beset with dangers unknown to the present generation. The little party passed the Indian lines in safety, and in due time arrived at Harod's Station, where they received their first intelligence of the happenings of the outside world. The decisive battle of King's Mountain had been fought and won, and Cornwallis was fleeing towards the seaboard. Bledsoe, in telling about it afterwards, said: "Both Robertson and I were a foot taller when we heard of the glorious work of Sevier and Shelby. We said to one another, "If they can so handle the British and Tories, can we not whip the Indians in the woods?"

At Harod's Station they found no ammunition, so they pushed on to Boonsborough, where they found Daniel Boone, who divided his ammunition with them. But it was not enough, and Bledsoe set out for Watauga, where he hoped to obtain a full supply from Sevier. Later he returned to his fort at Bledsoe's Lick, accompanied by a number of settlers.

In October, 1783, when Davidson county was organized, Isaac Bledsoe was elected first Major of the regiment of militia, of which his brother Anthony was Colonel. Previous to that time he had served as a Captain of one of the militia companies, and as such participated in many fights with the Indians.

After a long and useful career, Colonel Isaac Bledsoe was killed by Indians near his home at Bledsoe's Lick on the morning of April 9, 1793. At the time he was on his way to a clearing with his servants to mend the log heaps, when lurking foes shot him from ambush, and then scalped him. His remains were buried by the side of his brother Anthony.

The Indians gave to Isaac Bledsoe the name of "Tullitoska," the waving corn blade, or perpetual motion.

About 1772, Isaac Bledsoe married Katherine Montgomery, a member of a prominent family of that name in Southwestern Virginia. The family originally came from the northern part of Ireland, and was related to General Richard Montgomery, who was killed at the storming of Quebec. There were a number of Montgomery's in Southwest Virginia, but which one was the father of Katherine I do not know. Captain James Montgomery was a colonial officer. He was a justice of the peace in Washington county, and was sheriff in 1785. Alexander and Thomas Montgomery, of the same section of Virginia, served in the Indian wars. The most prominent of the name was Lieutenant-Colonel John Montgomery (probably a brother of Katherine). He commanded a regiment under General George Roger Clark in the Kaskaskia compaign, where he rendered distinguished service. He was born in Botetourt county; came to the Cumberland settlements with the Donelson expedition in 1780. He was the first sheriff of Davidson county. Soon after his appointment to that position he visited New Orleans, and was said to have been engaged in the Genet conspiracy, for which he was impeached in office. Soon after his return to Nashborough, he removed to what is now Montgomery county, which was so named for him. He founded Clarksville, which was so named in honor of his old commander, General George Roger Clark. His last public service was to command the troops on the Nickojack expedition in 1794. In the fall of that year he was killed by Indians while on a hunting expedition above Clarksville, in Kentucky.

Katherine Montgomery was born in what was at that time Augusta county, Virginia, then the extreme frontier. She was a woman of superior character and attainments. She bore the vicissitudes and confronted the dangers incident to a frontier life with bravery and fortitude unsurpassed by any. She was loved, honored and respected by all who knew her, and the memory of her gentle virtues is treasured by her descendants to this day.

There is a tradition in the family that Katherine

Montgomery on some occasion, during the Revolutionary War, carried important dispatches through the British lines to the patriot army, and while on the journey she was met by a British officer, who suspecting her, rode by her side and engaged her in conversation. He complimented her blooded horse, when she, with womanly tact, challenged him for a race, and out-distanced him to the extent that she was able to deliver her dispatches in safety.

GENEALOGY OF THE COLONEL ISAAC BLEDSOE LINE

FIRST GENERATION.
No. 1.

George Bledsoe.

SECOND GENERATION.
No. 2.

Abraham Bledsoe. Among other children he had three sons—
- Anthony Bledsoe.
- 4 Isaac Bledsoe.
- Abraham Bledsoe.

THIRD GENERATION.
No. 4.

Isaac Bledsoe, son of Abraham Bledsoe, was born in Culpepper county, Virginia, about 1735. Married Katherine Montgomery probably about 1772. Was killed by Indians near Bledsoe's Lick, Sumner county, Tennessee, April 9, 1793. Had children—

- 5 Margaret Bledsoe.
- 6 Sally Bledsoe.
- 7 Anthony Bledsoe.
- 8 Polly Bledsoe.
- 9 Katy Bledsoe.
- 10 Lytle Bledsoe.
- 11 Isaac Bledsoe, Jr.
- 12 Clarissa Bledsoe.

FOURTH GENERATION.

No. 5.

Margaret Bledsoe, daughter of Colonel Isaac and Katherine (Montgomery) Bledsoe, was born in Washington county, Virginia, on July 7, 1773. Came to what is now Sumner county, Tennessee, either in the fall of 1780, or the spring of 1781. Her father came in 1780, but possibly his family did not follow him until the next spring, when Colonel Anthony Bledsoe, with his family and several other families, came to the Cumberland country. Margaret married, on December 31, 1789, Joseph Desha. Margaret Desha was identified with the early, stirring events which transpired in Virginia, Tennessee, and Kentucky. She was one of the pioneer mothers, who helped make her State—were spinners of flax and weavers of linen, of whom James Lane Allen so eloquently writes. Her descendants refer with pride to the fact that Mrs. Desha spun the flax and wove the fine linen which her husband wore when a member of Congress. While her husband was filling the office of chief executive of the State of Kentucky, she, with rare ability, superintended his affairs at home, he having a large family of children and servants. She was the mother of thirteen children, and became famed as a notable housekeeper. After her husband retired from public life, they made a journey by carriage to visit relatives in Tennessee, also President Jackson, who was a personal and well-beloved friend of them both. Mrs. Desha died on May 20, 1849, and is buried beside her husband at Georgetown, Kentucky. Joseph Desha was a son of Robert Desha, whose ancestors were of French extraction, and were refugees after the revocation of the edict of Nantes, first probably stopping in Wyoming Valley, Pennsylvania, where Joseph

GENEALOGY OF COL. ISAAC BLEDSOE LINE 171

was born on December 9, 1768. His father emigrated to Kentucky in 1781, and the next year removed to Sumner county, Tennessee, and fixed his home about four miles east from Gallatin, where he died and was buried. His grave, and those of other members of his family, is enclosed by a rude stone wall in a field about one hundred yards from the Hartsville pike. Two of his sons were killed by Indians. In 1792 Joseph Desha returned to Kentucky and settled in Mason county. He served with distinction in the Indian wars under Wayne and Harrison in 1794. He was in the battle of the Thames with the rank of Major-General. He represented his county in the Kentucky Legislature from 1797 to 1807, serving in both houses. Between 1807 and 1819 he served several terms in Congress. In 1813 he was commissioned a Major-General of volunteers, and served as such until the close of the War of 1812. In 1824 he was elected Governor of Kentucky and served four years. At the expiration of his term he retired to his farm in Harrison county, and died at Georgetown, October 11, 1842. He had children—

13 Benjamin Desha, born December 24, 1790.
14 Rachael Desha, born July 7, 1794.
15 Robert Desha, born June 20, 1796.
16 Isaac Desha, born January 9, 1798. Died young.
17 Eleanor Desha, born February 20, 1800.
18 Isaac Bledsoe Desha, born January 1, 1802.
19 John Randolph Desha, born June 25, 1804.
20 Marcus Brutus Desha, born April 30, 1806.
21 Adelade D'Armely Desha, born May 31, 1808.
22 Alvira Desha, born April 26, 1810.
23 Lucius Junius Brutus Desha, born April 25, 1812.
24 Joseph Holmes Desha, born April 12, 1815.
    One child died in infancy unnamed.

FIFTH GENERATION.

No. 17.

Eleanor Desha, daughter of Joseph and Margaret (Bledsoe) Desha, was born in Mason county, Kentucky, February 20, 1800. Married James C. Pickett, who was at one time Secretary of the State of Kentucky, and afterwards Minister Plenipotentiary to the Columbian Confederation. He was born in Fauquier county, Virginia, February 6, 1793. In the War of 1812 he was an officer in the United States Artillery, and as such won a high reputation. From 1818 to 1821 he served in the regular army; then retired and practiced law. For one year he was editor of the *Maryville Eagle;* then served in the Legislature. In 1835 he was Commissioner of the Patent Office; then for three years was Fourth Auditor of the Treasury; then editor of the *Congressional Globe* at Washington. He died July 10, 1872.

While her father was Governor of Kentucky, Mrs. Pickett filled the place of hostess of the executive mansion. She is described as a woman of remarkable culture, dignity and refinement. Aside from her domestic and social duties, she found time to instruct her little son, Joseph Desha Pickett, who often referred to the fact that his earliest memories were of the Governor's mansion, at his mother's knee, learning to read the Bible. It was during her stay in the mansion that LaFayette visited Kentucky, and this little son carried through a long and useful life the memory of the distinguished General placing his hand on his head and blessing him. Mrs. Pickett is said to have been equal to every circumstance and occasion that came to her in those responsible times. She was devout, as well as accomplished, and left a record of unaffected piety and devotion to all that was good and true that came with-

GENEALOGY OF THE BLEDSOE FAMILY 173

in her sphere. She afterwards removed to Washington, D. C., where her husband held responsible positions under the Government. There she died, and was buried beside her husband in the Congressional Burial Ground. They had children—
25 Joseph Desha Pickett, born January 6, 1822.
26 John T. Pickett, born October 9, 1823.
27 Montgomery Pickett, died in infancy.
28 James Ellen Pickett, died in infancy.

No. 19.

John Randolph Desha, son of Joseph and Margaret (Bledsoe) Desha, was born in Mason county, Kentucky, June 25, 1804. Married at Cynthiana, in 1838, Mary Bracken Curry. Died at Lexington, July 27, 1878. His wife died at Versailles, March 23, 1875. Had children—
29 Ben Desha, born in 1841, died in 1855.
30 Issa Desha.
31 Adelaide Desha, born in 1845, died in 1860.
32 Mary Desha.
33 Ella Desha, born in 1852, died in 1860.

No. 21.

Adelaide D'Armely Desha, daughter of Joseph and Margaret (Bledsoe) Desha, was born in Mason county, Kentucky, May 31, 1808. Married, first, Dr. Harmon, of Georgetown. They had one son:
34 Bledsoe Desha Harmon.

After the death of Dr. Harmon, his widow married Colonel William Johnson, of Georgetown, grandfather of Hon. Tom Johnson, ex-member of Congress, and now Mayor of Cleveland, Ohio.

No. 23.

Lucius Junius Brutus Desha, son of Joseph and Margaret (Bledsoe) Desha, was born in Mason county, Kentucky, April 25, 1812. He was brought up on a farm and was early inured to hard labor; but his education was quite liberal, being obtained in the best schools of his time in the country. After finishing his education, in 1830, he chose farming as an occupation, and during the remainder of his life devoted his time and energy mainly to agricultural pursuits, his farm being one of the best and most productive in Harrison county. In 1844 he was elected to represent his county in the Legislature, and by re-election served three consecutive terms. He was a member of the Convention of 1849, which formed the Constitution of the State. In 1851, at the first election under the new Constitution, he was again elected to the lower house in the State Legislature, and served one term. In 1861 he was again elected. During the Civil War his sympathies were with the South, and notwithstanding he took no part in the great conflict, yet for several months he was one of the numerous civilian prisoners at Camp Chase, Ohio. In politics he was a staunch Democrat, and cast his first vote for Andrew Jackson, and his last, before the war, for John C. Breckinridge. He was a delegate to the Democratic National Convention at Baltimore in 1844, when James K. Polk was nominated; and in 1856 at Cincinnati, where James Buchanan was nominated; at New York in 1868, when Horatio Seymour was the nominee, and last, at St. Louis, in 1876, when Samuel J. Tilden was chosen as the standard bearer. In that year he was one of the three prominent candidates for Congress in the Sixth Kentucky District, when John G. Carlisle received the nomination. For a number of years he was Brigadier-General, and afterwards a Major-General in the old State militia service. For more than half a century he was one of the most prominent farmers and influential politicians in Kentucky, and one of the most substantial and

GENEALOGY OF COL. ISAAC BLEDSOE LINE 175

valuable citizens of his community. He was twice married; in 1832 to Julia Ann Moore, of Harrison county, who died in 1839; and in 1840 to her sister, Eliza Jean Moore. He died July 10, 1885. His last wife died May 6, 1902.

GOVERNOR JOSEPH DESHA, OF KENTUCKY

General Desha had two sons, who distinguished themselves in the Civil War; both were Captains in Morgan's command. One of them, Captain Jo. Desha, married Clarissa Rogan.

SIXTH GENERATION.

No. 25.

Joseph Desha Pickett, son of James C. and Eleanor (Desha) Pickett, was born in Mason county, Kentucky, January 6, 1822. Graduated from Princeton College in 1841; completed his course at Paris, France, and afterwards traveled extensively in Europe, Asia and Africa. Soon after his return home he became a professor in Bethany College. He was a member of the famous Secession Convention of Virginia in 1861. Joined the Confederate Army as chaplain; was chaplain of the Kentucky Orphan Brigade; then chaplain of John C. Breckenridge's Division. He was at Atlanta throughout the siege, ministering to the sick, wounded and dying. He was called "The Fighting Chaplain," and was loved and respected by the whole army. He was the founder of the Kentucky Relief Society, which did so much to alleviate the sufferings of the Southern soldiers. After the close of the war, he was at one time president of the Agricultural, Mechanical and Military College at Lexington. He was Professor of English Literature in the Kentucky University for many years; President of the College of Arts in 1877-78, and for a while was President of the Bible College. The last chair he filled was that of Professor of Metaphysics, Ancient and Modern Languages, in the Agricultural and Mechanical College, 1878-79. In the later year he was elected Superintendent of Public Instruction for Kentucky, which office he held by successive reelections for twelve years. In 1891 he retired and removed with his family to River Forest, near Chicago, his sons being located in business in Chicago. At the time of his death, in 1900, he was Chaplain-General Provis-

Hon. Joseph Desha Pickett

ional Department of the Northwest, Confederate Veterans. He married Elizabeth Jean Holton. Had children—

35 James C. Pickett. Died unmarried.
36 Eleanor Desha Pickett. Unmarried. Resides in Chicago.
37 William H. Pickett. Died unmarried.
38 John Desha Pickett. Resides in Atlanta.
39 Elizabeth Bacon Pickett.
40 Montgomery B. Pickett. Resides in Chicago.
41 Annie Glenn Pickett. Died unmarried.

No. 26.

John T. Pickett, son of James C. and Eleanor (Desha) Pickett, was born in Maysville, Kentucky. He received his early education in Scott county; was appointed to the Military Academy at West Point; afterwards studied law at the Lexington Law School. Was for many years United States Consular Agent at Vera Cruz, Mexico, and while there became interested in the "Manifest Destiny" movements along the Gulf, and soon distinguished himself as an active supporter of the principles of the "Ostend Manifesto." Yielding to his military penchant, he joined Lopez, Crittenden and others in the year 1850 in a crusade upon Cuba and personally commanded in a gallant fight, against heavy odds, at the battle of Cardenas; but the entire expedition, like most others of its kind, was a failure. He was commissioned by Louis Kossuth, as General in the Hungarian Army. He served with distinction in the Confederate Army as chief of staff to General Breckenridge, and represented the Confederate States at the opening contest, as Commissioner to the Republic of Mexico. Whilst holding this position he urged the Confederate Government to secure foreign intervention, and strengthen the military resources of the Confederacy by freeing the negroes, calling him to the field—a policy which was subsequently favored, though unsuccessfully urged, by General Robert E. Lee.

After the close of the war General Pickett engaged in the practice of law at Washington, D. C. He was an accomplished scholar, a graceful and vigorous writer, a superior linguist, a gentleman of commanding presence and captivating address. He married Katherine Keyworth, of Washington, D. C., where both died and are buried. He had children—

42   Eleanor Desha Pickett. Died unmarried.
43   Theodore John Pickett.

No. 30.

Issa Desha, daughter of John Randolph and Mary Bracken (Curry) Desha, married William Campbell Preston Breckenridge, at Lexington, Kentucky, September 19, 1861. Mr. Breckenridge was born near Lexington, August 28, 1837; graduated from Central College in April 1855, and from the law department of the University of Louisville in 1857. He was elected to Congress as a Democrat in 1885, and served four terms, distinguishing himself as an orator and for his great ability as a lawyer. Had children—

44   Eleanor Desha Breckenridge.
45   Sophonisba Preston Breckenridge.
46   Desha Breckenridge.
47   Campbell Breckenridge. Died in infancy.
48   Issa Desha Breckenridge. Died in infancy.
49   Robert J. Breckenridge.
50   Mary Curry Breckenridge.

No. 32.

Mary Desha, daughter of John Randolph and Mary Bracken (Curry) Desha, resides in Washington, D. C.; unmarried. She was one of the founders of the society of the Daughters of the American Revolution.

GENEALOGY OF COL. ISAAC BLEDSOE LINE   179

No. 34.

Bledsoe Desha Harmon, son of Dr. and Adelaide 'D Armely (Desha) Harmon, was born in Georgetown Kentucky. Married Mary Jane Lof-

MISS MARY DESHA

tin. They had children—
51   Adelaide Desha Harmon.
52   Helen Harmon.
53   Kate Harmon.
54   Irma Desha Harmon.

SEVENTH GENERATION.
No. 38.

John Desha Pickett, son of Joseph and Elizabeth Jean (Holton) Pickett, married Jessie M. Brownell. They reside in Atlanta, Georgia. Have children—

55 Desha Pickett.
56 Cornelia Francis Pickett.
57 Jean Montgomery Pickett.
58 Eleanor Desha Pickett.
59 Jessie Elizabeth Pickett.
60 Montgomery Pickett.

No. 39.

Elizabeth Bacon Pickett, daughter of Joseph Desha and Elizabeth Jean (Holton) Pickett, married Professor A. A. Bruce, who is Dean of the Law Department of the North Dakota University, at Grand Forks. They have children—

61 Glenn Bruce.
62 Edward McMaster Bruce.

No. 40.

Montgomery B. Pickett, son of Joseph Desha and Elizabeth Jean (Holton) Pickett, married Alma Morgan Osborn. They reside in Chicago. Have children—

63 Catherine Montgomery Pickett.
64 Elizabeth Pickett.

No. 43.

Theodore John Pickett, son of Colonel John T. and Katherine (Keyworth) Pickett, married Sallie V. Harris. They reside in Washington, D. C., where Mr. Pickett practices law. They have no children.

No. 44.

Eleanor Desha Breckenridge, daughter of William C. P. and Issa (Desha) Breckenridge, married Judge Lyman Chalkley at Washington City,

GENEALOGY OF COL. ISAAC BLEDSOE LINE 181

June 24, 1889. He is now Dean of the Law Department of the University of the South, at Sewanee, Tennessee. They have had four children, two of whom are dead, dying in infancy. The living are—
65 Lyman Chalkley, Jr., born June 1, 1898.
66 Issa Desha Chalkley, born March 5, 1900.

No. 45.

Sophonisba Preston Breckenridge, daughter of William C. P. and Issa (Desha) Breckenridge, is Vice-Dean of the Woman's Department of the University of Chicago.

No. 46.

Desha Breckenridge, son of William C. P. and Issa (Desha) Breckenridge, married on November 17, 1898, Madge McDowell, a great granddaughter of Henry Clay.

No. 51.

Adelaide Desha Harmon, daughter of Bledsoe Desha and Mary Jane (Loftin) Harmon, married Edward M. Kirtland. Had children—
67 Maude Harmon Kirtland.
68 Helen Desha Kirtland.

No. 52.

Helen Harmon, daughter of Bledsoe Desha and Mary Jane (Loftin) Harmon, married Colonel James A. Baret. No issue.

No. 53.

Kate Harmon, daughter of Bledsoe Desha and Mary Jane (Loftin) Harmon, married Clopton J. Hammond. Had one child—
69 Elizabeth U. Hammond.

EIGHTH GENERATION.

No. 67.

Maude Harmon Kirtland, daughter of Edward M. and Adelaide Desha (Harmon) Kirtland, married Perez Moier.

No. 68.

Helen Desha Kirtland, daughter of Edward M. and Adelaide Desha (Harmon) Kirtland, married Stuart Dean.

FOURTH GENERATION.

No. 6.

Sally Bledsoe, daughter of Colonel Isaac and Catherine (Montgomery) Bledsoe, married Rev. Samuel Gibson. No information.

No. 7.

Anthony Bledsoe, son of Colonel Isaac and Catherine (Montgomery) Bledsoe, was killed by Indians April 21, 1794, near the residence of General Daniel Smith, while boarding there and attending school.

No. 8.

Polly Bledsoe, daughter of Colonel Isaac and Catherine (Montgomery) Bledsoe, married William Read, of Sumner county. Had children—

28 Margaret Read.
29 Katherine Read.
30 Anthony Read.
31 Martha Lytle Read.
32 Francis Boyd Read.
33 Isaac de Brierleigh Read.
34 Clarissa Read.
35 Mary Read.
36 William Hadley Read. Died young.
37 Cornelia Read.

GENEALOGY OF COL. ISAAC BLEDSOE LINE 183

No. 9.

Katie Bledsoe, daughter of Colonel Isaac and Catherine (Montgomery) Bledsoe, married Thomas Scurry. Had children—

38 Clarissa Scurry.
39 Richard Scurry.
40 Susan Scurry. No information.
41 William Read Scurry.
42 Thomas Jefferson Scurry. No information.

No. 10.

Lytle Bledsoe, son of Colonel Isaac and Catherine (Montgomery) Bledsoe, married Miss Sanford. No information.

No. 11.

Isaac Bledsoe, Jr., son of Colonel Isaac and Catherine (Montgomery) Bledsoe. No information.

No. 12.

Clarissa Bledsoe, daughter of Colonel Isaac and Catherine (Montgomery) Bledsoe, married David Lauderdale. Had three sons. No information.

FIFTH GENERATION.

No. 28.

Margaret Read, daughter of William and Polly (Bledsoe) Read, married Anthony Bledsoe Neely. Had children—

43 Malvina Neely.
44 Katherine Prudence Neely.
45 Martha Ann Neely.
46 William Read Neely. Died in infancy.

No. 29.

Katherine Read, daughter of William and Polly (Bledsoe) Read, married Robert Rickman. Had children—

47 Katherine Rickman.
48 Henry Rickman.
49 Samuel Rickman.

No. 30.

Anthony Read, son of William and Polly (Bledsoe) Read, married Miss Sanford. No information.

No. 31.

Martha Lytle Read, daughter of William and Polly (Bledsoe) Read, was born in Sumner county, July 4, 1802. Married Francis Rogan, who was born in Sumner county, September 14, 1798, son of Hugh Rogan, pioneer. Had children

50 Ann Rogan. Died in infancy.
51 Hugh Rogan. Died in childhood.
52 Clarissa Rogan.
53 William Read Rogan.
54 Charles Brenard Rogan.
55 John Rogan.
56 James Leigh Rogan. Died in infancy.

No. 32.

Francis Boyd Read son of William and Polly (Bledsoe) Read, married Katherine Isam. Had children—

57 Nancy Jane Read.
58 Mollie Read.
59 Martha Read.

No. 33.

Isaac de Brierleigh Read, son of William and Polly (Bledsoe) Read, married, first, Teresa Bellemy, second, Eliza Branch, daughter of Governor Branch, of North Carolina, member of Jackson's cabinet, and afterwards Governor of Florida. After studying law in Gallatin he removed to Tallahassee, Florida, where he practiced, and where he became prominent in the 30s and 40s. He was a member of the Legislature and of the Convention which framed the first Constitution of the State of Florida. He took an active part in the Indian wars in that State, holding various

Genealogy of Col. Isaac Bledsoe Line

commanding offices. A brigade of cavalry was organized under orders of the Secretary of War and commanded by General Read. He engaged in several duels, and was assassinated on the streets of Tallahassee. He had one child, which died young.

No. 34.

Clarissa Read, daughter of William and Polly (Bledsoe) Read, married Joseph Aston. Had children—

60 John Aston. No information.
61 Wiliam Aston. No information.
62 James Aston. No information.

No. 35.

Mary Read, daughter of William and Polly (Bledsoe) Read, married Rev. Hugh Hill. Had children—

63 William Scurry Hill.
64 Mary Jane Hill.
65 Martha Hill.
66 James Hill. Died in infancy.

No. 37.

Cornelia Read, daughter of William and Polly (Bledsoe) Read, married Michael Duffy. Had children—

67 William Read Duffy. Never married. Died June 8, 1907.
68 Hugh Duffy.
69 Frank Duffy. Died in young manhood.
70 Micha Ellen Duffy.

After the death of Mr. Duffy, his wife married George Terry. Had one child—

71 Jefferson Davis Terry. Died in infancy.

No. 38.

Clarissa Scurry, daughter of Thomas and Katy (Bledsoe) Scurry, married Thomas Woodson. Had one daughter—

72 Katie Woodson.

No. 39.

Richard Scurry, son of Thomas and Katie (Bledsoe) Scurry, was born in Sumner county. Removed to Texas while a young man, and commanded a battery under General Sam Houston at the battle of San Jacinto. He served one term in Congress, 1851-53. Was for a time a member of the Supreme Court of Texas. While hunting he accidentally shot himself and died from the wound. He married and had one daughter—

73   Katie Scurry.

No. 41.

William Read Scurry, son of Thomas and Katie (Bledsoe) Scurry, was born in Sumner county. He learned the trade of printer; studied law and removed to Texas and practiced in Houston. In 1861 he entered the Confederate service as Lieutenant-Colonel of the Fourth Texas Mounted Infantry. Early in 1862 his regiment was in a brigade, which was sent to New Mexico. Colonel Scurry commanded the brigade in several engagements, and was the victor in every one of them. In September of the same year he returned to Texas and was commissioned a Brigadier-General. He commanded the land forces at Galveston on January 1, 1863. He was in the Red River campaign in 1864; and was in the battles of Mansfield and Pleasant Hill when General Banks of the Federal Army was so signally defeated. In the battle of Jenkins Ferry, April 30, 1864, he received a mortal wound. He was called "the gallant and daring Scurry." No information as to his marriage or descendants.

No. 43.

Malvina Neely, daughter of Anthony Bledsoe and Margaret (Read) Neely, married Richard Averett. No issue.

GENEALOGY OF COL. ISAAC BLEDSOE LINE 187

No. 44.

Katherine Prudence Neely, daughter of Anthony Bledsoe and Margaret (Read) Neely, married Wesley Blakemore. No issue.

No. 45.

Martha Ann Neely, daughter of Anthony Bledsoe and Margaret (Read) Neely, married Robert Bennett. Had one child—

73a Malvina Bennett, who married T. H. Mason, and had one child, Richard Jarvis Mason. No information.

SIXTH GENERATION.

No. 52.

Clarissa Rogan, daughter of Francis and Martha Lytle (Read) Rogan, married Joseph Desha. She now resides, a widow, on a part of the original tract of land belonging to her grandfather, Hugh Rogan. No children—

No. 53.

William Read Rogan, son of Francis and Martha Lytle (Read) Rogan, was born in Sumner county, February 7, 1837. In 1861 he answered the summons of his country and enlisted in the Confederate Army, in which he served to the close of the war, in Morgan's command. He was in the Ohio raid, and participated in all the hotly-contested engagements in which Morgan's brigade took part, with the rank of Captain. He was a brave and gallant soldier, and like his distinguished ancestor, Hugh Rogan, was ever ready for a brush with the enemy. He now resides in the old home of his father and grandfather, at Rogana. On October 19, 1858, he married Sarah Elizabeth Cecil, who was born in Kentucky, October 17, 1839. Had children—

74 Ann Augusta Rogan.

75 John Mathew Rogan.
76 Martha Lytle Rogan.
77 Frank Rogan. Died in infancy.
78 Charles Bernard Rogan, Jr.
After the death of his wife, Sarah Elizabeth, William R. Rogan married Mary Hill. Have one child—
79 Clarissa Rogan, born in November, 1901.

No. 54.

Charles Bernard Rogan, son of Francis, and Martha Lytle (Read) Rogan, was born in Sumner county, January 6, 1839. In 1861 he entered the Confederate Army and served to the close of the war with credit to himself and to his country, on the staff of General William B. Bate. He, like his brother, William R., proudly wears the Cross of Honor on his breast. On November 28, 1866, he married Fetoris Cecil, who was born in Kentucky, November 16, 1847. No issue.

No. 55.

John Rogan, son of Francis and Martha Lytle (Read) Rogan, was born in Sumner county, September 24, 1841. He enlisted in the Confederate Army at the beginning of the war, and served to June 20, 1862, when he died at Tupelo, Mississippi. Never married.

No. 57.

Nancy Jane Read, daughter of Francis Boyd and Katherine (Isam) Read, married Mr. Jones. No information.

No. 58.

Mollie Read, daughter of Francis Boyd and Katherine (Isam) Read, married Mr. Markham. No information.

No. 59.

Martha Read, daughter of Francis Boyd and Katherine (Isam) Read, married Mr. Seighman. No information.

Genealogy of the Bledsoe Family 189

No. 63.

William Scurry Hill, son of Rev. Hugh and Mary (Read) Hill, married Margaret Davis, sister of Sam Davis, the Confederate hero. No information.

No. 64.

Mary Jane Hill, daughter of Rev. Hugh and Mary (Read) Hill, married Mr. Robertson. No information.

No. 65.

Martha Hill, daughter of Rev. Hugh and Mary (Read) Hill, married Mr. Robertson. No information.

No. 68.

Hugh M. Duffy, son of Michael and Cornelia (Read) Duffy, married Fannie Desha. Had children—

80   Eliza Duffy.
81   Cornelia Duffy.
82   Frank Duffy.
83   Fanny Duffy.

No. 70.

Micha Ellen Duffy, daughter of Michael and Cornelia (Read) Duffy, married William H. B. Satterwhite. Have children—

84   Nellie C. Satterwhite.
85   James A. Satterwhite.

No. 72.

Katie Woodson, daughter of Thomas and Clarissa (Scurry) Woodson, married Mr. Yarbrough. Died in Texas. No information.

No. 73.

Katie Scurry, daughter of Richard Scurry, married Mr. Terril. She resides at Dallas, Texas. No information.

SEVENTH GENERATION.

No. 74.

Ann Augusta Rogan, daughter of William Read and Sarah Elizabeth (Cecil) Rogan, was born in Sumner county, August 23, 1859. Married Harris Brown, who has for many years been County Court Clerk for Sumner county, and who is one of its most prominent and useful citizens. He was born in Sumner county, March 18, 1858, and married June 18, 1895. No issue.

No. 75.

John Mathew Rogan, son of William Read and Sarah Elizabeth (Cecil) Rogan, was born in Sumner county, September 13, 1866. Married on April 26, 1899, Cecil Walton. Died July 31, 1899. No issue.

No. 76.

Martha Lytle Rogan, daughter of William Read and Sarah Elizabeth (Cecil) Rogan, was born in Sumner county, September 12, 1869. Married June 16, 1897, Dr. William James Morrison, D. D. S., of Nashville. Have children—

86   William Rogan Morrison, born February 6, 1899.
87   Mary Cecil Morrison, born September 12, 1900.
88   Andrew Lawrence Morrison, born May 12, 1902.

No. 78.

Charles Bernard Rogan, son of William Read and Sarah Elizabeth (Cecil) Rogan, was born in Sumner county, September 6, 1874. Married Mary Callan. He was commisisoned by President McKinley a Lieutenant in the Signal Corps in the war with Spain, and did service in Cuba, and then in the Philippines. After the close of the war he was made a Lieutenant in the Regular Army, and was later promoted to Captain, which rank he now holds. Have one child—

89   Augusta Cecil Rogan, born August 9, 1900.

THE CAGE FAMILY

William Cage, the head of the Sumner county Cage's, was born in Virginia in 1745; served in the Revolutionary War with the rank of Major. Married, first, Elizabeth Douglass, daughter of Colonel Edward Douglass; second, Ann Morgan. Removed to Sumner county, Tennessee, in 1785, and settled at Cage's Bend. When the Territorial Government was organized, in 1790, he was appointed by Governor Blount, Sheriff of Sumner county, and by successive appointments served to 1796, when he was succeeded by his son, Reuben Cage, who served to 1800, when he was in turn succeeded by James Cage. William Cage died at his home in Cage's Bend, March 12, 1811. His tombstone bears this inscription: "William Cage, a Major in the Revolutionary War. Died March 12, 1811.

GENEALOGY.

SECOND GENERATION.

1 William Cage and Elizabeth Douglass Cage had children—
2 Priscilla Cage married William Hale, of Sullivan county.
3 Wilson Cage married Polly Dillard, of Sumner county.
4 Reuben Cage married Polly Morgan, of Sumner county.
5 William Cage, Jr., married Fannie Street, of Sumner county.
6 Sally Cage, twin of William, married Jack Carr, of Sumner county.
7 James Cage, never married.
8 Edward Cage, married Elizabeth Jarrett, of Sumner county.
9 John Cage, married Thankful Morgan, of Sumner county.
10 Lofton Cage, married Nabury Gillespie, of Smith county.

192   HISTORIC SUMNER COUNTY, TENN.

11 Jesse Cage, married Polly Gillespie, of Sumner county.
    Children of second wife:
12 Richard Cage. No information.
13 Harry Cage, married Catherine Stewart, of Mississippi.
14 Albert Cage. No information.
15 Robert Cage, married Lucy Hunley, of Wilson county.
16 Elizabeth Cage, married Harman Hays. The celebrated Colonel Jack Hays, of the Texas Rangers, was their son.
17 Patsey Cage, married Thomas Morton.

THIRD GENERATION.
No. 2.

Priscilla Cage, daughter of William and Elizabeth (Douglass) Cage, married William Hale. Had children—

18 Cage Hale. No information.
19 Elizabeth Hale. No information.
20 Sallie Hale. No information.
21 Nicholas Hale. No information.
22 Richard Hale. No information.
23 Wilson Hale. No information.
24 James Hale. No information.
25 Douglass Hale. No information.
26 Priscilla Hale. No information.
27 Beasman Hale. No information.
28 Cyrus B. Hale, married Eliza Taylors.
29 William Hale. No information.

No. 3.

Wilson Cage, son of William and Elizabeth (Douglass) Cage, married Polly Dillard. Had children—

30 Leroy Cage, married Miss Moore, of Smith county.
31 Poleman Cage, married Miss Dillard, of Smith county.

GENEALOGY OF THE CAGE FAMILY

32 J. Overton Cage, married Miss Robo, of Smith county.
33 Elizabeth Cage, married Mr. Bradley, of Smith county.
34 Priscilla Cage, married Norval Douglass, of Sumner county.
35 Patsey Cage, married Mr. Rae.
36 Delia Cage, married W. C. Beck.
37 Harriet Cage, married Mr. Boyd.
38 William Cage, married Miss Watkins.
39 Harry Cage, married Miss Mulholland.
40 Adolphus W. Cage, married Miss Boyd.
41 Wilson Cage, married Miss Criswell.

No. 4.

Reuben Cage, son of William and Elizabeth (Douglass) Cage, married Polly Morgan. Had children—

42 Orville Cage, married, first, Louisa Douglass; second, Miss Watson.
43 Nancy Cage, married Fred Watkins.
44 Evaline Cage, married Mr. Abston.
45 Louisa Cage, married Mr. Abston.
46 Adeline Cage, married Mr. Gillespie.
47 Sophia Cage, married Dr. Jack Franklin.

No. 5.

William Cage, son of William and Elizabeth (Douglass) Cage, married Fannie Street. Had children—

48 George Cage. No information.
49 Maria Cage, married Foster Crutcher.
50 James Cage, married Sophia Wright.
51 Susan Cage, married Thomas Anderson.
52 Edward Cage. No information.
53 Marcus Cage. No information.
54 Lycurgus Cage, married Elizabeth James.
55 Rufus K. Cage, married Mary Boddie.
56 Wilson Cage. No information.
57 Corina Cage. No information.

No. 6.

Sally Cage, daughter of William and Elizabeth (Douglass) Cage, was a twin sister of William. She married Jack Carr, of Sumner county. Had children—

58 Betsy Carr, married Mr. Holt.
59 Priscilla Carr, married Mr. Murray.
60 William Cage Carr, married Miss Willis.
61 James C. Ca r, married Mrs. Belote.
62 Ann Carr, married R. Allen.
63 John Sewell Carr. No information.
64 Wilson Carr, married Miss Baskerville.
65 Reese Carr. No information.
66 Orvey Carr, married Mr. Crenshaw.
67 Martin Carr. No information.
68 Jesse Carr, married, first, Miss Brewer; second, Miss Woods.
69 Sarah Carr, married Samuel Wallace.
70 Patsey Carr. No information.
71 Name unknown. Died young.

No. 8.

Edward Cage, son of William and Elizabeth Douglass) Cage, married Elizabeth Jarrett. Had children—

72 Alva Cage.
73 Alfred Cage.
74 Edward Cage.
75 Priscilla Cage, married Mr. Noland.
76 Elizabeth Cage.

No. 9.

John Cage, son of William and Elizabeth (Douglass) Cage, married Thankful Morgan, of Sumner county. Had children—

77 William Clinton Cage, married Miss Lynch.
78 Minerva Cage, married Peter Hubbard.
79 Claiborne Cage, married Miss Stewart.
80 Jack Cage.
81 Edward Cage, married Miss Young.

Genealogy of the Cage Family

82 James Cage.
83 Elizabeth Cage, married Mr. Frazier.
84 Priscilla Cage, married David Barry.
85 Benjamin Cage.

No. 10.

Lofton Cage, son of William and Elizabeth (Douglass) Cage, married Nabury Gillespie. Had children—

86 Eliza Cage, married L. Coleman.
87 Selima Cage, married Mr. Elliott.
88 Albert Cage.
89 Fanny Cage.

No. 11.

Jesse Cage, son of William and Elizabeth (Douglass) Cage, married Polly Gillespie. Had children—

90 Elizabeth Cage, married Smith Franklin.
91 William C. Cage, married Julia Franklin.
92 Jack F. Cage, married Mary Cantrell.
93 Sophia Ann Cage.
94 Jane Cage.
95 Maria Cage, married Dr. James Franklin.
96 Caroline Cage, married Thomas Fletcher.
97 Minerva Cage, married Judge William Sharky, of Mississippi.

No. 13.

Harry Cage, son of William and Elizabeth (Douglass) Cage, married Catherine Stewart. Had children—

98 Penelope Cage. Died in infancy.
99 Duncan S. Cage, married Jane Connell.
100 Albert G. Cage, married Elvira Gayden.

No. 15.

Robert Cage, son of William and Elizabeth (Douglass) Cage, married Lucy Hunley. Had children—

101 Albert Cage, married Amanda Garrett.

196 HISTORIC SUMNER COUNTY, TENN.

102 Elizabeth Cage, married General Harry Hays.
103 Catherine Cage, married Mr. Taylor.
104 Minerva Cage, married Captain John Gidiere.
105 Rebecca Cage, twin of Minerva, died in childhood.
106 Lucy Cage, married, first, Mr. Witherspoon; second, Jack Ratcliff.
107 Jane Cage, married Judge William Holmes.
108 Harry Hays Cage, died during the Civil War.
109 Robert Cage, married Mary de Valcourt.

No. 16.

Elizabeth Cage, daughter of William and Elizabeth (Douglass) Cage, married Harman Hays. Had children—

110 Jack Hays, married Miss Calvert.
111 William Hays, married Miss E. Stephens.
112 Mary Ann Hays, married J. C. Lewis.
113 Sarah Hays, married Calvin Lea.
114 Harry Hays, married Bettie Cage.
115 Robert Hays.
116 Jane Hays.

No. 17.

Patsey Cage, daughter of William and Elizabeth (Douglass) Cage, married Thomas Morton. Had childrer—

117 Susan Morton.

No. 28.

Cyrus B. Hale, son of William and Priscilla (Cage) Hale, married Eliza Taylors. Had children—

117^1 William J. Hale.
117^2 Priscilla Hale, married D. J. Harper.
117^3 Ellar Hale, married J. B. Lipscomb.
117^4 James Cage Hale.

GENEALOGY OF THE CAGE FAMILY 197

FOURTH GENERATION.

No. 90.

Elizabeth Cage, daughter of Jesse and Polly (Gillespie) Cage, married Smith Franklin. Had children—

118 Blanche Franklin, married Hon. Stephen Archer.

No. 91.

William Cage, son of Jesse and Polly (Gillespie) Cage, married Julia Franklin. Had children—

119 Ann Cage, married James Bashaw.
120 John Hogg Cage.
121 Betsey Cage. Died young.
122 Martha Cage, married Isaac Guthrie.
123 Gertrude Cage. Died young.
124 Cora Cage.
125 Laura Cage, married William Seay.
126 Florida Cage, married John Scott.

No. 92.

Jack F. Cage, son of Jesse and Polly (Gillespie) Cage, married Mary Cantrell. Had children—

127 Jesse Cage, married Sallie Douglass.
128 Willie Cage. Died young.
129 Polly Cage, married Frank Douglass.
130 Fannie Cage.
131 James Cage, married Sallie Boddie.
132 Walter Bugg Cage.
133 Lou Cage, married W. C. Dismukes.
134 Jack Cage.

No. 95.

Maria Cage, daughter of Jesse and Polly (Gillespie) Cage, married Dr. James Franklin. Had children—

135 Mary Franklin, married Mr. Bondurant.
136 Carrie Franklin, married John Barry

198 HISTORIC SUMNER COUNTY, TENN.

137   Minerva Franklin.
138   Jessie Franklin.
139   James Franklin.
140   Jack Franklin.

No. 99.

Duncan S. Cage, son of Harry and Catherine (Stewart) Cage, married Jane Connell. Had children—

141   Leonora Cage, never married.
142   Harry Cage, married Jane Bisland.
143   Liza Cage, never married.
145   Albert Cage, son of Robert and Lucy (Hun- Hugh Connell Cage, married Madge Baldwin.
146   Duncan S. Cage, Jr., married Ellen Morgan.
147   Jane Cage, never married.

No. 100.

Albert Cage, son of Robert and Lucy (Hun-(Stewart) Cage, married Elvira Gayden. Had children—

148   Duncan Cage, never married.
149   Catherine Cage, married J. Baker Bisland.
150   Agrippa Gayden Cage, married Loula Lyle.
151   Mary Cage, married Judge John Clegg.
152   Harry Hays Cage.
153   Elvira Cage, married William McCollam.

No. 101.

Albert Cage, son of Robert and Lucy (Hunley) Cage, married Amanda Garrett. Had children:

154   Sallie Cage, married Will Powell.
155   Lucy Cage, married John Craig.
156   Harry Cage, married Miss Handy.
157   Emily Cage, married John Bobb.
158   Bessie Cage, married Dan Rose.
159   Isa Cage.
160   Albert Cage, never married.

No. 102.

Elizabeth Cage, daughter of Robert and Lucy (Hunley) Cage, married General Harry Hays. Had children—

161 Jack Hays. Died in January, 1888. Unmarried.
162 Lucy Hays, married Franklin Mix.
163 Kate Hays, married Harry Hays.
164 Minerva Hays, married Sydney Guyol.

No. 117a.

William J. Hale, son of Cyrus B. and Eliza (Taylors) Hale, married ———. He entered the Confederate Army in 1861, as Captain of a company in Bates' Second Tennessee Regiment, and was afterwards promoted to Lieutenant-Colonel. When W. B. Bate was commissioned Brigadier-General, Hale was promoted to Colonel of the regiment, and commanded it until the close of the war. He was a brave and gallant soldier and was loved and respected by all his men. After the war he engaged in merchandising in Hartsville, where he still resides and conducts a successful business. In 1883 he was elected to represent Trousdale, Sumner and Smith counties in the Legislature, and served two terms, with satisfaction to his people and honor to himself.

His son, W. B. Hale, served a term in the Legislature, and was afterwards a Captain in the war with Spain.

No. 103.

Catherine Cage, daughter of Robert and Lucy (Hunley) Cage, married Mr. Taylor. Had children—

165 Hunley Taylor. Died in 1880. Unmarried.

No. 104.

Minerva Cage, daughter of Robert and Lucy (Hunley) Cage, married John Gidiere. Had children—

166   Kate Gidiere, married Horace Reese.
167   Harry Gidiere.
168   Philip Gidiere.

No. 106.

Lucy Cage, daughter of Robert and Lucy (Hunley) Cage, married, first. Mr. Witherspoon; second, Mr. Ratcliffe. Had children—

169   Minerva Witherspoon, married Frank Hindman.
170   Jack Ratcliffe.

No. 107.

Jane Cage, daughter of Robert and Lucy (Hunley) Cage, married Judge William Holmes. Had children—

171   Robert H. Holmes.
172   Ethel Holmes.
173   William Holmes.
174   Harry Holmes, twin of William.
175   Maurry Holmes.

No. 109.

Robert Cage, son of Robert and Lucy (Hunley) Cage, married Mary de Valcourt. Had children—

176   Edith Cage.
177   Bessie Cage.
178   Mary Cage.
179   Robert Cage, Jr.

No. 127.

Jesse Cage, son of Jack F. and Mary (Cantrell) Cage, was born in Sumner county, January 30, 1841. The military records at Washington City show that on May 26, 1861, he enlisted as a private in Company E, Seventh Tennessee Infantry, Confederate Veterans. He was appointed Third Sergeant, April 20, 1862; Second Sergeant in April, 1864, and First Sergeant, February 24, 1865. The record shows that he was wounded in action before Petersburg, Virginia, April 2, 1865, and was captured and his leg amputated. He was then sent to Lincoln Hospital, Washington, D. C., where he was held until May 30, 1865, when he was released, after the surrender of General Lee. He then returned to his home in Sumner county. In 1869 he was appointed County Court Clerk for Sumner county. In 1870 he was elected to the same office for a term of four years. In August, 1874, he was reelected without opposition. In 1878 he declined to offer again for the office, and in 1884 removed to Nashville, and served as Chief Deputy under Colonel John T. Hillman, United States Revenue Collector under Cleveland's first administration. Since his term expired he has been with the Nashville Trust Company. He was called by the people of Nashville to, and was elected justice of the peace, and is now, 1908, holding that office.

On November 3, 1870, he married Sallie T. Douglass, daughter of Robert B. and Delia A. (Mitchell) Douglass. Has children—

180 Douglass Cage. Died in infancy.
181 Louisa Mitchell Cage.
182 Trousdale Cage.
183 Nellie Cage. Died at 18 months of age.
184 Maria F. Cage.
185 Mary Cage. Died at the age of five years.
186 Henry Cage. Died in infancy.

No. 129.

Polly Cage, daughter of Jack F. and Mary (Cantrell) Cage, married Frank Douglass. Had children—

187 Cage Douglass.
188 Mary Douglass.

189 Eastman Douglass.
190 Robert Douglass.
191 Ellen Douglass.
No. 131.
James Cage, son of Jack F. and Mary (Cantrell) Cage, married Sallie Boddie. Had children—
192 Lizzie Cage.
193 Charles Cage.
194 Mary Cage.
195 Sue Cage, twin of Mary. Died young.
196 Fields Cage.
197 Alice Cage.
198 Josephine Cage, twin of Alice.
199 Jessie Cage. Died young.

THE DOUGLASS FAMILY

The Douglass family has been prominent in Sumner county since 1785, when Edward Douglass, with all his children, settled on Station Camp Creek a few miles north from Gallatin. He was born in Farquier county, Virginia; married about 1740, Sarah George. He was a commissioned officer in the War for Independence, and a man of education, and a lawyer, though he had never practiced law. He, when called upon, gave legal advice to his friends and neighbors without fee or reward, always counseling them not to go into the courts. He was one of the first magistrates of Sumner county, and was active in all public affairs. His home was near Salem Camp Ground, on lands still in possession of his descendants.

GENEALOGY.
No. 1.

Colonel Edward Douglass and Sarah (George) Douglass had children—
2 John Douglass, killed by Indians while on a mission to them from Colonel Anthony Bledsoe.

GENEALOGY OF THE DOUGLASS FAMILY

3   William Douglass, married Peggy Stroud.
4   Elizabeth Douglass, married William Cage.
5   Elmore Douglass, married Betsey Blakemore.
6   Ezekiel Douglass, married May Gibson.
7   Sally Douglass, married Thomas Blakemore.
8   Edward Douglass, Jr., married Elizabeth Howard.
9   Reuben Douglass, married Elizabeth Edwards.
10 James Douglass, married Catherine Collier.

SECOND GENERATION.

No. 3.

William Douglass, son of Colonel Edward and Sarah (George) Douglass, married Peggy Stroud. Had children—

11 John Douglass, married Miss Gregory; moved to Arkansas.
12 Jesse Douglass. Drowned.
13 Elizabeth Douglass, married Matthew Scoby; moved to Arkansas.
14 Sally Douglass, married James Mays. No information.
15 Polly Douglass, married Abner Donent. No information.
16 James Douglass, married Miss Dobson. No information.
17 Alfred M. Douglass, married Cherry Ferrell.

No. 4.

Elizabeth Douglass, daughter of Colonel Edward and Sarah (George) Douglass, married William Cage. (See genealogy of the Cage family.)

No. 5.

Elmore Douglass, son of Colonel Edward and Sarah (George) Douglass, married Betsey Blakemore. Had children—

18 John Douglass.
19 Celia Douglass, married John Pages.

20 Sally Douglass, married Isaac Hooks.
21 Nancy Douglass, married Moses Pincton.
22 Elizabeth Douglass, married Mr. Cooper.
23 Edward Douglass, married Miss Green. Went to Mississippi.
24 Elmore Douglass, Jr.
25 Burchet Douglass, married Patsey McGee.
26 Ily Douglass, married —— Harris.
27 Eunis Douglass, married Mr. Harris.
28 Asa Douglass, married Fannie Barksdale.
29 Delia Douglass, married Mr. Brooks.

No. 6.

Ezekiel Douglass, son of Colonel Edward and Sarah (George) Douglass, married Mary Gibson. Had children—

30 John Douglass, married Polly Kellum. Moved to Arkansas.
31 James Douglass, married Rina Hunt.
32 Sally Douglass, married Mr. Joselin.
33 George Douglass, married Mrs. White.
34 Robert G. Douglass.
35 Tempy Douglass.

No. 7.

Sally Douglass, daughter of Colonel Edward and Sarah (George) Douglass, married Thomas Blakemore. Had children—

36 James Blakemore, married Patsey Taylor.
37 William Blakemore.
38 John Blakemore, married Miss Rankin.
39 Reuben Blakemore, married Miss Bentley.
40 Tourblen Blakemore.
41 Edward Blakemore, married Miss Murray.
42 George Blakemore.
43 Lee Blakemore, married Charlotte Johnson.
44 Wesley Blakemore, married Kitty Neely.
45 Albert Blakemore.
46 Elizabeth Blakemore, married William Dickerson.

GENEALOGY OF THE DOUGLASS FAMILY 205

47 Coena Blakemore, married John Black.
48 Ann Blakemore, married Mr. Taylor.
49 Matilda Blakemore, married Henry Hart.
50 Fielding Blakemore, married Rebecca Johnson.

No. 8.

Edward Douglass, Jr., son of Colonel Edward and Sarah (George) Douglass, married Elizabeth Howard. Had children—

51 William Howard Douglass, married Sallie Edwards.
52 Harry Lightfoot Douglass, married, first, Miss P. Shelby; second, Miss Z. Allcorn; third, Miss J. Crabb.
53 Patsey S. Douglass, married John Hall.
54 Delia Douglass, married Edward Douglass.
55 Elmore Douglass, married, first, Eliza Fulton; second, Eliza Houston.
56 Norval Douglass, married Priscilla Cage.
57 Eliza G. Douglass, married C. Grandison Sanders.

No. 9.

Reuben Douglass, son of Colonel Edward and Sarah (George) Douglass, married Elizabeth Edwards. Had children—

58 Willie J. Douglass, married, first, Eliza Watkins; second, Lucy Grimm.
59 Sophia Douglass, married Charles Watkins.
60 Peggy Douglass, married Lewis Green.
61 Evalina Douglass, married William Franklin.
62 Malissa Douglass.
63 Bennett Douglass.
64 William Douglass.
65 Patsy Douglass, married Mr. Partee. Moved to West Tennessee.
66 Emma Douglass, married William Clark.

No. 10.

James Douglass, son of Colonel Edward and Sarah (George) Douglass, married Catherine Collier. Had children—

67 Alfred H. Douglass, married, first, Lucy Bennett; second, Rebecca Fulton.
68 Matilda G. Douglass, married, first, J. Cook; second, Joel Parrish.
69 Edward L. Douglass, married Delia Douglass.
70 Isaac C. Douglass, married Eliza Baker.
71 James S. Douglass, married Luck Scarlock.
72 Harry C. Douglass, married Elizabeth Elliott.
73 Young N. Douglass, married Miss B. Rawlings.
74 Robert G. Douglass, married Elizabeth Blythe.
75 William C. Douglass, married Lucy Seawell.
76 Thomas C. Douglass, married Francis Cantrell.
77 Louisa F. Douglass, married G. W. Allen.

THIRD GENERATION.

No. 11.

John Douglass, son of William and Peggy (Stroud) Douglass, married ———— Gregory and moved to Pulaski county, Arkansas. Had children—

78 Thomas Douglass.

No. 13.

Elizabeth Douglass, daughter of William and Peggy (Stroud) Douglass, married Matthew Scoby. They removed to LaFayette county, Arkansas. Had children—

79 Jesse Scoby.
80 Patima Scoby.
81 Josephine Scoby.

No. 17.

Alfred Douglass, son of William and Peggy (Stroud) Douglass, married Cherry Ferrell. Had children—

GENEALOGY OF THE DOUGLASS FAMILY 207

82 James Douglass, married Mary Rogers.
83 Alfred W. Douglass, married Mourning H. Boddie.
84 Louisa Douglass, married Burchett Ferrell.

No. 19.

Celia Douglass, daughter of Elmore and Betsey (Blackmon) Douglass, married John Pages. Had children—

85 Seawell Pages.
86 Thomas Pages, married Miss Ledbetter.
87 Douglass Pages.
88 Norval Pages.
89 Louisa Pages.
90 Nancy Pages, married Thomas Watson.
91 Betsey Pages, married Mr. Donald.
92 Polly Pages.
93 Martha Pages, married Dick Shalton.

No. 30.

John Douglass, son of Ezekiel and Mary (Gibson) Douglass, married Polly Kallum, and removed to Arkansas. Had children—

94 Polly Douglass, married Jared C. Martin.
95 A. Gibson Douglass.
96 Sophia Douglass.
97 James Douglass.
98 John Douglass.
99 Emily Douglass.
100 Patsey Douglass.
101 Earl Douglass.

No. 31.

James Douglass, son of Ezekiel and Mary (Gibson) Douglass, married Rina Hunt. Had children—

102 Patsey Douglass.
103 Mary Ann Douglass, married Merry C. Aston.
104 Robert B. Douglass, married Delia A. Mitchell.
105 Albert G. Douglass, married Dorotha Turner.

106 Evaline Douglass, married Charles Boddie.
107 Sarah T. Douglass.
108 D. W. Clinton Douglass, married Martha Ann Murray.
109 William Douglass.
110 Harry Douglass.

No. 33.

George Douglass, son of Ezekiel and Mary (Gibson) Douglass, married Mrs. White. Had children—

111 George Douglass, Jr.
112 Mary Abston Douglass.
113 Washington LaFayette Douglass. Died young.

No. 36.

James Blakemore, son of Thomas and Sally (Douglass) Blakemore, married Patsey Taylor. Had children—

114 William Blakemore.

No. 43.

Lee Blakemore, son of James and Sally (Douglass) Blakemore, married Charlotte Johnson. Had children—

115 Mary Blakemore

No. 50.

Fielding Blakemore, son of James and Sally (Douglass) Blakemore, married Rebecca Johnson. Had children—

116 Jesse Thomas Blakemore, married Mary E. Darnell.
117 William Blakemore, married Ann Thermon.
118 Sally Blakemore.
119 Clinton Blakemore.
120 Ann Elizabeth Blakemore.
121 Fielding Driskill Blakemore.

Genealogy of the Douglass Family

No. 51.

William Howard Douglass, son of Edward Douglass, Jr., and Elizabeth (Howard) Douglass, married Sally Edwards. Had children—

- 122 Henry L. Douglass, married Mary Hall.
- 123 Elizabeth H. Douglass, married Dr. James Mitchell. Moved to Texas.
- 124 William E. Douglass. Died in Austin, Texas. Never married.
- 125 Sarah E. Douglass, married Dr. James Glass. Moved to Mississippi.
- 126 Cullen E. Douglass, married, first, Harriet Bain; second, Mary Estes.
- 127 Robert B. Douglass. Never married.

No. 52.

Harry Lightfoot Douglass, son of Edward, Jr., and Elizabeth (Howard) Douglass, married Priscilla Shelby, and after her death, Miss Z. Allcorn, and after her death, Jane Crabb. Had children—

- 128 Priscilla Douglass, married Dr. R. C. K. Martin. (See Colonel Anthony Bledsoe genealogy.)
- 129 William R. Douglass.
- 130 Elizabeth H. Douglass.

One child by each wife.

No. 53.

Patsey S. Douglass, daughter of Edward, Jr., and Elizabeth (Howard) Douglass, married John Hall. Had children—

- 131 William M. Hall, married Jane Allcorn.
- 132 Elizabeth E. Hall, married John B. Forrester.
- 133 Cornelia T. Hall, married, first, E. D. Hicks; second, James I. Guion.
- 134 Delia Ann Hall, married William Crenshaw.
- 135 Robert J. Hall, married Mary Sharkey.
- 136 Julia P. Hall, married Dan R. Russell.
- 137 Edward D. Hall.

No. 54.

Delia Douglass, daughter of Edward and Elizabeth (Howard) Douglass, married Edward Douglass. Had children—

138 William Howard Douglass.

No. 55.

Elmore Douglass, son of Edward and Elizabeth (Howard) Douglass, married, first, Eliza Fulton. Had children—

139 Edward Douglass. Drowned in 1834.
140 David Fulton Douglass, married S. Helen Rice. No issue.
141 Norvell Douglass, married, first, Mourning Miller; second, J. Dillon.
142 George Bell Douglass.
143 Catherine S. Douglass.
144 Elizabeth S. H. Douglass, married John A. Reed.
145 Cynthia E. Douglass.
146 Sophia Ann Douglass, married Dr. James Pitts.
147 Nedella Douglass, married Richard Fondolan.
148 J. J. White Douglass.

After the death of his first wife, Elmore married Miss J. Dillon. Had children—

149 Martha A. Douglass, married William D. Haggard.
150 H. Louis Douglass.
151 Susan M. Douglass.

No. 56.

Norval Douglass son of Edward, Jr., and Elizabeth (Howard) Douglass, married Priscilla Cage. Had children—

152 Elmore Douglass.
153 Granderson S. Douglass.
154 Mary P. Douglass.
155 Edward H. Douglass.
156 John Forrester Douglass.

Genealogy of the Douglass Family

157   Wilson Cage Douglass, twin of above.
158   Harry Norval Douglass.
159   Ellen E. Douglass.

No. 57.

Eliza G. Douglass, daughter of Edward J. and Elizabeth (Howard) Douglass, married C. Grandison Sanders. Had children—

160   James D. Sanders.
161   Elizabeth H. Sanders, married William E. Elliott.
162   Mary S. Sanders.
163   Delia A. Sanders, married Mr. Briscoe.
164   Martha Sanders.
165   Cornelia A. Sanders.
166   Norval D. Sanders.
167   David M. Sanders.
168   Edward D. Sanders.
169   Eliza G. Sanders.

No. 58.

William J. Douglass, son of Reuben and Elizabeth (Edwards) Douglass, married, first, Eliza Watkins; second, Lucy Grimm. Had children—

170   William W. Douglass, married Miss Bell.
171   Jane A. Douglass, married Dr. J. Franklin.
172   Richard E. Douglass, married Sarah Walton.
173   Guy M. Douglass, married Miss Harris.
174   Reuben Douglass, married Mrs. Turney.
175   Charles W. Douglass.

By second wife—

177   Elizabeth Douglass, married Joseph Miller.
178   Willie J. Douglass, married, first, Helen Doubleday; second, Eliza B. Douglass.
179   Walter Douglass, married Clara Doubleday.
180   Evaline Douglass, married John Brown.

No. 60.

Peggy Douglass, daughter of Reuben and Elizabeth (Edwards) Douglass, married Lewis Green. Had children—

181 William Green.
182 Reuben D. Green, married Kate Royston.
183 Sarah Green.
184 Elizabeth Green, married Clinton Bledsoe.
185 Edward D. Green.
186 Sophia Green, married Thomas Bell.
187 Peggy Green, married Mr. Gordon.

No. 61.

Evaline Douglass, daughter of Reuben and Elizabeth (Edwards) Douglass, married William Franklin. Had children—

188 Mary Franklin, married Kleber Miller.
189 Elizabeth Franklin.
190 Margaret Franklin.
191 Jane Franklin.
192 Ben Franklin, died in the Confederate Army.

No. 65.

Patsey Douglass, daughter of Reuben and Elizabeth (Edwards) Douglass, married Mr. Partee. Had children—

193 Reuben D. Partee.
194 Bennett D. Partee.

No. 66.

Emma Douglass, daughter of Reuben and Elizabeth (Edwards) Douglass, married William Clark. Had children—

195 Jane Clark, married Mr. Bone.
196 Reuben Clark. Killed in the Confederate Army.
197 Charles Clark, married Martha Brown.
198 Elizabeth Clark, married Ben Harris.
199 Malissa Clark.
200 William Clark.
201 David Clark.
202 Ellen Clark, married Dr. Alfred Brown.
203 Edward Clark.

Genealogy of the Douglass Family

No. 67.

Alfred H. Douglass, son of James and Catherine (Collier) Douglass, married Lucy Bennett; second, Rebecca Fulton. Had children—

204 James S. Douglass, married Caroline Mills.
205 Alexander H. Douglass.
206 Caroline Douglass, married Thomas Miller.

Children of second wife—

207 Alfred H. Douglass, Jr.
208 David F. Douglass.
209 Catherine C. Douglass.
210 Elizabeth S. Douglass, married Andrew Edgar.
211 Young Elmore Douglass.

No. 68.

Matilda G. Douglass, daughter of James and Catherine (Collier) Douglass, married, first, J. Cook; second, Joel Parrish. Had children—

212 Catherine C. Cook, married Dr. Walker.
213 (Name unknown, married Mr. Farmer.)
214 Adeline Cook, married Mr. Mitcher.
215 Marcus Cook.
216 James D. Cook.
217 Henry C. Cook, twin of James D.

No. 70.

Isaac C. Douglass, son of James and Catherine (Collier) Douglass, married Eliza Baker. Had children—

218 Louisa Douglass, married O. Cage.
219 Loucelia Douglass, married J. Franklin.
220 James Douglass, married Sarah Donovan.
221 Mary Kate Douglass, married John F. Anderson.
222 Caroline Douglass, married George Cook.
223 Sophis Ann Douglass.
224 Alice Douglass.
225 Isaac B. Douglass.
226 Amanda F. Douglass.

No. 71.

James S. Douglass, son of James and Catherine (Collier) Douglass, married Lucy Searlock. Had children—

227 William A. Douglass, married Caroline Vinson.
228 Rebecca Louisa Douglass.
229 Feliciana Douglass.
230 Isaac Douglass.
231 Thomas S. Douglass.

No. 72.

Harry C. Douglass, son of James and Catherine (Collier) Douglass, married Elizabeth Elliott. Had children—

232 Melissa Douglass.
233 Ellen Douglass.
234 Edward Douglass.
235 Harry Fagan Douglass.
236 Young A. Douglass.
237 George W. Douglass.
238 Inman Julian Douglass.
239 Robert P. Douglass.

No. 73.

Young N. Douglass, son of James and Catherine (Collier) Douglass, married Miss B. Rawlings. Had children—

240 Washington R. Douglass.
241 James Rufus Douglass.
242 Charles S. Douglass.
243 Margarett L. Douglass.
244 Mary Caroline Douglass.
245 Young N. Douglass, Jr.

No. 74.

Robert G. Douglass, son of James and Catherine (Collier) Douglass, married Elizabeth Blythe. Had children—

246 Andrew B. Douglass.
247 Catherine C. Douglass.

GENEALOGY OF THE DOUGLASS FAMILY 215

248 Alfred Hicks Douglass.
249 Martha Douglass.

No. 75.

William C. Douglass, son of James and Catherine (Collier) Douglass, married Lucy Seawell. Had children—

250 William Douglass.
251 Matilda Douglass.
252 Ann Douglass.

No. 76.

Thomas C. Douglass, son of James and Catherine (Collier) Douglass, married Francis Cantrell. Had children—

253 Mary Douglass.
254 Kate Douglass.
255 James Douglass.
256 William Douglass.
257 Robert Douglass.
258 Matilda Douglass.
259 Young N. Douglass.
260 Larilda Douglass.
261 Fannie Douglass.
262 Ida Douglass.

No. 77.

Louisa F. Douglass, daughter of James and Catherine (Collier) Douglass, married G. W. Allen. Had children—

263 John Allen.
264 Catherine C. Allen.
265 Young D. Allen.
266 Loutilda A. Allen.
267 Camella Allen.

FOURTH GENERATION.

No. 103.

Mary Ann Douglass, daughter of James and Rina (Hunt) Douglass, married Merry C. Abston. Had children—

268 Charles Abston.

269 Kemmie Abston, married James Bostick.
270 Ann Abston, married John Cantrell.
271 Jennie Abston.
272 Sallie Abston, married Larrey Maney.
273 Virginia Abston.
274 Henry Abston, married Miss Turner.
275 Mollie Abston, married Harry McClain.
276 Liza Abston.
277 Martha Abston, married John A. McFerrin.

No. 104.

Robert B. Douglass, son of James and Rina (Hunt) Douglass, married Delia A. Mitchell. Had children—

278 Ellen Douglass, married, first, Harvey E. Topp; second, S. H. Hayes.
279 Jennie Douglass, married Dr. W. H. Haggard.
280 John Douglass.
281 Frank Douglass, married Polly Cage.
282 Sallie T. Douglass, married Jesse Cage.
283 DeWitt Clinton Douglass, married Belle Bender.
284 Henry L. Douglass.
285 James Douglass, married Mrs. Scofield.
286 Mollie Douglass.
287 Eva Douglass.

No. 105.

Albert G. Douglass, son of James and Rina (Hunt) Douglass, married Dorotha Turner. Had children—

288 Seaton T. Douglass, married Selina Matthews.
289 Willie Douglass, married Lady McKinnie.
290 Eliza Douglass.
291 Albert Douglass.
292 Stephen Douglass.
293 Jessie Douglass.

GENEALOGY OF THE DOUGLASS FAMILY 217

No. 106.

Evaline Douglass, daughter of James and Rina (Hunt) Douglass, married Charles Boddie. Had children—

294 Martha Boddie, married Henry Davis.
295 Elmore Boddie.
296 Eliza Boddie.
297 Lizzie Boddie, married William H. Baber.
298 Sallie Boddie, married James Cage.
299 George Boddie.
300 Maria Boddie.

After the death of his first wife, Charles Boddie married Sue Maney. Had children—

301 Mag Boddie.
302 May Boddie.
303 Fannie Boddie.
304 Monie Boddie.
305 Susie Boddie.
306 Ella Boddie.

No. 108.

D. W. Clinton Douglass, son of James and Rina (Hunt) Douglass, married Martha Ann Murray. Had children—

307 Martha Douglass.
308 James Douglass, married Bettie Bright.
309 Mina Douglass.
310 Susie Douglass.
311 William Douglass.
312 Robert Douglass, twin of William.

No. 278.

Ellen Douglass, daughter of Robert B. and Delia A. (Mitchell) Douglass, married Harvey E. Topp, then S. H. Hayes. Had children—

313 Robert Topp, married Bettie Walker.
314 Harvey Topp.
315 Anna Hayes.
316 John Hayes.
317 Frank Hayes.

No. 149.

Martha A. Douglass, daughter of Elmore and (J. Dillon) Douglass, married Dr. W. D. Haggard, of Nashville. Had children—

318   Louisa Haggard, married Dr. J. Y. Crawford. After the death of his first wife, Dr. Haggard married—

No. 279.

Jennie Douglass, daughter of Robert B. and Delia A. (Mitchell) Douglass, married —— Haggard. Had children—

319   William Haggard.
320   Robert Haggard. Died in infancy.
321   Douglass Haggard.

No. 288.

Seaton T. Douglass, son of Albert G. and Dorothea (Turner) Douglass, married Salina Matthews. Had children—

322   Nellie Douglass.
323   Timmie Douglass.
324   Seaton Douglass.
325   Seline Douglass.

No. 297.

Lizzie Boddie daughter of Evaline (Douglass) and Charles Boddie, married William H. Baber. Had children—

326   Mary Baber.
327   Kimball Baber.
328   Lucy Baber.
329   Sarah Baber.
330   Will Baber.
331   Eva Baber.
332   Charles Baber.

ABRAHAM

Another name that deserves to be remembered is that of Abraham, a mulatto belonging to Colonel Anthony Bledsoe. General Hall said of him: "He was a brave, active and intelligent fellow, and indeed a good soldier and marksman." He seems to have been a general favorite with the whites. He was ever ready and anxious for a brush with the Indians, and more than one of them met death before his unerring rifle. What became of him I am unable to say. Doubtless his remains were mingled with the soil he so bravely helped to defend, and from which he helped to clear the primitive forest. General Hall gives, in his "Narrative," the following example of the bravery of Abraham: "He was passing one evening from the Lick fort up to Greenfield, when right in the thick canebrake he met two Cherokee chiefs of note, "Mad Dog" and "John Taylor," the latter a half-breed, well known in Nashville before the war broke out, and who could talk good English. They had been on a visit to the Shawnees; and having sent on their warriors, they were on their way by themselves to steal horses and murder any settler who might fall in their way. Abraham met them about ten paces off, and instantly drawing up his gun, he shot the Mad Dog dead in his tracks, turning himself at once and fleeing after his exploit.

SOME SUMNER COUNTIANS

SAMUEL R. ANDERSON.

Brigadier General Samuel R. Anderson was born in Sumner County in 1804. He was a son of Robert Anderson, a Virginian, and an officer in the war for independence. He received a good education, married a Miss Trousdale of the same county, served as Lieutenant Colonel of the famous First Tennessee, "The Bloody First," in the war with Mexico. On May 9, 1861, he was commissioned a Major General in the State troops and Brigadier General in the provisional army of the Confederate States on July 9, and on August 5 was assigned to the command of a brigade, which included the First, Seventh and Fourteenth Tennessee Regiment of infantry for service in the mountains of West Virginia under General Loring. Later he served under Lee, Jackson, Magruder and Archer. On November 4, 1864, he was recommissioned Brigadier General. After the close of the war he returned to Tennessee, and died in Nashville in 1883.

DR. REDMOND D. BARRY.

Redmond D. Barry was a native of County Kildare, Ireland; was a graduate of Trinity College, Dublin, with the degrees of A. M. and M. D. He was a classmate of General Packingham, commander-in-chief of the British forces at the battle of New Orleans, and was killed. Dr. Barry practiced medicine in Liverpool for some time and was distinguished for his skill in surgery. While there he attracted the attention of Fox, who secured for him an appointment as surgeon in the British navy, but his party feeling was so intense that he soon resigned and came to America. He first settled in North Carolina, then went to Kentucky and read law under John C. Breckinridge. He came to

Sumner County, where he married Miss Jane Alexander, who was known as the "Cumberland Beauty." She was a member of the family of Alexanders, six of whom were signers of the Mecklenburg Declaration of Independence. After coming to America Dr. Barry studied law and was for many years regarded as one of the greatest lawyers in Tennessee. He accumulated a large fortune and left many descendants, some of them now living in Sumner County.

To Dr. Barry is given the honor of introducing blue grass into Sumner County in 1800, but not much of it was grown until in 1836, when General Joseph Miller introduced it into general cultivation. Dr. Barry may be said to have been the pioneer in raising blooded stock in Sumner County, or in Tennessee. In 1804 he brought from Virginia the first thoroughbred stallion that appeared in the Valley of the Cumberland—Gray Medley. For more than a century the Barry family has been one of the most prominent in the county.

JUDGE THOMAS BARRY.

Thomas Barry, son of Dr. Redmond D. Barry, was born in Sumner County July 2, 1807. He received a classical education, studied law and became eminent in his profession. He was a personal friend of Andrew Jackson, for whom he cast his first vote. He married Sarah H. Peyton, who was born in Sumner County in 1812. Early in the fifties he was the Democratic candidate for Congress, but was defeated. He served two terms in the lower house of the State Legislature. When the war broke out in 1861 his sympathies were with the Union, and while he took no part in the Civil War, he contributed very much toward ameliorating the condition of the families of men who had espoused the cause of the South. In 1865 he was appointed by Governor Brownlow Chancellor of his division, a position he filled to the entire satisfaction of the public until 1869. He died on May 23, 1891.

GENERAL WILLIAM B. BATE, TWENTY-THIRD GOVERNOR.

William Brimage Bate, soldier and statesman, was born near Castalian Springs (Bledsoe's Lick), Octo-

SENATOR W. B. BATE

ber 7, 1826. He was educated at Rural Academy, working on his father's farm during his vacations. When he, the eldest son, was 15 years of age his father, James H. Bate, died. After a few years' work on the farm, when he was 18 years of age he determined to make his own way in the world. His first employment was as clerk on the steamboat Saladin, the principal owner of which was "John Bell of Tennessee," plying between Nashville and New Orleans. In 1846, when the war with Mexico began, Mr. Bate was in New Orleans and enlisted in a Louisiana regiment, six months' troops. When his time expired he joined the Third Tennessee and was made First Lieutenant and served until the end of the war. He then returned to Sumner County and to the farm. Soon afterwards he became editor of the *Tenth Legion*, published at Gallatin. In 1849 he was elected to the Legislature. He then entered the law school at Lebanon, graduated in 1852, and began practice at Gallatin. 1854 he was elected Attorney General and served two terms. On January 17, 1856, he married Miss Julia Peete, of Huntsville, Ala. In 1860 he was an elector on the Breckinridge ticket. The day after the opening gun at Fort Sumpter was fired, April, 1861, he enlisted as a private in Company 1, Second Tennessee, Confederate, and was elected Captain, and later was made Colonel, then a Brigadier General, and finally a Major General, serving until the end of the war. In the battle of Shiloh he was desperately wounded. In that battle his cousin, Dr. Humphrey Bate, was wounded; his brother, Captain Humphrey Bate; Captain Tyree, brother-in-law of Captain Bate, and his cousin, James McDaniel, were killed. In the battle of Chickamauga General Bate was distinguished for gallantry and had three horses killed under him. He was also conspicuous for his bravery in the battle of Mission Ridge, and in the campaigns under Johnston in Georgia, in 1864. From 1862 to the end of the war General Bate remained in active duty in the field on crutches. He was three times wounded and had six horses killed under him in battle. In 1863 he was tendered the nomination for Governor, but declined in a telegram that is historic: "No, sirs; while an armed foe treads our soil and I can fire a shot or draw a blade, I will take no civil honors." After the close of the war General Bate returned to Nashville and resumed the practice of law. In 1882 he was elected Governor and re-elected in 1884. In 1887 he was elected United States Senator, and, by re-election, served until his death, March 9, 1905.

The Bate family originally came from Saxony and settled in Yorkshire, England, early in the sixteenth century. Humphrey Bate, the ancestor of the American branch of the family, came to America at an early date and settled in Bertie County, North Carolina. He married Sarah Legate, who bore him five children. The eldest, James, born in 1747, served throughout the Revolutionary War. In 1876 he married Mary Spiva. Their second child, Humphrey Bate, who was born in 1779, came to Tennessee in 1803 and settled near Bledsoe's Lick, on lands a part of which are still in possession of the family. He married Elizabeth P. Brimage; they had five children. After the death of his first wife he married Anna F. Weathered, a daughter of Frank Weathered, who bore him nine children. James Henry Bate, a son of his first marriage, was born in 1804 and died in 1842. He married Amanda F. Weathered in 1825. Of this union William Brimage Bate was born. Senator Bate's daughter Mazie married Thomas F. Masten and resides in Texas. Susie married O. W. Childs. They reside in Los Angeles, California, the other two children, both daughters, died young.

JUDGE B. D. BELL.

Bennett D. Bell was born in Sumner County in 1852. In 1873 he graduated from Emory and Henry College, then studied law at Cumberland University, graduating in 1878. The following summer he was elected Attorney General of the Ninth circuit, and after eight years returned to practice his profession. In 1900 he was appointed to the judgeship of the Ninth circuit to fill the unexpired term of Judge Mumford, deceased. In 1902 he was elected to the same office, and continued to fill that position until August, 1908, when he was elected to the Supreme Court of Tennessee. Judge Bell is a nephew of the late General Tyree Bell of the Confederate army.

GENERAL TYREE H. BELL, CONFEDERATE.

Tyree H. Bell was born in Cincinnati, Ohio, September 6, 1815, moved with his father to Tennessee in 1817 and settled on the headwaters of Station Camp Creek, in Sumner County, where he was reared and educated. His education was received in an old log school-house, under the tutorship of Seth Thomas, a noted teacher in his day. He followed the occupation of farmer, stock raiser and trader and became a man of prominence in his county. He married, in October, 1841, Mary A. Walton, of the same neighborhood, a daughter of Josiah Walton. In 1857 he removed to Dyer County and settled near Newbern, where he resided until November, 1875, when he moved to California. He died in New Orleans, La., August 30, 1902, and was buried at his home in Fresno County, California, on the anniversary of his birth, September 6, 1902.

General Bell entered the Confederate service as Captain in the Twelfth Tennessee Infantry, June 4, 1861. He commanded the regiment at the battles of Belmont and Shiloh, and had two horses shot under him. In July, 1862, he was made Colonel of the regiment, and led it in the Kentucky campaign. In 1864 he was placed in command of a brigade in General Forrest's division. In the latter part of that year he was commissioned Brigadier General. He was in many engagements, and everywhere conducted himself with gallantry and won the praise of his superior officers, including the peerless Forrest.

COUNTESS EUGENIE BERTINATTI.

The most distinguished woman Sumner County has produced was Miss Eugenie Bate, daughter of Colonel

COUNTESS EUGENIE BERTINATTI (EUGENIE BATE)

Humphrey Bate, great-granddaughter of Frank Weathered, sister of Major Henry C. Bate, of Nashville; of Dr. Humphrey Bate, of Sumner County; William Weathered Bate, of St. Augustine, Texas, and of Mrs. Agnes Elizabeth Wright, of Murfreesboro, and cousin of the late Senator William B. Bate.

She was born near Bledsoe's Lick on September 6, 1826. She was a woman of great intellect, personal beauty and charm of manner. She received a liberal education and married Council Rogers Bass, a wealthy Missisippi planter. Four children were born of this union, one of whom, Miss Ella, married the Marquis Incisa, an Italian nobleman, and died a year later. The other two daughters died before reaching the years of maturity. Her son, Council R. Bass, Jr., joined the Confederate army when a mere boy and served under General Forrest in his last campaign. He died on the home plantation early in 1879. After the death of her husband Mrs. Bass spent most of her time in Washington City, where she reigned as a belle and was famous for her beauty and her mental accomplishments, and where she met and married the Italian Ambassador, Chevalier Bertinatti. She returned with him to Italy, where they lived in the ancient castle of his family, Castella le Monte, near Turin. Count Bertinatti represented his country at several courts in Europe, and in Turkey, and everywhere his Countess was a social favorite. She was a personal friend of the mother of the present Queen of The Netherlands, and of the ill-fated Carlotta, wife of the unfortunate Emperor of Mexico, Maximilian, and received from her a decoration in recognition of the efforts of Count Bertinatti in behalf of her husband. While residing in Italy Madame Bertinatti cultivated her native talent for art, and through that means added to her fame. After the death of her husband Countess Bertinatti made her home in Italy, but made several visits to her native land, which she always loved. She left Italy in 1905 for a final visit, and after spending several months with her brother and sister, she took up her residence in Nashville, where she died on December 9, 1906, and now rests with her children in Oak Hill Cemetery, at Georgetown, D. C. During the last nine years of her life her niece, Miss Pearl Wright, was her constant companion. She was with her in Italy, and after the death of her husband returned to America with her, and was with her when she died. Miss Wright now resides in Nashville.

GEORGE DAWSON BLACKMORE.

George Dawson Blackmore was born near Hagerstown, Maryland, in the month of February, 1762, and died in Sumner County, Tennessee, September 27, 1833. He was a soldier in the Continental army in the Revolutionary War, enlisted December 19, 1776; was a corporal in Captain Calmer's company, Second Virginia, commanded by Colonel Spotswood and by Colonel Febiger; was a Sergeant in March, 1779; was ensign July 4, 1779, and Lieutenant in February, 1781, and served till the close of the war. He was a prisoner at Charleston in May, 1780. The war records of the United States War Department show that he resigned April 1, 1782. This may be true, yet he continued in the service elsewhere.

He married Elizabeth Neely in Sumner County, Tennessee, on December 25, 1786. She died December 13, 1833. She was a daughter of Captain Alex. Neely, who was killed by Indians near Bledsoe's Lick. Her mother was Elizabeth Montgomery, a sister of Catherine Montgomery, wife of Colonel Isaac Bledsoe, the pioneer. He served in the Indian warfare in the settlement of Sumner County; was a Captain and commanded a company at Nickajack. George Dawson and Elizabeth (Neely) Blackmore had ten children — four sons and six daughters. Two of the daughters, Polly and Margaret, died in infancy. One, Elizabeth, never married. Rachel married James Charlton and reared a large family in Sumner County. Three of her sons removed to Mississippi, where they died. Two removed to Texas and one to South Carolina. Catherine Montgomery Dawson married Judge Joe C. Guild and reared a family of sons and daughters. Major George Blackmore Guild and

Mrs. Colonel Baxter Smith of Nashville, and Mrs. Kittie G. Young of Gallatin are her children now living. Emaline married James Hadley and reared two sons, both dead. Charles Neely Blackmore reared a large family in Sumner County. Three of his sons, Andrew J., James A. and William M. Blackmore, are yet living. Dawson Blackmore died at the age of thirty-six and was unmarried. Dr. James A. Blackmore lived in Sumner County and reared three children, all of whom are dead. He died in 1863. William Montgomery Blackmore lived in Gallatin and had three sons, two of whom died in infancy. The other, and youngest, is Hon. James W. Blackmore of Gallatin, a prominent lawyer, and one of the most useful and beloved citizens of the county. He has served as Mayor of Gallatin several terms, and two terms, 1883-87, as State Senator. William M. Blackmore married Rachel Jackson Barry, daughter of Redmond Dillon Barry. He served as a Captain of Company I, Tenth Legion, First Tennessee Regiment, Colonel W. B. Campbell, in the war with Mexico, 1846-47.

Captain George Dawson Blackmore came to Sumner County with the Bledsoes, or soon afterwards. After the Indian wars had ceased he settled on a farm about four miles from Gallatin, on the Bledsoe Lick road. In 1792 and 1793 he was a Captain in the service of the territory south of Ohio River. John Carr, a contemporary, says of him: "He commanded a company of and was also employed as Quartermaster in supplying provisions for the troops stationed at the various forts. He was active, sprightly and energetic and as brave a man as I ever saw." He was a man of prominence in Virginia before coming to the Cumberland country. His fort was the lowest down on Clinch River, at the mouth of Stony Creek, in what is now Scott County. It was an important place, and is frequently mentioned as early as the time of Dunmore's war.

COLONEL JAMES BOWIE.

James Bowie, reputed inventor of the Bowie knife, and one of the heroes of the Alamo was a son of Reason Bowie, who came from Maryland to Sumner County about 1793. On November 10 of that year he purchased from James and George Winchester 640 acres of land on Station Camp Creek, about one mile west from Gallatin. Two months later he sold 217 acres of the land to James Odom, founder of the Odom family of Sumner County. Bowie built his house on the banks of a small creek, and in that house, the only vestige of which remains are the ruins of the stone chimney, it is claimed that Colonel James Bowie was born. Some writers say that he was born in Maryland, and others give Georgia the credit. There seems to be no record as to when the Bowie family left Sumner County. The lands on which they had their home passed to the ownership of James Odom, whose son, Harris Odom, in 1827, built his home about fifty yards south from the Bowie house. The Harris Odom home, a commodious story and a half brick, is still standing, and is in a perfect state of preservation, and is occupied by the present owner of the farm, W. A. Hewgley. Harris Odom died in the fifties, and the farm passed to Captain Walton, who later sold it to James Alexander, who, in 1897, sold it to Mr. Hewgley.

The Bowie family went to Louisiana, where they were wealthy planters, and where James and his brother, Reason P., became noted for reckless daring and for being dangerous men. They fought a number of duels, and each had more than one "notch on the handle of his pistol." They were men of superior education, over six feet high, with fair complexion and blue eyes; said to have been remarkably handsome and fascinating men, with the manners of a Chesterfield; brave, fearless and daring; devoted to their friends and a terror to their foes. Some time before the revolt of Texas against Mexico James Bowie went to Mexico, where he married Ursulita de Veramendez, the only daughter of Governor Veramendez, of one of the Mexican States. She was born in Monclova, Mexico, but was of pure Castilian blood. General Santa Anna was her godfather. When Texas seceded from Mexico, Bowie espoused the cause of the former and was a Colonel in the army of the new republic. He commanded a detachment in the battle of Conception, the "Texas Bunker Hill," and in other engagements, distinguishing himself for bravery. He was one of the heroic band of 150 as brave men as ever faced a foe, which, on March 6, 1836, made the victory of General Santa Anna and his army of 4,000 Mexicans "cost them dearer than defeat." The Alamo never surrendered. There were none of its defenders left alive to surrender it. As long as there was a man able to fire a gun or draw a blade they held the fort. When the Mexicans entered the garrison there were none left to oppose them, none left to tell the story of how they died fighting to the very last. Colonel Bowie's wife and child died before he did. His brother, Reason P., died in 1838, aged 40 years. Bowie County, Texas, was so named for James Bowie.

THE BOWEN FAMILY

Moses Bowen and his wife, Rebecca Reece Bowen, emigrated from Wales to the American colonies in 1698 and settled in Chester County, Pennsylvania. John Bowen, their son, married Lily McIlhaney and in 1730 moved to Virginia. They had twelve children, one of whom, Captain John Bowen, was the father of Captain William Bowen, who was the first to emigrate to Tennessee.

Captain William Bowen was born in Fincastle County, Virginia, then Augusta County, in 1742. He was a very active, enterprising man, and by the time he was 35 years of age he had accumulated quite a handsome estate for that day by adding to the portion given to him by his mother. He took part in several campaigns against the French and Indians as a member of the Colonial Army of Virginia before the Revolution of 1776. He was a First Lieutenant in Captain William Russell's company in the campaign against the Shawnee and other Indian tribes in 1774, the confederation being commanded by "Cornstalk," a noted chief of the Shawnees. He was in the hotly contested battle of Point Pleasant on October 10, 1774. He was also with Captain Russell while that officer was in command of Fort Randolph, when that garrison was ordered to be disbanded by Lord Dunmore in July, 1775, fearing the fort might be held by the rebel authorities. Prior to this date he was with Russell's Rangers when they assisted in relieving the beseiged fort at Watauga.

Captain Bowen was principally engaged in the partisan warfare on the border of Virginia and Tennessee during the Revolution. He was in the cavalry service, employed in scouting and protecting the frontiers from the inroads of the British, Indians and Tories. At the termination of the long struggle for independence he, with fifteen other soldiers of the Continental army, traveled all through Kentucky and the Cumberland country, as Middle Tennessee was then called, prospecting for favorable places to locate their land warrants, which had been received for services in the war of independence. Captain Bowen was so pleased with the country that he located some of his lands in what is now Smith County, Tennessee, but the larger portion in Sumner County, about twelve miles from Nashville. He moved his family from Virginia in the early autumn of 1784 to Sumner County, where he built a double log house in which he lived for two years; then built a two-story brick, which is still standing near Goodlettsville and in good preservation, though it was built in 1787, when what is now Tennessee was a part of North Carolina. It is said to have been the first brick house built in Tennessee. General Daniel Smith, his friend and fellow soldier, built a stone house, known as "Rock Castle," in the same vicinity. The two sent to Lexington, Ky., for stone and brickmasons to erect the two houses.

Captain William Bowen, in 1777, married Mary Henley Russell, daughter of General William Russell and his wife, Tobitha Adams, in Augusta County, Virginia, now Washington County, near where Abingdon now stands. He died in Sumner County on December 15, 1804. He left eight children. Tobitha married Colonel Armstead Moore of Virginia. They moved to Smith County, Tennessee, where they died, leaving eleven children.

Colonel John Bowen, son of Captain William Bowen, was born in Virginia in 1780; came with his parents to Sumner County in 1784. At the age of 16 years he was sent to Lexington, Ky., to school. About the year 1800 he commenced the study of law in the office of John Breckinridge in Lexington. After two years he returned home and began the practice of law in Gallatin and soon rose to prominence.

In 1813 Mr. Bowen was elected to Congress as a Democrat and served one term, at the expiration of which he returned to the practice of his profession at Gallatin. In 1815 he married Elizabeth Allen, daughter of Grant Allen and his wife, Tabitha Marshall, of the Dixon Springs neighborhood. They had four children; two died in youth and two reared large families. The eldest, Mary, married Judge Jacob S. Yerger of Greenville, Miss., a member of the famous Yerger family formerly of Lebanon. They had three sons killed in the Confederate army. William G. Yerger, a prominent lawyer of Greenville, is the only living son. Henry Yerger, another son, died at his home near Greenville, leaving a family. Grant Allen Bowen, son of John H., married Amanda Yerger. They left two children, John H., Jr., and Mary.

Colonel John H. Bowen died on September 25, 1822. He was an accomplished scholar, a just and upright man, a great lawyer, a pure statesman and a true friend. The brick house which he erected for his home in Gallatin is still standing. It was bought after his death by Governor William Trousdale, and from him it passed to his son, the Hon. Julius A. Trousdale, and after his death was presented by his widow, Mrs. Anne Berry Trousdale, to the Daughters of the Confederacy.

Levisee Bowen, daughter of Captain William Bowen, married Colonel James Saunders. They had their home in Wilson County, where six children survived them.

William, son of Captain William Bowen, married Mary Rankin, and after her death, Polly McCall. They removed to LaGrange, Texas, where they died, leaving seven children.

Samuel, son of Captain William Bowen, married Amanda Stone. They removed to Missouri, where they died, leaving seven children.

Mary Bowen died young. Celia married Rev. Barton W. Stone, a noted divine, and one of the founders of the "Campbellite" Church. They lived in Kentucky and Missouri; left six children.

Catherine Bowen, third daughter of Captain William Bowen, was born in Sumner County in March, 1785. She was married in 1807 to David Campbell, who was born in Washington County, Virginia, on March 4, 1781, and died near Leeville, Wilson County, Tennessee, on June 18, 1841. She died at "Campbell," the home of her eldest son, Governor William B. Campbell, March 7, 1868. They lived in Sumner County for some years after their marriage, then moved to Carthage, Smith County. They had six children—William B. Campbell, who married Frances Owen and left seven children; John H. died unmarried; Mary R. H. married E. P. Scales; Margaret died unmarried; Virginia T. I. married Rev. William Shelton; David H. R. married Lucy Goodall.

THE CAMPBELL FAMILY

The Virginia Campbells were descended from the ancient family of that name in Argyleshire, Scotland. Alexander Campbell lived at Inverary, in that shire; his son, William Campbell, married Mary Byers. They emigrated from Scotland to the north of Ireland, near Londonderry, in Donegal township, Ulster district, and there lived for some years, and then came with their eight children to America—the exact date is not known. The father was an honorable, upright gentleman; the mother was a woman of remarkable intelligence, possessed of all the womanly virtues—a good wife and a good mother. They children were: David, William, Elizabeth, Martha, Alexander, Robert, Jane and Mary.

David, was called "Black David" because of his dark hair and complexion, and to distinguish him from his distant cousin, "White David," who was fair, with yellow hair and blue eyes. These two married half sisters. Black David, who was born in 1710, married Jane Cunnyngham. They came from Ireland with their parents and settled in Virginia, it is thought, first in Culpepper County; later they removed to Augusta County, which at this time was the extreme frontier. They had four children: William, Mary, Martha and David.

William Campbell, the eldest son of David, married Mary Ellison. He inherited the whole of his father's property, which left the other children to take care of themselves. His youngest brother, Captain David Campbell, who was born in 1753, married his cousin, Margaret Campbell, daughter of White David and his wife, Mary Hamilton. On July 29, 1799, Captain

David Campbell lost his wife, by whom he had eight children, four of whom died in childhood. Jane married Colonel Wright, of the United States army. They left no issue. Mary married her cousin, David Campbell, afterwards Governor of Virginia. They had no children. John entered the regular army and served until the close of the War of 1812, when he retired with the rank of Lieutenant Colonel. He left no children. The youngest son, David, was born on March 4, 1781. He married Catherine Bowen, daughter of Captain William Bowen and granddaughter of General William Russell. Captain David Campbell, after the death of his wife, Margaret, married a second time, and by this wife had one child, Margaret Lavinia, who married Rev. John Kelly. In 1823 Captain David Campbell removed to Middle Tennessee and lived for a time in Sumner County; then bought a farm in Wilson County, where he died August 18, 1832. It was at their old homestead on Mansker's Creek that their eldest son, William Bowen Campbell, was born.

GOVERNOR WILLIAM B. CAMPBELL.

William B. Campbell was born in Sumner County, on Mansker's Creek, February 1, 1807; was reared on a farm; completed his education at Abingdon, Va., under his uncle Governor David B. Campbell, with whom he studied law; commenced practice at Carthage in 1829. In 1831 was elected by the Legislature Attorney General for the Fifth District. He resigned the same year and moved to Sparta; returned to Carthage in 1835 and was elected a member of the Legislature. He married Miss Fannie I. Owen. In 1836 he was elected Captain of a company for the Creek War. During the seven months he was in command of his company he fully sustained the reputation for courage and skill of his distinguished ancestors and other members of the Campbell family at King's Mountain and elsewhere. In 1837 he defeated William Trousdale for Congress, and again defeated him in 1839; re-elected in 1841 without opposition, and at the end of his term retired to private life and the practice of law. Soon afterwards he was made Major General of militia. When the war with Mexico began he was elected Colonel of the First Tennessee.

Governor William Bowen Campbell

In that war he won distinction, as did his regiment at Monterey, Vera Cruz, Cerro Gordo and other engagements. The regiment was called the "Bloody First," and well it merited the title. Soon after the return of the troops from Mexico Colonel Campbell was by unanimous vote elected to succeed Judge Abram Caruthers as Circuit Judge. In 1851 he was nominated by acclamation as the Whig candidate for Governor. In this election he was again opposed by William Trousdale, and again defeated him. At the end of his term he refused renomination. In 1853 he moved from Carthage to Lebanon and accepted the presidency of the Bank of Middle Tennessee. In 1861 he canvassed the State in opposition to secession. On July 23, 1862, he was commissioned a Brigadier General in the Union Army, which office he resigned two months later. In 1865 he was elected to Congress, but was not permitted to take his seat until in June, 1866. He died at Lebanon August 19, 1867.

For two centuries the Campbell family has been prominent in Virginia and Tennessee. They participated in the early Indian wars, the French and Indian war, Dunmore's war, and in the Revolution. In the battle of King's Mountain were eight members of the family, one of whom was the commander-in-chief. In the War of 1812, in the Mexican War, and in the Civil War they were conspicuous for their bravery.

Governor Campbell left seven children. The eldest, William B., died unmarried just after leaving college. The eldest daughter, Mary O., married D. C. Kelly. They left one son, David C. Kelly, who married Jane Cowan of Hendersonville, Sumner County. The second daughter, Margaret H. Campbell, married James S. Pilcher, an attorney at law, practicing at Nashville. They have three children: Stuart, Campbell and Frances Pilcher. The third daughter, Fannie A. Campbell, married J. M. Bonner, a Nashville lawyer; they have three children: Campbell, Moses and Mary Bonner. The three living sons of Governor Campbell are: Joseph A., who married Alice Hall; they have three daughters, Frances, Mary and Jessie B. Campbell. They live near Lebanon, at "Campbells," the old homestead that has been in the family for many years. I. Owen Campbell married Susie Towson. They live on a farm four miles from Lebanon. The youngest child of Governor Campbell—Lemuel R. Campbell—married Johnnie Marshall. They have three sons: William B, Matthew M. and Russell Campbell. Lemuel R. Campbell is a lawyer, practicing in Nashville, but resides on his farm, four miles from the city.

E. W. CARMACK

Edward Ward Carmack was born near Castalian Springs, in Sumner County, November 5, 1858. His father, a Christian minister, died while he was an infant, leaving a widow and children with a scant endowment of worldly wealth. Edward early began his struggles with the world, working on a farm, in a brickyard and at other occupations, attending the country schools and receiving instructions from his mother when the time could be spared from his labors. He studied law and was licensed to practice in Columbia. He became editor of the *Columbia Herald,* and in 1884 was elected a member of the Legislature from Maury and Williamson Counties. In 1886 he became one of the editors of the *Nashville American,* and later was editor-in-chief of the *Democrat.* In 1892 he moved to Memphis to accept the position of editor-in-chief of the *Commercial Appeal,* and while occupying that position gained much prominence by his vigorous and forceful editorials. He had opinions on all public questions and earnestly and boldly expressed them. In 1896 he resigned from that paper and was elected a member of Congress as a Democrat. His opponent, Josiah Patterson, contested the election, but the House, "though strongly Republican, decided in favor of Mr. Carmack amid one of the most dramatic scenes ever witnessed in Congress." "Members stood on their seats that they might not lose a syllable of his logic, while with breathless attention they listened to his thundering appeals in behalf of the South that burned their way into the hearts of all." Never before was such a speech heard in Congress; it attracted attention

Senator Edward Ward Carmack

Some Sumner Countians 241

from all parts of the Union and fixed the speaker's position as an orator and logician high in public estimation. In 1898 he was re-lected, and in 1901 he was elected a United States Senator. As a debater Mr. Carmack had few equals in the Senate. What he conceived to be right he advocated; what he considered wrong he condemned with vigor. Few adversaries cared to meet him in debate. Senator Carmack was bold, frank and fearless. He was a student, an orator and a statesman. In intellect he had no superior in the Senate. In April, 1890, Mr. Carmack married Miss Elizabeth Cobey Dunnington, a daughter of one of the most distinguished families of Maury County. They have one child, Edward W., Jr. In 1906 he was defeated for re-election to the Senate. A writer in the *Knoxville Journal and Tribune*, signing himself "Observus," said of Senator Carmack:

"In my humble opinion, the greatest and most brilliant intellect in Tennessee today is a Democrat. Not only so, but in my humble opinion he is the greatest and most brilliant intellect today in the Senate of the United States. If Edward W. Carmack were a Senator from one of the Northern States, and belonged to the dominant party, and had one-half the length of service of some of his colleagues from those States, he would stand today without a peer in that great body. He has all the facility with the King's English that John J. Ingalls had; but while Ingalls was a mere partisan free lance, tilting in the arena of words for his own occasional amusement, Carmack is a broadminded, philosophical statesman. Nothing finer was ever uttered on the political rostrum than his explanation of the reasons why there have always been two great contending political parties since the dawn of Anglo-Saxon history. It is merely the contention of two great ideas. The one idea stands for the strength of a centralized government; the other stands for the liberty of the individual. The one carried to an extreme means despotism; the other carried to an extreme means anarchy; but the two balancing and checking each other, mean the very government which we enjoy today—a government which is an evolution of all the centuries since the Witanagemote of the Saxons. All my life I have been a student of the history of our race, and this one great dominant fact has influenced every line of that history, and yet I never learned it until it fell from the lips of this man of transcendent perception and genius."

In 1908 the temperance element of the Democratic party in Tennessee urged Mr. Carmack to become a candidate for the nomination for Governor, which he reluctantly did, making a most brilliant campaign, in which he engaged in fifty joint debates with his opponent, who was backed by the saloon element of the party. Mr. Carmack was defeated in the primary by a little over 6,000 votes. Soon after the election he became editor-in-chief of the *Tennessean*, a daily paper published at Nashville. His brilliant editorials soon attracted the attention of the people all over the country.

On the afternoon of November 9, 1908, while on his way from his office to his rooms, he was shot and instantly killed while in the act of raising his hat and bowing to a lady acquaintance. With the exception of the three Presidents who were assassinated, the death of no man in America ever attracted such widespread indignation and horror. In every county and almost every town in Tennessee memorial exercises were held and resolutions passed condemning the murder and eulogizing the dead man.

TRIBUTE FROM BISHOP HOSS.

To the *Nashville Tennessean:*

It is impossible for me to write much. My heart is broken. Senator Carmack's death overwhelmed me. He was by all odds the greatest Tennessean that has appeared in public life in this generation. As a Senator he commanded the admiration of the nation. In his whole career there is not the slightest trace or stain of dishonor. No dirty dollar ever touched his fingers. He came out of the Senate poor, and his friends knew it and were proud of it. He never engaged in bargain and intrigue; he never compromised principle for preferment; he never turned aside one hair's breadth from the straight path of truth and courage. Defeat did not break his spirit nor sour his temper. When Tennessee turned her back on him, the noblest of her sons, he kept his head erect and moved right onward. The evil forces that were banded against him did not dismay him; the slanders that were circulated to ruin him utterly failed to alter or modify the inflexibility of his purpose. Much as I loved him living, and unspeakable as is my grief over his death, I should rather see him wrapped in his shroud than to have him alive again and enjoying place and prominence at the expense of bartered manhood. Being dead, he yet speaketh. Human as he was, compassed with customary infirmities as he was, he yet had a heart as warm as a summer sea and a transparent simplicity of nature like that of a child. O my dear, dear friend! Shall I ever look upon his like again? E. E. Hoss.

From the *Nashville Banner:*

"Lawyer, statesman, patriot, orator, able and fearless leader, editor, friend, gentleman, was Edward Ward Carmack, who met such a tragic and sudden death on the streets of Nashville Monday afternoon. The State, the nation, mourn the loss of one of their ablest sons; the widowed wife and fatherless boy are grief-stricken over the death of a faithful husband and considerate, kind father; his personal friends are bowed down over the death of one who was faithful; the cause he represented feels keenly the loss of a fearless leader; the entire country is shocked over the sad tragedy which took from life into death a man."

Senator Carmack's tribute to the South:

"The South is a land that has known sorrows; it is a land that has broken the ashen crust and moistened it with its tears; a land scarred and riven by the plowshare of war and billowed with the graves of her dead; but a land of legend, a land of song, a land of hallowed and heroic memories. To that land every drop of my blood, every fiber of my being, every pulsation of my heart is consecrated forever. I was born of her womb; I was nurtured at her breast, and when my last hour shall come, I pray God I may be pillowed upon her bosom and rocked to sleep within her tender and encircling arms."

JOHN CARR.

John Carr, "Uncle Jackie," as he was familiarly called, was born near Ramshouse's Mill, in South Carolina, September 5, 1773. While he was an infant his father moved with his family to Houston's Fort, on Big Moccasin Creek, about twenty miles below Abingdon, Va. His father died in 1782, leaving a widow and eight children. In 1784 the widow and her children, the eldest son being married, set out for the Cumberland country, and arrived in Sumner County the next year, locating at Mansker's Station. The next year they removed to Hamilton's Station, on Drake's Creek, a short distance above Shackel Island. As a boy and as a young man, John Carr participated in the Indian wars and was a brave and fearless soldier. He was a devout Christian, a member of the Methodist Episcopal Church, a good citizen, a kind neighbor and a true friend. He was the author of a very interesting little volume, now very scarce, "Early Times in Middle Tennessee." He married Miss Cage. Many of the descendants of Mr. Carr and of his brothers are still living in Sumner County and elsewhere. "Uncle Jackie's" home was four miles east of Gallatin, where he died in 1857. His younger brother, William, who was born on January 29, 1776, at Houston's Fort, Virginia, and died in

Cannon County, Tennessee, on December 12, 1856, fought in the Indian wars and in the War of 1812. He was a local Methodist preacher, and for many years had his home on Goose Creek, near Hartsville.

ISAAC CLARK.

The first book of a literary character published in Nashville or in Middle Tennessee was "Clark's Miscellany," a small volume of prose and verse, published by Bradford in 1812. Its author was Isaac Clark, a citizen of Sumner County. He was a lawyer and was a candidate for Congress about 1810, but was defeated.

ANDREW J. DONELSON.

A. J. Donelson was born in Sumner County, August 25, 1799, son of Samuel Donelson. His elder brother, John, served in the Creek war under Jackson and died soon after its close. His younger brother, Daniel L., was a Brigadier General and died in the Confederate service. Their father, Samuel Donelson, died while they were quite young. Their mother, the only daughter of General Daniel Smith, after the death of her husband, married James Sanders of Sumner County. Upon this second marriage, Andrew Jackson Donelson was adopted by Andrew Jackson, with whom he remained until he entered Cumberland College. In 1816 he was appointed in the first class at West Point, from which he graduated three years later. He was then commissioned in the engineers' corps, and was appointed on the staff of General Jackson, where he served until after the close of the Florida campaign, when he resigned. He then entered Transylvania University to study law. In 1823 he began practice at Nashville with Mr. Duncan, but soon abandoned the law and became a farmer. About that time he married Emily, the youngest daughter of Captain John Donelson, by whom he had four children—A. J., who died while a lieutenant of United States engineers; Emily, who married General John A. Wilcox, who was a member of Congress from Mississippi; Capt. John S., who was killed at the battle of Chickamauga, and Rachel J., who married General William B. Knox.

When Andrew Jackson was elected President he appointed Mr. Donelson his private secretary, Mrs.

HON. ANDREW JACKSON DONELSON

Donelson doing the honors of the White House. In 1836 she died, and in 1841 he married Mrs. E. A. Randolph, daughter of James G. Martin. From this union he had eight children—Daniel S., who was a prominent Confederate and was murdered in Memphis in 1864; Martin, a planter in Mississippi, as was also his third son, W. A., near the Hermitage; Catherine, who died in 1868; Captain Vinet Donelson, who was a merchant in Nashville; Lewis R., who resided in Memphis; Rosa E., and Andrew J.

In 1844 Mr. Donelson was appointed charge d'affaires to the republic of Texas, and secured its annexation to the United States. He was afterwards appointed Minister to Prussia. At the same time he represented his country at the court of Germany. He was afterwards transferred entirely to Germany, in which position he continued until the German mission was abolished. He was a delegate to the. Southern Convention at Nashville in 1850. In April, 1851, he became the editor of the *Washington Union*. In 1856 he was nominated for Vice President on the ticket with Filmore. He died at his home in Memphis, June 26, 1871.

CAPTAIN H. C. ELLIS.

Captain H. C. Ellis was born in Sumner County, near Fountain Head, in 1818. He was related to the Gwin family, from which Senator William Gwin was descended. In 1843 he removed to Hartsville, where he engaged in merchandising until the beginning of the Civil War, when he entered the Confederate army as Captain of a company in the Ninth Tennessee Regiment of Cavalry under General John H. Morgan, with whom he served, and was captured on Morgan's Ohio raid, and was in prison with the officers of Morgan's command at Columbus, Ohio. From Columbus he was sent to Fort Delaware, where he was held prisoner until exchanged in 1864, when he rejoined his command and served until paroled in North Carolina after the surrender of General Lee. As a citizen he was public spirited and was foremost in every enterprise for the good of his town and county. He was successful in business and accumulated a considerable fortune, and was at his death one of the wealthiest men in Trousdale County.

248   HISTORIC SUMNER COUNTY, TENN.

Captain Ellis married Miss Josephine Towson, with whom he lived over half a century, and to whom he clung with a beautiful devotion until the last ray of reason was gone. Mrs. Ellis survives her husband and spends much of her time in travel and in visiting her many friends and relatives, ever keeping in mind the sacred memory of her honored and noble husband. Captain Ellis was one of the founders of the first bank in Hartsville, and was its president from its organization in 1884 to his death, October 17, 1903. Captain Ellis left no children.

WILLIAM S. FULTON.

W. S. Fulton was born in Cecil County, Maryland, June 2, 1795; received a classical education, and in 1815 moved to Sumner County, where his father, David Fulton, engaged in banking. He read law in the office of Felix Grundy in Nashville and commenced practicing in 1817. In June, 1820, he moved to Florence, Ala., and the next year was elected Judge of the County Court. He served in the War of 1812. In January, 1818, he became the private secretary of Andrew Jackson and served in that capacity during the Seminole campaign. In 1825 he married Matilda F. Noland of Florence, Ala. From May, 1829, to March, 1835, he acted as Secretary of the Territory of Arkansas, and on the 9th of March, 1835, was appointed Governor of the Territory, in which office he continued until the admission of Arkansas as a State, in 1836, when he was elected to the United States Senate, serving until 1844. He died August 15, 1844.

GEORGE S. GAINES.

George S. Gaines was a younger brother of General Edmund Pendleton Gaines of the United States army. He was born in Virginia. In 1794 he came to Tennessee and located in Gallatin, where he resided until 1804, when he went to Alabama, having been appointed assistant factor for the Choctaw Indians at St. Stephens, then the capital of the Territory of Alabama. In 1807 he was made principal factor. It was from letters from Mr. Gaines that General Jackson and Governor Willie Blount first received the information of the massacre at Fort Mims in the autumn of 1813. When Aaron Burr was arrested and sent up to St. Stephens by Captain (afterwards General Gaines), Mr. Gaines was sick. Burr prescribed for him and was otherwise exceedingly kind to the invalid, and the two became very much attached to each other. He continued to hold the position of Indian agent for many years, but later in life made his home in Mobile. He was a man of high intelligence, good education, sterling honesty, and was without fear. He was honored and respected by all who knew him. It was at Mr. Gaines' suggestion that the colony of distinguished French refugees, officers and soldiers under Napoleon selected the site at White Bluff for the location of their colony and the town of Demopolis.

JUDGE JOE C. GUILD.

Joseph Conn Guild was born in Stewart (now Houston) County December 14, 1802. In 1810 his father removed with his family to Sumner County and settled near the headwaters of Bledsoe's Creek, where both he and his wife died a few years later, leaving two sons, the elder of which, James Guild, became a noted physician in Tuscaloosa, Ala., and the subject of this sketch, who in 1821 began the study of law in the office of Foster & Brown, in Nashville. In 1822 he began the practice of law in Gallatin. In 1836 he enlisted for the Seminole war, and was commissioned Lieutenant Colonel of the regiment, of which William Trousdale was Colonel, and served with signal gallantry. In 1852 he was an elector on the Democratic ticket. In 1859 he was elected Chancellor for the Seventh division and served until the breaking out of the Civil War. Soon after the close of the war he removed to Nashville, where, in 1870, he was elected

Judge of the Law Court, serving until 1877. In 1878 he published his "Old Times in Tennessee," an octavo volume replete with interest. He served three terms in the State House of Representatives and one term in the State Senate. He died in Nashville on January

JUDGE JOE C. GUILD

8, 1883. On December 19, 1826, Judge Guild married Catherine Blackmore, a daughter of Major George D. Blackmore, a pioneer of Sumner County. They had five children: George B. Guild, a lawyer, who now resides on Woodland street, Nashville; Bettie, who married Colonel Baxter Smith, one of Nashville's most prominent lawyers; Florence, who married Captain

T. L. Dodd; Kitty, who married John M. McKee. The second son was Walter J. Guild.

COLONEL SAMUEL GWIN.

Samuel Gwin was a brother of Senator Gwin. He also located in Mississippi, where he became prominent, though less so than his brother, and less is known of him. The following letter, copied from "Claiborne's History of Mississippi," will give some idea of Colonel Gwin:

"WASHINGTON, October 14, 1831.

"*Hon. George Poindexter, United States Senator:*

"SIR—My recent appointment, Register of the Land Office at Mount Salus, makes it my duty to explain to you why I sought the position, and to say something of my antecedents. I am a native of Tennessee; was a volunteer under Jackson in his Indian campaigns; was in Coffee's brigade in the assault and capture of Pensacola in 1814, and in all the engagements with the British below New Orleans. I lost my health by long protracted exposure, and to this day am a habitual sufferer. In 1829 the Postmaster General was good enough to give me a clerkship in his department, since which time I have never been absent from my post. My beloved wife is now threatened with consumption, and I am advised that the only hope for her is to take her to a warmer climate. Under this advice, and with this hope, and for the happiness of a young family, I submitted the case to the President, and, with the noble sympathies of his nature, he conferred on me the Mount Salus appointment.

"I do not apprehend that anyone will doubt my qualifications or character, but I fear my non-residence may be considered an objection. For this I must ask indulgence. I have never resided in Mississippi, but have shed my blood on her soil in her defense, as the records of our battles will attest.

"My venerable father and his six brothers were soldiers of the Revolution. Respectfully, your obedient servant, SAM'L GWIN."

Senator Poindexter bitterly resented the appointment of Colonel Gwin, and from that time on made vigorous war on President Jackson. He succeeded in the Senate in having the nomination of Colonel Gwin rejected, and he was appointed to the new Land Office at Chocchuma, a more profitable position. The Gwins succeeded in defeating Senator Poindexter for re-election. The canvass resulted in a duel between Judge Isaac Caldwell, Poindexter's law partner, and Colonel Gwin. Both parties fell. Caldwell expired in two hours. Gwin was shot through the lungs and survived about a year.

WILLIAM M. GWIN.

William M. Gwin was a native of Sumner County, born near the present town of Fountain Head, on October 9, 1805. His father, Rev. James Gwin, was a distinguished Methodist minister, who removed from North Carolina in 1790. He was a man of pronounced ability; a soldier in the War for Independence; helped to defend the frontier against the attacks of the Indians; a friend of Andrew Jackson, and his chief chaplain in his Louisiana expedition. He was in the fight at Horseshoe Bend, at Caney Fork, in November, 1792; at Nickojack in 1794, and at New Orleans in 1815. When he first came to Sumner County he stopped one year at Hamilton Station, "But the wickedness of the place was such that he determined to build a cabin in the woods, and trust in God for protection, and did so accordingly, and was preserved by a most indulgent God from the merciless savages." He was a personal friend of Bishop McKendree, and for him named his son, William McKendree Gwin.

William M. Gwin, after receiving a classical education, qualified himself in Gallatin for the practice of law, but abandoned it almost before beginning its practice. He then turned his attention to medicine, and in 1828 took his degree at Transylvania University. He soon afterwards removed to Clinton, Mississippi, where he soon had an extensive practice. In 1833 he retired from practice on being appointed by President Jack-

SENATOR WILLIAM M. GWIN

son United States Marshal for the District of Mississippi; was re-appointed by VanBuren. When President Harrison went into office Dr. Gwin resigned.

Dr. Gwin was elected to Congress in 1841 and served one term, declining renomination. Previous to his election he extensively speculated in lands, and had amassed a large fortune, much of which was dissipated during his term of office. He is said to have spent $75,000 a year during his term in Congress in high living and entertaining. Tradition has it that on the occasion when General Jackson was in financial distress his friend Gwin offered to buy the Hermitage, which he proposed to present to his father for a residence. In 1845 he was defeated for the United States Senate, and the same year removed to New Orleans to superintend the construction of the custom-house. He laid the foundation of the building, and proceeded with the work until General Tyler was elected President, when he resigned and set out for California, where he arrived on June 4, 1849. The establishment of a State Government was the absorbing topic, and Mr. Gwin immediately entered into the discussion. He was elected to the convention which met at Monterey in September to frame a Constitution.

The first Legislature met in the ensuing December, and elected John C. Fremont and William M. Gwin United States Senators. He was said to have been the first to propose a railroad to connect the Atlantic and the Pacific. In 1853 he introduced a bill in the Senate appropriating $200,000 for the survey of a transcontinental railway. On January 18, 1858, he reported a bill for the construction of the Pacific road, but owing to the agitation of other questions no action was taken. He served two terms in the Senate, and closed his political career, which had been a useful one, on March 5, 1861. He acted as intermediary between Secretary Seward and the Commissioners of the Confederate Congress, to confer with the incoming administration on terms of peace and reconciliation. In 1863 Mr. Gwin was in Paris, and while there, on the invitation of the Minister of Foreign Affairs, drew up a plan for the colonization of the Northern States of Mexico from the States of the American Union. For two years the intrigueing continued, but nothing came of it. Dr. Gwin was a strong sympathizer of the Confederate States of the South, and rendered valuable service to the cause while in Europe. After the close of the war he returned to California and engaged in agricultural pursuits. He died in New York on September 3, 1885.

WILLIAM HALL, SEVENTH GOVERNOR.

In the June number of the *Southwestern Monthly,* published in Nashville in 1856, now very scarce, and accessible to but few readers, was published "Hall's Narrative," from which I take the following:

"I was born in Surry County, North Carolina, in the year 1775, and my father sold his possessions in North Carolina in 1779, and started for Kentucky. He came on to New River, in Virginia, and purchased a tract of land and remained there to 1785. He did this in consequence of the times being so perilous and troublesome that he could not then get through the wilderness with his family. He sold his plantation there in the fall of 1785 and moved to Sumner County, which was made a county that year, arriving here on the 20th of November, 1785. He settled near Bledsoe's Lick, on the spot where I am at present residing. Leaving his family at Bledsoe's Fort, he came out during that winter, put up buildings and moved his family to the place. In the spring of 1786 the Indians came and stole all his horses, twelve or fifteen in number. He then moved his family back to the fort, and continued there until the next fall. He then returned and lived here until in the summer of 1787, the Indian war having broken out during the summer of that year. My brother James was killed on the 3d of June, in 1787, at this place, being the first white person killed in this section after the war broke out. The circumstances are these:

"James and myself went to a field at Mr. Gibson's, about a quarter of a mile from my father's houses, we having put our horses up there, and the Indians, fifteen in number, had ambuscaded the road, ten lying

behind some logs on the roads, and five, about fifty
yards further up in a treetop, at the gap in the pasture
fence. The ten Indians behind the log let us pass them
—I suppose because we were boys, probably intending
to quietly tomahawk us. But after we passed the ten
rose up with their tomahawks in their right hands and

Governor William Hall

their guns in their left. I was not noticing them, and
my brother was close behind me. As I turned to speak
to him about some corn with which to catch the horses,
as we were near the fence, I saw the whole ten hem-
ming us in. The case looked so hopeless that I never
dreamed of resistance, and had concluded at once to

surrender. But the next thing I saw two of them struck my brother as he turned around, each striking their tomahawks into his brain one on each side of the forehead. Instantly seeing the case was hopeless, I sought to dodge the ten, when up rose the other five from the treetop, and as I fled past them, I was so near to them that some of them raised their tomahawks to strike me down. Dashing into the thick canebrake, close by which the road ran, two of them rushed after me. Being about thirteen years of age, and, of course, slimmer than they were, and withal very active, I soon found that, unencumbered with a gun or anything else, I could make my way through the thick cane faster than they could. The first misstep that befell me, a grapevine caught me by the neck, threw me over backwards, and took off my hat; but, recovering myself, I still fled onward, gaining on them at every jump. I feared, at last, that they would cut me off at the point of a ridge which I had to cross to get to my father's houses, since the thick cane terminated a little distance below, and I should there be compelled to leave it. Watching one fellow, who was running along the hillside where the cane was thickest, as Heaven ordered it, a large tree had fallen right in his path, crushing the cane about in all directions, and forming an insurmountable obstacle, thus compelling him to go around at one end or the other. Fortunately, he took down towards me to get around the top. and by the time he had got to the end of it, I had already passed it, and consequently I had them the whole tree behind me. They, however, ran me to within 100 yards of the house. They killed and scalped my poor brother, and then fled. As I got to the house half a dozen young men and as many young women were coming on a visit to my father's. The young men were all armed, and they at once jumped off their horses and ran back with me to where my brother was lying, and brought him in. The word was immediately given out, the fort being only about a mile distant, and five men under Major James Lynn instantly went in pursuit of of the Indians. The latter had taken a buffalo trace from Bledsoe's Lick to Dickson's Lick through the canebrake, and the Major, being an old Indian fighter, told his men that they would not pursue directly after them for fear of an ambush, but as they, the whites, were the fewest, they would take another trace, which led on to Goose Creek, ahead, and where the trace crossed, they could there find out whether the gang had passed. Pursuing this plan, they came upon the Indians right in the creek, and, firing upon them, they fled, two of them being wounded, leaving their baggage behind them. The whites brought back my poor brother's scalp, which had been tied to a pack, and likewise one of the tomahawks with which he had been killed, the blood still upon it.

"My father was not at home when my brother was killed, having been summoned to Nashville to attend a council General Robertson was holding with Little Owl and others of the Cherokee chiefs.

"After my father returned from Nashville, three families of us residing out from the fort held a council as to whether we should spend the summer at the farms or go to the fort at Bledsoe's Lick. Our two neighbors were Messrs. Gibson and Harrison, and the former having no white family, it was agreed that the three should combine and hire each two young men to guard the farms through the season. From the 3d of June, accordingly, the day after my brother was killed, to the 2d day of August, we had no alarm, but on that day the spies came in and advised my father to pack up at once and move to the station; that the Indians were at least thirty in number. We accordingly loaded up a sled and started for the fort. We started with the first load in the morning, my sister being alone on horseback, going to the fort to arrange things at the cabins as fast as they should arrive, and we had two men along also, my brother and a Mr. Hickerson, to guard us. When about half a mile from my father's house, and crossing Defeated Creek, the horses became alarmed, the two I was driving turning so suddenly around as to nearly run over me. I said to the young men that I was sure the horses smelt the Indians, but my brother insisted upon going onward, which we did, making four trips during the day. When we came late in the evening to make the last trip and take the family to the fort, five men went along to guard the family thither. We packed up when the sun was about two hours high, whites, negroes and all, I still driving the horses, my little brother behind me on one of them. We had arranged it that we should go ahead as we had been doing all day, the two young men in advance of me and the sled. The Indians, forty or fifty in number, had arranged an ambuscade on both sides of the road for about 100 yards, and as we went on, my brother and Hickerson in advance, a little dog belonging to my brother showed violent alarm on approaching the top of a large ash tree that had fallen in the road. My brother was just in advance, and as he stopped a moment I stopped the horses to see what was the cause of the alarm evinced by the dog. My brother took a step forward towards the tree top, when immediately I saw a gun poked out from amongst the leaves, which, being fired at once, my brother was shot right through the body with a couple of bullets. He instantly turned and dashed back into the woods and fell dead about 100 yards off, while the Indians, finding themselves discovered, rose all together, yelling like demons, and charged upon our party. Hickerson took his stand unwisely right in the road instead of treeing, and his gun missing fire, he next attempted to use my gun, which he had in his hand, but in the act of firing it he was shot with six or seven bullets, and running a little distance, he also fell and expired. At this I jumped off the horse, and taking my little brother John, and my sister Prudence, I ran back and placed them behind the men, who, advancing, kept the Indians a few moments at bay. My mother was mounted upon a large, powerful horse, and he, scared quite ungovernable, dashed right along the entire line of the Indians, whilst she holding to his mane was carried about a mile distant to the fort.

"My father and Mr. Morgan, my brother-in-law, kept the Indians in check until the whites and negroes scattered into the woods, and Morgan was then wounded by the Indians, who, flanking around, shot him very dangerously through the body. He, however, succeeded in escaping, my father keeping the savages back for some little time longer, but finally, after firing his heavy rifle, which I could mark distinctly from the report made, so different from that by the Indians' guns, he turned and ran about forty yards, when he fell, pierced by thirteen bullets. The Indians scalped him and hastily fled, not stopping to take anything but his rifle and shot pouch, and in their hot haste they did not even pick up the things scattered by the overturning of the sled, the horses having dashed it against a tree as they broke clear of it at the first alarm. Meanwhile, I had directed my little brother and sister to run back to the house, I awaiting behind a tree upon the hill above the result of the fight, and when I heard my father fire and the Indians raise the yell, thereupon I started for the fort. My little brother and sister ran back to the house, but the alarmed dogs barking at them they ran back to the scene of battle. Here they found Mr. Rogan's hat, which the little boy picked up, and coming to the sled, my little sister picked up also a small pail of butter, and the two thoughtlessly walked on towards the fort, along the road, meeting the men directly who were coming from thence. The children were placed in charge of a negro man, who took them safely back.

"After my father was killed my mother concluded to move to Greenfield Fort, her two sons-in-law living there, and so I moved her there soon after, where we remained until the December following."

SOME SUMNER COUNTIANS   261

It was amid such scenes that William Hall grew to manhood. He assisted in repelling many attacks of the Indians, and more than one fell before his unerring rifle. He served as Sheriff of Sumner County, was a Brigadier-General in the Creek War, and was in the war of 1812; served as Major-General of militia, was

OLD HOME OF GOVERNOR WILLIAM HALL

elected to the State Senate in 1821, re-elected in 1823 and again in 1825 and again in 1827, and was chosen Speaker. On the 16th of April, 1829, when Governor Houston resigned, he became Governor, serving to the end of the term, October 1, the same year. In 1831 he was elected to Congress as a Democrat. He died at his home, Green Garden, on the 7th of October, 1856.

Mrs. Hall, before her marriage, was Miss Thankful Doak, a native of North Carolina. Their son, William, afterwards Governor, married Miss Mary B. Alexander; they ,had children—Richard A., William H. Thankful J., Martha, Mary, Alexander and John A., all of whom left Sumner County except Richard and William. Richard left no children. William married Catherine Barry, who left one son. His second wife was Miss S. W. McDaniel, grandniece of General James Winchester. By this marriage he had one son. Judge William H. Hall, now cashier of the First National Bank of Gallatin, and three daughters.

JOHN HALLUM.

Judge Hallum was descended from William Hallum, who came from England about 1760 and settled at Hagerstown, Md. During the War of Independence he removed to South Carolina, where he became a wealthy planter and slave owner. His sons, William and Henry, emigrated to Tennessee in 1790 and located near Carthage. Bluford, a son of Henry, married Minerva Davis and settled at Ca Ira (Cairo), Sumner County, where the subject of this sketch was born in January, 1833. In 1837 his father and grandfather built a flatboat, in which, late in the autumn, they embarked with their families, and after a voyage of six weeks, moored their craft in Wolf River, near Memphis. His father located twenty miles west from Somerville, where he remained until 1840, then removed to a farm which he had bought, eighteen miles north from Memphis. In 1844 the family returned to Sumner County.

John Hallum was self-educated; he taught school in Sumner County; removed to Memphis and there taught; studied law and practiced with success; served in the Confederate army, and a part of the time was held a prisoner by the Federals. After the war he removed to Arkansas; later to Arizona; lived for a time in Missouri; then in Texas; finally drifted back to Arkansas, where he died on July 11, 1906. His death was the result of a fall from the steps of a hotel at Pine Bluff. He had been twice married, but survived both his wives. He was the author of "Diary of an Old Lawyer," "Reminiscences of the Confederacy," "Bench and Bar of Arkansas," and "History of Arkansas."

ROBERT HATTON, STATESMAN AND SOLDIER.

Robert Hatton was born November 2, 1826, at Youngstown, Ohio, where his father, a Virginian and a Methodist preacher, was located. In 1835 the family moved to Nashville, Tenn., where Robert attended school for two years, when the family moved to Sumner County. In 1842 the father became pastor of a church in Gallatin. Robert Hatton began his career as a clerk, then taught school; then, in 1845, entered Cumberland University, graduating in 1847; then acted as tutor in the same institution for one year, and then entered the law department. He was admitted to the bar in 1850 and formed a partnership with Jordan Stokes at Lebanon. In 1853 he dissolved the partnership and formed another with Nathaniel Green. In 1852 he was married to Miss Sophie Rielly of Williamson County. In 1855 he was elected a member of the Legislature from Wilson County as a Whig, was an elector on the Fillmore ticket in 1856, was the Whig candidate for Governor in 1857, and was defeated by Isham G. Harris. In 1859 he was elected a member of Congress. He was opposed to secession, but when his State joined its fortunes with its Southern sisters he felt that it was his duty to stand by his own people. At the commencement of the war he raised a company for the Confederate service and was elected Captain, and then Colonel of the Seventh Tennessee. He served in Virginia under Lee and Jackson. On May 23, 1862, he was made Brigadier General and placed in command of the Fifth

Brigade, First Division and First Army Corps of the Army of Virginia. He was killed while gallantly leading his men in the battle of Seven Pines, May 31, 1862. His widow now resides in Nashville.

THE HEAD FAMILY.

The Head family has been prominent in Sumner County for several generations. The original founder of the Tennessee branch of the family was Henry Head, who was born in Albemarle County, Virginia, in 1770. His mother was descended from the same family as Chief Justice John Marshall of the Supreme Court of the United States. He married Elizabeth Sanford and removed to Sumner County about 1812 and settled near Cairo. A few years later he bought a farm near Bledsoe's Lick, where he spent the remainder of his life, dying in 1853. His wife, who was of Scotch descent, was also born in Albermarle County, in 1777, and died in Sumner County in 1873. They had twelve children, ten sons and two daughters. John W., the youngest of the twelve, was born in 1821. He studied law and became one of the most prominent members of the Gallatin bar, noted at that time for its men of talent. In 1858 he was elected Attorney General and Reporter, and served until the breaking out of the Civil War. He published three volumes of "Head's Reports." In 1873 he was a member of the Court of Arbitration. In October, 1874, he was elected a member of Congress, and died one week after his election, October 10, 1874. Mr. Head married in 1822, Evaline Brooks of Smith County. She survived him many years. Their sons, Chares R. and Lee Head, both became prominent lawyers. Charles R. married first Sophia Childress of Nashville, who died in 1870, leaving a daughter, Adrian C. In 1874 Mr. Head married again, Alice Burford, a native of Smith County, born in 1849. They had six children: John W., David, Lee, Elizabeth, Allen and Alice. Lee was born in 1849; he received a classical education, studied law and practiced in Gallatin. In 1873 he was elected a member of the Legislature and re-elected in 1875. In 1878 he was elected Judge of the Sumner County Court, which position he held for a number of years. In 1881 he married Nannie Gillespie, a native of Sumner County, daughter of R. G. Gillespie. To them were born two children, Graham and Charles R.

Dr. James M. Head, Sr., was the eleventh of the twelve children of Henry and Elizabeth Head. He received his education at old Rural Academy at Bledsoe's Lick, then studied medicine with Dr. Sharpe; then took a course in Transylvania Medical College at Lexington, Ky. In 1841 he married Berthenis P. Branham, who was born in 1825 and died in 1885. Eight children were born to them, of whom two died in infancy. Milton E. married Elizabeth Yager in 1868. Florence married Dr. J. L. Vertrees in 1869. Dr. John B. married Virginia Perkins in 1871. James M. married Minnie Cherry of Nashville, in which city he has since had his home, and of which he served two terms as Mayor. Alice married a Mr. Simpson. Lucy, the eldest, married Matthew Johnson of Sumner County. Penelope, the youngest, married William A. Lauderdale of Sumner County. Clara married J. Y. Robb of the same county, and who was Clerk and Master of the Chancery Court for many years. To them were born five children: Dr. C. W. Robb of Goodlettsville; William S. Robb of Gallatin; Joseph, who died in infancy; Nellie, who married Dr. B. P. Gilbert of Louisville, now of Nashville; and Bessie, who married Dr. A. H. Holder of Gallatin. Lucy, the youngest daughter of William and Penelope Lauderdale, married Dr. Thomas Kennedy of Louisville, who at the time of their marriage was practicing medicine at Castalian Springs. Of the other members of the

Head family no record has been obtained. Dr. Head entered the Confederate army in 1861 as surgeon of the Thirtieth Tennessee and served two years.

J. W. JUDD.

Judge John Walters Judd was born in Sumner County on September 6, 1839. He is a son of Rev. John W. Judd, who was born in Brunswick County, Virginia, February 8, 1812, and died at Tullahoma, Tenn., February 20, 1861, where he was stationed by the Tennessee Conference of the M. E. Church, South. On his mother's side Judge Judd is descended from James Stark, who came from Scotland long before the Revolutionary War and settled in Stafford County, Virginia, where his son, Jeremiah, was born. John, the son of Jeremiah, was born in Stafford County on November 22, 1744. On January 4, 1769, he married Sarah English. They came to Tennessee in 1811 and settled near Hendersonville, where he died on May 16, 1814. Sarah English Stark was born in King George County, Virginia, July 4, 1749, and died in Sumner County, Tennessee, September 28, 1820. Jeremiah Stark had five sons in the War for Independence. John, son of John and Sarah English Stark, was born in Stafford County, Virginia, on May 8, 1788; he married Margarett Primm, who was born on October 1, 1787. Their daughter, Lydia, who was so named for her great-grandmother, Lydia, sister of General Daniel Smith, was born in Sumner County on April 14, 1816, and married Rev. John W. Judd on November 12, 1835, and died in Sumner County on July 28, 1840. General John Stark of New Hampshire, a celebrated officer in the Revolutionary War, was a member of the same family as the Sumner County Starks. Judge C. B. Stark of St. Louis is a son of the late Judge Joel Stark of Springfield, Tenn., and an uncle of Judge Judd.

JUDGE JOHN W. JUDD

Judge Judd learned the trade of coachmaker at Gallatin, and subsequently used the means derived from this trade in educating himself. He began reading law in the office of his uncle, Judge Stark, in Springfield, in January, 1861. The war coming on, he enlisted in Company C, Forty-ninth Tennessee Infantry. He was taken prisoner when his regiment surrendered at Fort Donelson, February 16, 1862; was exchanged and joined his regiment at Vicksburg, September 16, 1862. When the regiment was reorganized he re-enlisted for three years, or during the war. On account of a wound in his knee he was, in the spring of 1863, transferred to the Ninth Tennessee Cavalry, in Morgan's command. He was with Morgan in his raid through Kentucky, Indiana and Ohio in 1863. Escaping capture with a small part of the command, he crossed the Ohio and made his way to Tennessee and joined the army at Knoxville. He was in the battles of Chickamauga, Mission Ridge, Wytheville, and on the 9th of June, 1864, was severely wounded and left for dead at the battle of Mt. Sterling, Ky. He was there captured and taken to Camp Chase, Ohio, where he remained until the close of the war.

After returning home he resumed the practice of law in partnership with his uncle at Springfield. This partnership continued until Judge Stark was elected Judge in 1878. Later he formed a partnership with the late Lewis T. Cobb, which connection continued until 1888, when Judge Judd was appointed by President Cleveland Associate Justice of the Supreme Court of Utah, which position he resigned in 1889. In 1893 President Cleveland appointed him United States Attorney for the District of Utah. He held that position until 1896, when Utah was admitted to statehood, when he was reappointed and held until 1898. He then returned to Tennessee and located in Nashville, and in 1899 was appointed Assistant District Attorney for the Louisville & Nashville Railroad, which position he held until January 1, 1907, when he resigned, and has since devoted his time to his law classes in the law department of Vanderbilt University.

Judge Judd was commissioned special Supreme Judge by Gov. Porter in 1878, to sit in trial in some cases in which Judge Cooper was incompetent. He has several times been commissioned as Circuit Judge and as Chancellor in special cases. Judge Judd first married Mrs. Lee G. Miller (Gilbert) at Springfield, on May 11, 1870. She died April 8, 1878. On January 4, 1881, he married Miss Eliza H. Bayless, of Shelbyville, Ky. In 1904 Judge Judd purchased "Bellwood," one of the finest farm in Sumner County, one mile west of Gallatin. It is a part of one of the tracts of land originally claimed by Thomas Sharp Spencer. The residence was built in 1827 by Colonel George Elliott, the founder of the Elliott family in Sumner County. It was then known as Elliott Spring. Later it passed to the possession of Colonel Wall and became known as Wall Spring. The name Bellwood was given the place by Judge Bell of Gallatin, from whom Judge Judd purchased it.

THE LAUDERDALES.

The original name of the Lauderdale family was "Maitland," but many generations back the "Laird of Maitland" was made Earl, or Lord, of Lauderdale, for military services rendered his country, and a landed estate was given with the title. James Maitland was the grandfather of Isabella Marr, who married Robert Bruce, King of Scotland, and Helen Marr, Isabella's sister, who married Sir William Wallace.

Sir Richard Maitland, an early Scotch lawyer and poet, wase born in 1496. His father, William Maitland, of Lethington, fell at Flodden. His mother was a daughter of George, Lord Seton. He studied law at the University of St. Andrew and afterwards in France. He was knighted about the year 1552, and about 1554 was made an Extraordinary on Session. In 1561 he was admitted an Ordinary Lord of Session by the title of Lithington. In 1562 he was nominated Lord Privy Seal, which office he resigned in 1567 in favor of John, Prior of Codingham, his second son. He died in 1586, aged 90 years, seventy of which had been spent in public life. His son John was made a Lord of Parliament in 1590, by the title of Lord Maitland, in which he was succeeded by his son John, who was made Earl of Lauderdale in 1624. His son John became Duke of Lauderdale. One of Sir Richard's daughters, Mary, assisted her father in his literary work and also wrote verses. Their works were collected in two large volumes, a folio written by Sir Richard and a quarto by his daughter. These volumes are now in the Pepysian library, Cambridge.

John Maitland, Earl and afterwards Duke of Lauderdale in the peerage of Scotland as a great-grandson of Sir Richard. In his early life he was a Presbyterian, and was a party to the surrender of Charles I to the English army in 1645. Soon afterwards he became a supporter of the royal cause. He was taken prisoner at the battle of Warchester, and after being liberated accompanied Charles II to Scotland. From 1682 he was virtually ruler of Scotland. In 1672 he was made Duke of Lauderdale and a Knight of the Garter, and he had also an English peerage conferred upon him with the title of Earl of Guildford in 1674. He was one of the administrative council known as "the Cabal." His dukedom and his English title expired with him. The earldom of Lauderdale passed to his brother Charles and is still in possession of his descendants. One branch of his family settled in Ireland. In 1714 one of them came to America and located in Southeastern Pennsylvania, but soon afterwards removed to Botetourt County Virginia. He had a large family, seven sons and three daughters. The daughters married with the McClellans, Logans,

DeShas, Franklins, Gillespies, Alcorns and Henrys. The sons, John, James and William, all served in the Revolutionary War, one of them as a commissioned officer.

James Lauderdale, mentioned above, was the founder of the Sumner County branch of the family. He

HOME OF THE LAUDERDALES

married a Miss Mills and moved to Tennessee about 1794, and acquired a large body of land adjoining the Greenfield tract, upon which he built his home. A part of this land is still in possession of some of his descendants. He had six sons and one daughter. Five of his sons served as commissioned officers under

Jackson in the Indian wars and in the War of 1812. William was Quartermaster, with the rank of Major. James was commissioned a Major in a regiment in Coffee's brigade, and later was commissioned Lieutenant Colonel of a regiment of mounted infantry. He fell at the first battle of New Orleans, December 23, 1814, while gallantly leading his regiment in a charge against the British. He was a brave and gallant soldier, and his death was lamented throughout the army. He was never married.

Sam D. Lauderdale, son of James, was a Colonel in the Creek War under Jackson, and had the confidence and esteem of his commander and his men. When the term of enlistment of his men had expired he was placed in command to lead them back to Tennessee. When the Choctaw Indians were removed to the West in 1833, Colonel Lauderdale was placed in command of the transportation without asking for the place. When the war with Mexico broke out, though past three score and ten, he was, with no little difficulty, persuaded from volunteering his services.

In 1830 Major William Lauderdale, with his Tennesseans, carried his country's flag farther into the Indian country than anyone else had done up to that time, and established Fort Lauderdale in Southeastern Florida.

In 1836 James Shelby Lauderdale, son of Colonel Sam D., was an ensign in a company of mounted rifles from Mississippi, which marched to join General Jessup's command on the Texas frontier to stop the Mexicans in case of the defeat of General Sam Houston. In the Mexican War William Lauderdale was a Lieutenant in Captain Blythe's company, Second Mississippi Rifles, from Lowndes County. John Lauderdale raised a company, but it was not accepted, because more troops were offered than were needed. He then served in the ranks. Gallant Sam Lauderdale, who fell at Cerro Gordo, was a son of Major William Lauderdale.

Tennessee, Alabama, Mississippi and Texas have counties named in honor of these Lauderdale heroes.

When the Civil War broke out the Lauderdales rallied to the defense of their beloved land and bravely sustained the ancient reputation of the family. The bones of more than one of them were left to bleach on bloody battle fields. James Shelby Lauderdale, before mentioned, raised the first company in Texas for the Confederate service. He gave his company its first drill on Christmas day, 1860. His company formed a part of the Tenth Texas Infantry and did gallant service. But few of the one hundred men who marched out with him in 1861 ever returned. Captain Lauderdale was taken prisoner and confined at Camp Chase, and then at Johnson's Island. During the latter part of the war he served on the staff of General Ashbet Smith, and then on the staff of General J. B. Robertson. He now resides at Somerville, Texas, and though well advanced in years, is in the full enjoyment of all his faculties and in the esteem of his fellow citizens. (Captain Lauderdale died at the home of his son, J. W. Lauderdale, in Somerville, Texas, January 27, 1909, aged 93 years and 6 months.)

The Lauderdales have been quiet, peaceable, law-abiding citizens, farmers and professional men. They have lived unostentatious lives, but when grim-visaged war appeared they sniffed the battle from afar and hastened to the front, where danger and honor were found.

The names of the children of James Lauderdale, the founder of the Sumner County family, were:

John Lauderdale, who married Miss Wood and had six sons and three daughters.

J. Franklin Lauderdale, who married Miss Sewell.

William Lauderdale, who married Miss Head.

Sam H. Lauderdale, who married Miss Winchester.

Harry Lauderdale, who first married Jane Malone; second, Nancy Crenshaw.

Josiah Lauderdale never married, went to Texas, where he was a surveyor and Indian fighter. "A better, braver and nobler soul never lived."

Sallie Lauderdale married J. H. Brittain of Lebanon. Elizabeth Lauderdale married John Patterson.

Clarinda Lauderdale never married.

Sam D. Lauderdale, son of James, married Miss Hawkins. Had five sons and one daughter.

James Shelby Lauderdale married Miss Adams and had seven sons and three daughters.

William C. Lauderdale married Miss Turner. No issue.

John Lauderdale married Miss Dodson, and after her death, Miss Jeffreys. Had a son and a daughter.

Andrew J. Lauderdale married Miss Givens; had one son and one daughter. Samuel B. Lauderdale died at the age of ten years.

Cornelia Lauderdale married J. J. Lewis, and after his death, Benjamin Seale. Had a son by each; both served in the Civil War. The Lewis son was killed in battle.

David Lauderdale, son of James, married Miss Bledsoe; had three sons.

William Lauderdale, son of James, married Miss Hart.

Josiah Lauderdale, son of James, married Miss Hanna; had five sons and three daughters.

The daughters of James Lauderdale married John Hawkins; had five sons and three daughters: James Hawkins, Benjamin Hawkins, Harry Hawkins, John Hawkins (never married), Sam Hawkins; Patsey Hawkins married Wesley Malone; Ella Hawkins married Dr. William Welsh; Harriett Hawkins never married.

Harry Lauderdale, son of John W. Lauderdale, who married Jane Malone, daughter of Hal Malone of

Sumner County, had a son, John, who went to West Tennessee, where he married a Miss Ferguson. Their daughter, Miss Jennie Lauderdale, was for some years State Librarian, and is now Librarian of the University of Nashville.

After the death of his first wife, John Lauderdale married Miss Tipton of West Tennessee. They had two children, Amelia, who married Charles L. Davison of Nashville, and Harry, who married Miss Pilkering of Clarksville. They now reside in Beaumont, Texas, where he is treasurer of the S. C., N. O. & P. Railroad.

After the death of his wife, Jane (Malone), Harry Lauderdale married Nancy Crenshaw. They had one daughter, Mary J., who married Judge George E. Seay of Gallatin. Their son, Hon. Ed T. Seay, formerly Speaker of the State Senate, is now Assistant District Attorney for the Louisville & Nashville Railroad for Tennessee.

John Wood Lauderdale married Jane Sewell and moved to West Tennessee. Their granddaughter, Amelia, married John Skeffington, a lawyer of Dyersburg, for several years Attorney General for that district. Their daughters, Misses Mary and Jane, are respectively Librarian and Assistant Librarian of the State of Tennessee.

Josiah Lauderdale, who married Miss Hanna of Sumner County, moved to Wellington, Mo. Their sons, James, William and Bledsoe, bore a conspicuous part in the Civil War. Bledsoe was cruelly murdered by Federal soldiers after he had been wounded and had surrendered.

Kimberland Spring, near the old Lauderdale home, and from which the family procured its water, was a noted muster ground during the early days of Sumner County. It was a rendezvous for the people, and a place where the local militia met for drill and parade.

The old stone spring house is still standing and in good state of preservation.

The Lauderdale graveyard, now overgrown with weeds and bushes, is an interesting spot. Beneath the wide-spreading branches of a mammoth ash tree reposes the remains of John Lauderdale, born September 16, 1768; died September 29, 1853. Cornelia Lauderdale, born 1769; died 1854. Jane Malone Lauderdale (daughter of Hal Malone), born January 13, 1811; married January 13, 1834; died January 16, 1836. Near her grave is that of her husband, Harry B. Lauderdale, born 1811; died 1847.

Hallery Malone sleeps in the same lot. Many of the old grave stones are now prone upon the ground, and the secret spot shows a sad degree of neglect. In another generation the tooth of time will have obliterated the marks on most of the older tombs.

ISAAC LINDSEY.

Isaac Lindsey was one of the stout-hearted pioneers of Sumner County. He came from Virginia in 1780 and settled at Eaton's Station, on the east side of the river, at the first headlands below Nashville. He was one of the signers of the Cumberland Compact, May 13, 1780, and was one of the first justices of the peace of Davidson County, elected January 7, 1783. In the same year he removed to Sumner County and located near Saundersville, at Lindsey's Bluff. In 1786, when Sumner County was organized, he was elected one of its first magistrates. In that year he embraced religion, connected himself with the Methodist Church and soon afterwards began to preach. He was a man of the first order of talent, a good man and a useful citizen. He died at his home in Sumner County at an advanced age, loved, honored and respected by all who knew him. Of his descendants no facts have come to the author.

HALLERY MALONE.

"Hal" Malone, son of Isom and Judy Cole Malone, was born near Petersburg, Va., on December 13, 1758. The family was of Scotch-Irish origin and Methodist in religion. As to when the first of the name came

OLD HOME OF HALLERY MALONE

to America no records have been found. Hallery was a Revolutionary soldier, and was with Washington at the crossing of the Delaware, when the patriot army could be tracked by the blood from the barefooted soldiers upon the frozen ground. He was at that time only eighteen years of age and was wounded. To the day of his death he refused a pension, declaring that every man owed service to his country. Soon after the close of the Revolution he married Katie Lyon, daughter of Peter and Bettie Norvill Lyon. At an early date he removed to Tennessee and settled about two miles north from Bledsoe's Lick. His old home, built more than a century ago, is still standing on a beautiful eminence overlooking one of the forks of Bledsoe's Creek, on land which was originally part of the Greenfield track. There he reared a large family, and from that old house he and his faithful wife were, after long and useful lives, carried to Lauderdale's graveyard. "Uncle Hal" died on June 17, 1854, aged 96 years.

The late Senator William B. Bate, in writing of Hallery Malone in one of the Gallatin papers soon after his death, said:

"A kinder husband, father and neighbor it has never been our fortune to know. No one ever met him that he did not wear a smile, or entered his home unless greeted with an open-handed hospitality peculiar to the men of the olden time. The poor loved him for the charity which came from his liberal hand; the rich loved him for his warm, honest heart that never envied, for he was their friend; they exalted, for they felt him their equal."

Hallery Malone was the father of five sons and three daughters, all of whom became useful citizens, married and left large families. Wesley married Betsey Hawkins; William L. married Sarah Shelby Weathered, a granddaughter of Colonel Anthony Bledsoe; Jack married Bettie Hanna; James Norvill married Katurah Hanna; Charles B. married Louisa Zimmerman; Nancy married James Essex; Sallie married McLinn Harper; Jennie married Harry Lauderdale.

KASPER MANSKER.

Kasper Manscoe, or Mansker, was a German and spoke English with a strong accent. He was one of the earliest and most energetic of the explorers of what is now Tennessee. He probably came from Pennsylvania, a State that gave to Tennessee some of its best citizens during its early period. In the summer of 1769 he was one of a party of daring adventurers who spent several months in the Cumberland country, hunting and exploring. They spent most of their time on Roaring River and Obed's River. In the spring of 1770 some of the party returned home. Mansker, with several others, made canoes, in which they loaded the proceeds of their hunt, and descended the Cumberland, the Ohio and the Mississippi to Natchez, where some of the party located, the others, including their leader, Mansker, made their way back to New River, Va. It is believed that they were the first white men to navigate the Cumberland River. In the autumn of 1771 Mansker led another party to the Cumberland.

They made their headquarters at a place since known as Station Camp, about ten miles west of Gallatin. This party was called the "long hunters." They spent the winter in huts made of buffalo skins and returned to the settlements in the spring of 1772. Mansker again came to the Cumberland in 1779 and built a fort near Mansker's Lick, on Mansker's Creek. Three years later he built another fort about one mile east of the first named, and there made his home until he died, an old man, respected and beloved by all. He was a Colonel of militia. His remains lie in an unmarked grave near his old home in Sumner County He had no children.

Andre Michaux, a French scientist, who was sent to America by his government to report on the flora and fauna of the United States, in his diary in 1796, says: "The 25th (February) started to return to Carolina and slept ten miles away at the house of Colonel Mansko, a decided enemy of the French because, he said, they had killed their king. Although I had not dined, I would not accept his supper, believing that a Republican should not be under obligations to a fanatical partisan of royalty. I was greatly mortified that the night and the rain should compel me to remain in his house. But I slept on my deer skin and paid for the maize he supplied me with to cross the wilderness."

It is not probable that the old hunter Mansker, had any love for French royalty, but that he hated the French nation because it had, only a short time before, overrun his own native Germany.

WILLIAM M'KENDREE.

William McKendree, the famous Methodist preacher and bishop, for some years had his home—if it can be said that he had a home—in Sumner County. He was born in King William County, Virginia, July 6, 1757. He was converted at the age of 30, and soon afterwards entered the ministry, preaching in Virginia, Maryland and the Carolinas. In 1801 he was appointed presiding elder of the Western Conference, embracing East and Middle Tennessee, Southwestern Virginia, Kentucky and portion of Ohio. He came West in the fall of 1800, and from that time on until his death, March 5, 1835, he was probably the most prominent figure in the Methodist Church in Tennessee. He continued to hold the position of presiding elder until 1808, when he was elected bishop. His father's family had removed to Sumner County and settled near Fountain Head, and there the bishop called his home, and there, at the house of his brother, Dr. James McKendree, he died and was buried in the family graveyard beside his father.

CAPT. JOHN MORGAN.

Captain John Morgan, a Revolutionary soldier, came to Sumner County in 1784 with his father-in-law, Major William Hall, whose eldest daughter, Mary, he had married before leaving North Carolina. He built his fort on an eminence in the vicinity of Rogana, on lands now owned by Dr. Jesse Johnson. Some of the logs of which the fort was constructed are now in the walls of a barn on the farm of Dr. Johnson. Captain Morgan's father, 'Squire John Morgan, came with him and was killed by an Indian warrior while returning from the spring under the hill. The Indian rushed upon him and sank his tommyhawk deeply into his brain, where it was left, being too tightly wedged into the skull to be withdrawn. He also lost a brother, Armistead, a fine young man, and very popular with the settlers. He was killed from ambush at Southwest Pass, on the route from Knoxville, while piloting a party of emigrants.

Captain Morgan's eldest daughter, Nancy, married James Bright of Kentucky, who was a surveyor, and settled at Fayetteville, Lincoln County, about 1803, and where Captain Morgan also settled about the same time. On the breaking out of the Creek War he raised a company of mounted troops and joined General Jackson at the rendezvous at Huntsville, Ala. He was a large, handsome man, with noble features and gray hair that hung down on his shoulders, and when he rode through Fayetteville at the head of his company, his appearance and the occasion were never forgotten by those who witnessed it, and is one of the traditions of the town. He was well advanced in years, but he said: "A man should never get too old to fight the British and Indians."

He died some time in the 30's and was buried near Mulberry. His wife survived him until 1850 and is buried in the old cemetery at Fayetteville. General

John Morgan Bright, one of the most honored citizens of Fayetteville, is a grandson of Captain John Morgan. Colonel E. L. Drake of Winchester is his great-grandson. In a letter to the writer he says: "I remember my great-grandmother Morgan (Mary Hall) very distinctly—how her black eyes flashed at the mention of the British or Indians."

RT. REV. J. B. MORRIS, BISHOP.

John B. Morris was born near Hendersonville, Sumner County, June 29, 1866; was educated at St. Mary's College in Kentucky, graduating with the highest honors, and in the American College in Rome, where he won distinction. After returning from Rome he was connected with St. Mary's Cathedral and St. Joseph's Church in Nashville. In 1894 he was appointed Chancellor of the diocese of Nashville, and subsequently pastor of the cathedral and Vicar General. In December, 1905, the title of Monsignor was conferred on him by Pope Pius X. On April 16, 1906, he was created Bishop of Acomonia, in the archepiscopal province of Laodicea, in the province of Phrygia, Asia Minor, and Coadjutor Bishop of Little Rock, with the right of succession on the death of Bishop Fitzgerald. Bishop Morris has the distinction of being the first native Tennessean to be exalted to that high dignity. Bishop Morris is a son of Mr. John Morris, who was born in Ireland in 1837, and there received his early education. At the age of 12 years he came to America and located in Wheeling, W. Va., where he later worked on various railroads. He came to Sumner County in 1855, and in 1865 married Ann Morrisey of Nashville. She is a native of Canada, born in 1847. Of this union were born John B. (Bishop), Mary E., Margaret, Ellen Agnes, Martin J. and Edna.

SOME SUMNER COUNTIANS 283

THE ODOM, ELLIOTT AND BODDIE FAMILIES.

In the closing years of the eighteenth century there came to Sumner County two families who represented the highest type of what Roosevelt calls "the backwoodsman," the Elliotts and the Odoms. The Elliotts were of English descent. The family consisted of three sons and one daughter. The Odoms were from South Carolina and were Huguenots. There were the father and mother, James and Rhoda Odom, and two sons, Harris and Eli, and three daughters, Elizabeth, Mary and Sarah. These two families settled on Station Camp Creek and owned all the land from the town of Gallatin to about three miles west, extending from the Nashville pike north to the Douglass pike. It was inevitable in those pioneer days that the families should intermarry, and hence, the record goes, that Charles Elliott married Elizabeth Odom and settled at Walnut Grove, on the creek a mile west of Gallatin. Across the creek at Wall's Spring, lived George Elliott, who married Mary Odom. A mile farther up the creek was the home of James Odom, the father of the family, at Maple Grove. His wife was Rhoda Gibson, whose father was scalped by the Indians, but who lived to be the hero of many a small boy descendant. Here Harris Odom lived with his wife, Adeline Elliston, the step-daughter of his sister, Elizabeth, who married, as her third husband, Joseph T. Elliston of Nashville. Eli Odom married a niece of his brother-in-law, George Elliott, Katie Phagan, who was the mother of Ellen Odom, Mrs. Charles Trousdale.

We are amazed at the rapidity with which fortunes are made today. But the success of these pioneers, under conditions that would seem to prohibit the accumulation of money, is far more remarkable. George Elliott was a Colonel under General Coffee in the Creek War and at the battle of New Orleans. For many years his was the most celebrated racing stud in the South. Leviathan, Albion, Pocolet and Haynies Maria were a few of the giants of the turf that made his stables famous. Men came from all parts of the United States to see what blue grass could do for the blooded horse. Mrs. Elliott used to say that she never knew if she would have one or twenty guests at a meal. When Colonel Elliott was reproached in those earnest, early days of the circuit rider and camp meeting for horse racing he would say: "The first race horse I ever owned I won from the General." General Jackson was an intimate friend and frequent guest at the Elliott home, "Wall Spring," so named for a fine, bold spring on the creek, which was famous as a camping ground for "movers" and Indians. Colonel Elliott accumulated a large fortune and dispensed a liberal, old-time hospitality. The ambition of his later years was to have the finest thoroughbred stock of every kind. At the county fairs it was said "only let old Jarret, the Colonel's head groom, lead an animal in, if it were a butting ram, a grunting pig, or a thoroughbred stallion, it always bore off the prize." This splendid estate is now owned by Judge John W. Judd, who makes his home in the original Elliott mansion. Colonel Elliott was a man of most noble mein. In character he was simple, strong, generous and honest. He lived to see his country rent by Civil War. His son, Eli Elliott, fought gallantly for four years for the land his father loved, and came home at the close of the war to find devastation where all had been delight.

Walnut Grove, the home of Charles Elliott and his wife, Elizabeth Odom, consisted of a square mile of land, devoted almost entirely to groves and meadows. About 1795 was built there the stone house which stands today in a perfect state of preservation—a model of early colonial architecture. The only child of this marriage was a daughter named Maria. Charles Elliott died in 1808, and after a few years his widow was married to a famous young Methodist preacher, Leaner Blackman. In 1815 the couple went to a general conference at Cincinnati. As they were returning home, crossing the ferry on the Ohio River, the lead horses became frightened (they were driving

RESIDENCE OF JUDGE JOHN W. JUDD. FORMER HOME OF COL. GEORGE ELLIOTT. ERECTED IN 1827

a coach and four). Mr. Blackman caught the bridle to quiet them, but rearing up, they threw him overboard and he was drowned before his wife's eyes. She returned to Cincinnati and had him buried there. The family have a portrait of her painted about this time. She is seated, dressed in black, under a weep-ing willow, leaning on a tombstone, on which is inscribed: "Leaner Blackman, drowned in the Ohio River, May 16, 1815." In 1816 her daughter, Maria, was married to Elijah Boddie, a young man of a wealthy and distinguished family of North Carolina. His grandfather, Nathan Boddie, of Edgecombe, was a member of the Mecklenburg Congress. The young man came to Sumner County to see some property he had inherited, fell in love with the beautiful Maria, and with the splendid country, and never returned to his native State. Being a man of wealth, he was able to indulge his taste in the development of his splendid estate. It used to be said that "there was not a weed on the Boddie farm." Elijah Boddie was a lawyer who never took a fee and a politician without ambition. He was a philanthropist of the highest order. He was a leader in the Democratic party in Tennessee for many years, and could have held any office in the gift of his party, but he said he could not spare the time from home duties. He had eleven children, seven of whom lived to be grown. He died in 1851 at the age of 64 years. He left Walnut Grove to his eldest son, Charles Elliott Boddie, a man of the highest type, but who lost it in the disastrous wind-up of the Civil War. It was bought by Mr. Dismukes, who occupied it for a number of years. It is once more the home of the Boddies. Its owner is Miss Katie Trousdale, a granddaughter of Eli Odom, and it is occupied as a summer home by Mrs. Carrington Mason of Memphis, the only living child of Elijah Boddie and Maria Elliott.

NATHANIEL PARKER.

The first of the Parker family came to America in about the second ship after the Mayflower landed at Plymouth Rock. Thomas Parker espoused the cause of Roger William and went with him to the Hartford Plantations. One of his descendants emigrated to Pennsylvania, and afterwards he, or one of his descendants, removed to Hampshire County, Virginia. From this line sprang John Parker, the father of Nathaniel Parker.

Nathaniel Parker was born in Hampshire County, Virginia, about 1730. He served under Washington in his attack on the French at Fort Duquense. He also served under Captain Jack against the Indians. He was fond of adventure, as were most men of his day, and wandered through the wilderness of Pennsylvania and Northwestern Virginia, fearless of Indian foes. He may be classed with the "long hunters," as he spent much of his time hunting and exploring, being out often by himself for long periods of time. He made several journeys from his native State to the Cumberland country and back. While in Sumner County he spent most of his time at Greenfield. Before the Indian troubles ceased he removed his young children (his wife being dead) to Sumner County and built a house near Greenfield. That house is still standing and is occupied by Mr. Robert Bryson. Five years after the death of Colonel Anthony Bledsoe, Mr. Parker married his widow, he being at the time 63 and she 60 years of age. He died in 1803 and was buried near the site of the old Morgan fort, on lands now belonging to Dr. Johnson.

Nathan Parker had seven sons. The three eldest, John, Thomas and Richard, married sisters, Misses Rogers, members of the same family as General George Rogers Clark. The eldest, John, never came to Tennessee. The other sons were: Nathaniel, Jr., Isaac, Aaron and Robert. From these sons of Nathaniel Parker have descended many prominent people of Sumner County and elsewhere. George W. Parker was a lawyer of eminence at Gallatin. He went to Missouri, where he died. His wife was a sister of Hon. Balie Peyton. Hon. James M. Head, former Mayor of Nashville; Dr. Head of Sumner County;

Prof. A. J. Hibbett of Pikeville; Hon. John H. De-Witt, a Nashville lawyer, are descendants of Mr. Parker.

THE PEYTON FAMILY.

"The Peyton family is of high antiquity in the mother country. It is said that its founder was

Hon. Balie Peyton

William de Malet, one of the great barons who accompanied William the Conqueror to the conquest of England, and as a recompense received, among other grants, the lordship of Peyton's Hall in Norfolk. Sir Henry Peyton was knighted by James I, and was a gentleman of the Privy Chamber of Prince Henry in

1610, and was a member of the London company to whom King James granted a charter "to make habitations in that part of America commonly called Virginia." John, son of Robert Peyton of this family, is supposed to have been the first who made the voyage to Virginia in 1622, and to have settled in the colony in 1644. He married Ellen Packington and left two sons, Henry Peyton of Acquia, Westmoreland County, and Valentine Peyton of Nominy, the same county, a Colonel in the British army. From Henry Peyton was descended the Sumner County Peytons.

Ephraim Peyton married a daughter of Jonathan Jennings. He was one of the party that accompanied James Robertson across the mountains from the Watauga to the Cumberland. His wife came with the Donelson party by water in one of the boats of her father. While on the voyage, on the 7th of December, 1779, she gave birth to a child, which was accidentally killed in the confusion incident to an attack on Jennings' boat by Indians. Mr. Peyton settled in Sumner County and was killed by the Indians at Bledsoe's Lick. He was the father of Balie Peyton and Joseph H. Peyton, both of whom were members of Congress.

Jonathan Jennings selected a site for his home opposite the head of the first island above Nashville, and was just beginning improvements on the place when he was killed by the Indians in 1781. He was one of the signers of the "Cumberland Compact," and was a man of some prominence. He was born in Virginia, and was a descendant of the English nobility, whose homes were Edrington Castle and Acton Place. A member of the family, Sarah Edrington Jennings, married the Duke of Marlboro, and as Duchess of Marlboro was the bosom friend and confident of Queen Anne. Three brothers Jennings emigrated to America in the reign of George II and settled in Virginia. The Bledsoes, Jennings, Lusks, Prices and Grants of Kentucky are descended from one of these brothers. Several generations after the migration of these brothers one of their descendants, Lillian Jennings Price, of New York, married John, Duke of Marlboro, the direct descendant of Sarah Jennings and John Churchill, the favorite soldier nobleman of Queene Anne. Thus through their grandmother, the daughter of Jonathan Jennings, the Peytons of Sumner County were connected with the Churchill family of England. Then again, another Duke of Marlboro the reigning Duke, married Consuela Vanderbilt, a great-great-great-granddaughter of Colonel Anthony Bledsoe, one of the founders of Sumner County.

JOSEPH H. PEYTON, CONGRESSMAN.

Joseph H. Peyton was born in Sumner County in 1813. He received a liberal education, studied medicine and practiced for a short time, then entered the political field. He held various local offices, and in 1841 was elected State Senator. In 1843 he was elected a member of Congress as a Whig. Was re-elected in 1845, and died November 12 of the same year.

BALIE PEYTON, CONGRESSMAN.

Balie Peyton was born in Sumner County November 26, 1803. He received a limited education; studied law and commenced practice at Gallatin in 1824. In 1833 he was elected to Congress as a Jackson Democrat; was re-elected in 1835. In 1837 he moved to New Orleans, where he practiced his profession. Among his first cases was the famous suit of Mrs. Myra Gaines against New Orleans,. which was not terminated until after the death of Peyton. In 1840 he stumped the State of Tennessee, Kentucky, Ohio and Indiana in favor of General Harrison. After the election of Harrison to the Presidency he appointed Mr. Peyton, United States District Attorney at New

Orleans. When the Mexican War broke out he recruited a regiment of six months men, but before seeing any service the regiment was recalled, but Mr. Peyton remained with the army as chief of General Worth's staff. In 1848 he canvassed Louisiana for the Taylor and Filmore ticket, and received as a reward the appointment of Minister to Chili. In 1852 he went to San Francisco, where he practiced law until 1855, when he returned to Gallatin. In 1862 he was elector for the State at large on the Bell and Everett ticket. His last public service was in 1869-70, when he represented Sumner and Smith Counties in the State Legislature. He died August 18, 1878.

HUGH ROGAN.

During the early years of the Cumberland Settlement, whenever and wherever there was "trouble" with the Indians, Hugh Rogan was to be found. He was a "raw Irishman," whatever that may mean. He was born at Glentourn (now Glentown), County Donegal, Ireland, on September 16, 1747. Married Ann Duffy of Lisduff, County Tyrone. One son, Bernard, was born to them at Lisduff in 1774, and died at Rogana, Sumner County, Tenn., in the month of February, 1873, aged 99 years and 3 months. Hugh served under the patriot Grattan in his native land, and when his chief's cause failed he fled to America, arriving a few days after the battle of Bunker Hill was fought. He enlisted on the first ship built by the colonists in the War of the Revolution, and served in various capacities until the colonists had gained their independence. He then made his way to the southwestern frontier and came with the Donaldson party down the Tennessee and up the Cumberland to French Lick. He first located at the mouth of Stone's River, but at the breaking up of that settlement he went to Mansker's Station, in Sumner County. He participated in all the battles and campaigns against the

Indians; he was with Robertson on the Coldwater expedition and was severely wounded near the mouth of Duck River. He defended Bledsoe's fort when attacked by the Indians; he was with General Daniel Smith in 1782, when he was attacked near where Cragfont now is. He was a man without fear, with a big, kind heart, and was a general favorite among the pioneers. He was one of the signers of the Cumberland Compact.

From Mansker's Station, after a short time, he went to the fort of Colonel Isaac Bledsoe, where he made his home. After there were no more Indians to fight he started back to Ireland to bring his wife and son over, but reaching Virginia, he was told that his wife, believing him dead, had married again. Greatly disappointed, he returned to Sumner County, but years later he received a direct message from his wife that the story of her marriage was false. In 1796 he again set out for the old country after an absence of twenty-one years. As soon as possible he returned to Sumner County, where he owned valuable lands, which are still owned and occupied by his descendants. He died at Rogana in 1814. Francis, second son of Hugh and Ann Rogan, was born in Sumner County in 1798 and lived all his life and died, in 1886, on the farm at Rogana now owned by his son, William.

A. A. C. ROGERS, CONGRESSMAN, ARKANSAS.

Anthony A. C. Rogers was born in Sumner County, February 14, 1821. He became a merchant, and in 1854 moved to Arkansas. In 1861 he was arrested for treason against the Confederate Government. In 1862 he was elected to Congress, but was not allowed to take his seat, the State not having gone through the ordeal of reconstruction. In 1868 he was again elected as the People's candidate. In 1870 he was the Democratic candidate but was defeated.

GEN. GRIFFITH RUTHERFORD.

Griffith Rutherford was born in Ireland about 1731. "His family were originally Scotch, and for centuries were classed among the most ancient and powerful families in Teviotdale." Some of the family removed to Ireland, where John Rutherford married a Miss Griffith, a Welsh lady. Their son, Griffith Rutherford, sailed from Ireland for America in 1739, accompanied by his wife and only son, Griffith. The parents died either on the voyage or soon after their arrival in America, and young Griffith was taken by an old German couple. About 1753 he went to Rowan County, North Carolina, and in 1758 purchased from James Lynn two tracts of land on Grant's Creek, about seven miles southwest from Salisbury, and adjoining the land of James Graham, whose sister, Elizabeth, he married about that time. Their son, James Rutherford, was a Major in the Revolutionary Army, and was killed at the battle of Eutaw Springs.

General Rutherford was a man of strong character, resolute and determined, and of unusual capacity, and early in life attained a position of prominence. He was a member of the North Carolina Assembly as early as 1769, and about that time he was Sheriff of Rowan County. He was in the Assembly of 1770 and 1771, and at the same time was Captain of militia. He continued to represent his county in the Assembly, and was a member of the Legislature of 1773 and 1774. In 1775 he was elected a member of the Provincial Congress, and was appointed a member of the Committee of Safety for Rowan County and Colonel of militia. He was in all the subsequent Provincial Congresses and assisted in forming the State Constitution. For years he was one of the most prominent men in North Carolina. In April, 1776, he was appointed Brigadier General for the Western District, and was Senator from Rowan County from 1777 to 1788, except when a prisoner of war in 1780-1781.

During the Revolution he was among the most active and enterprising military men in the State. He led the Rowan regiment to South Carolina in the "Snow Campaign" in December, 1775, and conducted the expedition against the Indians in September, 1776. In 1779 he marched with his brigade to Savannah to aid General Lincoln. In June, 1780, he suppressed the Tories at Ramseur's Mills, threatened Lord Rawdon in South Carolina, and dispersed the Tories on the Yadkin. He marched with Gen. Gates to Camden, where he was badly wounded and taken prisoner. He was confined in St. Augustine until the summer of 1781, when he was exchanged, and at once calling his brigade together, he marched on to Wilmington, driving the Tories before him. Before he reached Wilmington the British Commander at that place had learned of the surrender of Cornwallis and hurriedly evacuated the town.

In 1792 General Rutherford moved to Sumner County, Tennessee, but where he located I have been unable to learn. His numerous descendants knows but little of him. His will, dated in Rowan County, North Carolina, on July 14, 1792, and recorded in Transcript of Wills No. 1, Sumner County, gives personal property and slaves to his wife, Elizabeth, and "my two sons, John and Griffith W., and my daughter, Elizabeth," who was unmarried. The executors named were Henry Rutherford, Robert Weakley and John King.

In most of the accounts of General Rutherford it is stated that he came to Tennessee in 1786, but this is evidently an error, for his will, mentioned above, was dated in North Carolina in 1792. Governor Blount, in a letter to General James Robertson, dated May, 1792, published in the American Historical Magazine, says:

"General Rutherford and W. F. Lewis will leave in September with thirty wagons, so they write me. The General has actually exchanged all his lands in North Carolina for lands on the Cumberland."

Upon the organization of the territory of the United States south of the Ohio River, in 1794, President Washington appointed General Rutherford a member of the Legislative Council, and he was chosen President of that body. Six years later, in 1800, he died, but where, and when his body was buried, there is no record, and the remembrance has faded from the memory of men.

Rutherfordton and Rutherford County, North Carolina, and Rutherford County, Tennessee, were so named for General Rutherford.

HUBBARD SANDERS.

Hubbard Sanders was a native of Virginia; is said to have married a daughter of Colonel William Russell, of Abingdon, Washington County, that State. He removed to Tennessee and located in Sumner County at an early period, and lived to an advanced age. He was a Methodist preacher, a man of wealth and culture, and did much for the cause of Methodism in Sumner County. On his land was erected a church which was called Sanders' Chapel, and around it grew up the village of Sandersville. He reared a large family, and some of his descendants are still living in the vicinity of Sandersville.

WILLIAM LEWIS SHARKEY.

Judge William L. Sharkey, twenty-third Governor of Mississippi, was born in Sumner County in 1797. When 6 years of age he was taken by his parents to Warren County, Mississippi, where he grew to manhood. He received his education at Greeneville, and in law at Lebanon, Tennessee. In 1822 he was admitted to the bar at Natchez, and in 1825 removed to

Vicksburg. He served one term in the Legislature. In 1832 he was elected Chief Justice of the Court of Errors and Appeals, and held that position for eighteen years, then resigned and resumed the practice of law at Jackson. He was the President of the Southern States' Convention, which met in Nashville in June, 1850. In 1851 he declined both the Consulship at Havana and Secretary of War under President Fillmore. He was one of the Commissioners to frame the Mississippi Code in 1857. In 1865 he was appointed by Gov. Clark a Commissioner with William Yerger to go to Washington to confer with President Johnson in behalf of his State. Mr. Johnson appointed him Provisional Governor on June 29, 1865; served until October, when the military assumed charge of the State. He died at Washington City, April 29, 1873.

Judge Sharkey was not a man of liberal education, and when he was elevated to the Supreme bench he was not well learned in the law. But his intellect was vigorous, and his sagacity almost unerring. His conclusions, as well of law, as of fact, were generally correct, and he extracted the true principle from the most discordant and irreconcilable authorities. As presiding Judge he was affable and patient. The most prosy speaker was assured of an attentive hearing, and his manner was such as to seldom give offense. He presided in the court for nearly twenty years, and at last resigned a place which seemed to be his by right. In political life he was timid, wavering, inconsistent and wholly unreliable.

Judge Sharkey married Miss Minerva Cage, of Sumner County.

DANIEL SMITH.

Daniel Smith, son of Henry and Sarah Crosby Smith, of English origin, was born in Stafford County, Virginia, on October 28, 1748, and died at his home, Rock Castle, in Sumner County, Tennessee, on June 6, 1818. Upon coming from England the family first settled in Somerset County, Maryland, but later removed to Virginia. He was educated at William and Mary College, and, like many of the young men of talent of his day, became a surveyor. On June 10, 1773, he married Sarah Michie, of the eastern shore of Maryland, and soon afterwards settled in the western country. He was appointed Deputy Surveyor of Augusta County in 1773. At that time this county embraced nearly all of Southwestern Virginia; Mr. Smith settled in that part of the county, which later formed Botetourt, then Fincastle, then Washington and finally Russell County. His place was on Clinch River, twelve miles below Blackmore's Fort, at Maxwell's Hill. It was known as Smith's Station, though the fort was called Fort Christian. As early as 1774 he was a Captain in the Colonial troops, and was one of the most active company commanders in Dunmore's war. The correspondence which passed between him and his superior officers shows him to be a man of education beyond most men of his day. He participated in the battle of Point Pleasant in October, 1774, and in many of the engagements with the Indians. He aided in defending the frontier against the Indians during the Revolution. He was a member of the Committee of Safety for Fincastle County in 1775, and of a committee that sent resolutions to the Continental Congress July 15, 1775, in which they declared that they would "never surrender their inestimable privileges to any power on earth but at the expense of their lives."

When Washington County was organized Captain Smith was appointed one of the Justices of the Peace by Governor Patrick Henry—December 21, 1776.. On the same day he was appointed Major of Washington County militia. In 1780 he was appointed Sheriff of Washington, and the next year upon the reorganization of the militia, he was commissioned Colonel in the Second Battalion. In 1779 he was appointed with Dr. Thomas Walker to extend the line between Virginia and North Carolina, which line had been run by Jefferson and others. He was in the battle of King's Mountain, and soon after the close of the War, in 1783, with the Bledsoes, Shelbys, Blackmores, Neeleys, and others, came to Tennessee. He

ROCK CASTLE; HOME OF GEN. DANIEL SMITH
ERECTED 1791

located a large body of valuable land near the present town of Hendersonville, in Sumner County, and in 1784 began the building of Rock Castle, but owing to the depredations of the Indians the house was seven years in being completed. It is constructed of cut stone, has seven large rooms and is as sound today as when built, and has been "the roof tree" of five generations, and is now the property of Mrs. Horatio Berry, a great-great-granddaughter of General Smith.

Two carpenters engaged in the construction of the house left work in one Saturday afternoon to fish in Drake's Creek nearby and were killed by the Indians. Two youths, one a son of Colonel Anthony Bledsoe, and the other a son of his brother, Colonel Isaac Bledsoe, who were living at General Smith's and attending school near Hendersonville, were killed by prowling Indians. Samuel Donaldson, who married Geenral Smith's only daughter, was killed by Indians.

In 1790 General Smith was appointed by President Washington Secretary of the ceded territory south of the Ohio. He was elected by the first Legislature of Tennessee one of the four Presidential Electors. In 1798 he succeeded Andrew Jackson in the Senate of the United States, and was again elected in 1805 and served until 1809. In 1793, in the absence of Governor Blount, he acted as Governor of the Territory. He was a member of the Constitutional Convention of 1796. He made the first map of Tennessee, published by Carey, of Philadelphia, and used by Imlay in 1794. Michaux, a French botanist, who passed through this section of the county in 1792, and after his return to France, published an interesting book of travel, speaks of his visit to General Smith, of the beautiful fields of cotton and corn which surrounded his house, of the translations of foreign works his library contained, and of the quiet, studious and exemplary life led by a retired public servant. Living at a time when many public men were justly or unjustly the object, not only of censure, but of official accusation, it is worth while to publish the following from Jefferson's paper:

"Daniel Smith was a practical surveyor, whose work never needed correction. For intelligence, well cultivated talents, for integrity and usefulness, in soundness of judgment, in the practice of virtue and in shunning vice, he was equalled by few men, and in the purity of motive excelled by none."

Smith County was so named in honor of General Smith.

General Smith had two children, a son, George, who was born in Virginia, May 12, 1776, married Tabitha Donelson, and Mary, who was born in Virginia April 26, 1781. She married Samuel Donelson, Andrew Jackson's law partner, who was later killed by Indians. There was quite a romance connected with their marriage, it being an elopement. Andrew Jackson made a rope ladder and helped his partner to steal his bride from an upper room in the old Rock Castle homestead of the family. After the death of Samuel Donelson his widow married James Sanders of Sumner County, by whom she had several children.

George Smith had a son, Harry, who was the father of Mrs. Horatio Berry, who inherited the Rock Castle estate, where she now resides.

THOMAS SHARP SPENCER.

Thomas Sharp Spencer, called the "Chevalier Beyard of the Cumberland Valley," was a native of Virginia, and a bold, daring hunter, who at an early day went to Kentucky in search of adventure. From Kentucky he came to what is now Tennessee, in 1778, with a party of hunters, who made their camp at Bledsoe's Lick. After a time all of the party returned to the settlements except Spencer and one other, whose name is given in some of the histories and as Holliday in others, as elsewhere stated in this story as Drake. He was a man of gigantic size and great physical strength, and never knew the meaning of the word fear. Many stories are told of his prowess and of his adventures with the Indians, and if they were all collected they would fill a volume which would read more like romance than fact. He helped to build the first cabin, make the first clearing and plant the first corn in Middle Tennessee. He was a nephew of that Judge Samuel Spencer, who issued the warrant for the arrest of John Sevier for high treason in 1788, and who was killed by a turkey gobbler.

In 1794 Spencer made a journey to Virginia to collect some money that was due him from an estate.

SPENCER'S CHOICE. FORMER HOME OF DAVID SHELBY ERECTED IN 1798

Returning, he was shot from ambush by Indians, at what is now called Spencer's Hill, in Van Buren County. The seat of justice of that county was so named in his honor. So, also, were Spencer's Creek and Spencer's Lick.

After the death of Spencer, the body of land containing 640 acres, lying one mile south of Gallatin, and known to this day as "Spencer's Choice," passed to the ownership of his brother, William, and his sister, Elizabeth. The latter purchased her brother's interest, and then sold the entire tract to David Shelby, who, in 1798, built the stone residence still standing and occupied by A. P. Howisson, the present owner.

GENERAL WILLIAM TROUSDALE, THIRTEENTH GOVERNOR

William Trousdale was born in Orange County, North Carolina, September 23, 1790. In 1796 his father, Capt. James Trousdale, moved to Tennessee, and settled on a grant of 650 acres of land on which the town of Gallatin was afterwards located. He was educated in the common schools of the county. In 1813 he volunteered for the Creek war, and was elected Third Lieutenant. Took part in the battles of Talladega and Tallahatchie. Re-enlisted in 1814, and was at the capture of Pensacola, and in the battle of New Orleans, under Jackson. After the close of the war he returned home and resumed his studies. Admitted to the bar in 1820. In 1827 married Miss Mary Ann Bugg. In 1835 he was elected to the State Senate. In 1836 he was made Major General of Militia. He was Colonel of the Second Regiment of Mounted Volunteers in the Seminole War, in 1836. After the close of that war he declined to accept the appointment as Brigadier General in the Regular Army, tendered by President Jackson. He was a Democratic elector in 1840. In 1847 he was appointed by President Polk, Colonel of the Fourteenth United States Infantry, and as such participated in the battles of Contreras, Cherebusco, Molina del Rey and Chepultepec, in the war with Mexico. In this last battle he commanded a brigade. He was twice wounded, but refused to leave the field. On August 23, 1848, he was made Brigadier General by brevet. In 1849 he was elected Governor of Tennessee, and served two terms. In May, 1853, President Pierce appointed him Minister to Brazil, which office he held four years. Died in Gallatin, March 27, 1872, leaving many descendants.

WILLIAM WALTON.

Captain William Walton was not for many years a citizen of Sumner County, but long enough to deserve

GOVERNOR WILLIAM TROUSDALE

mention here. He was born in Bertie County, North Carolina, a county that has given to Tennessee many of her prominent men, in 1760. He was of English Cavalier descent; attained his early manhood about the beginning of the Revolutionary war, and at the age of 17 enlisted in Major Hardy Murfree's battalion as a private. Later he was commissioned a Lieutenant, and then Captain. He was in many of the most important engagements of the war, and demeaned himself as a brave and gallant soldier. He was twice taken prisoner. In December, 1783 he was married to Sarah Jones, and in 1785 removed to what is now Sumner County Tennessee and settled at Mansker's Station near Goodlettsville. The next year he located a body of land in what is now Smith County, on a part of which the county seat was afterwards located (Carthage.) Captain Walton continued to reside in Sumner County until 1796, when he removed to his new home. At that time Smith County was a part of Sumner. When Smith County was formed he was one of its first magistrates, a position he had held in Sumner County. When the question of a county seat came up, through his influence it was located on his land, he giving a square in the center of the town for a courthouse and other public buildings.

Captain Walton inaugerated the plan, and was the contractor who built what is known as "Walton's Road," which connects the Cumberland country with Knoxville and East Tennessee, and was for many years one of the most traveled roads in the State. The construction of this road was a great achievement at that day. The Tennessee Central Railroad closely follows its course from Lebanon to Kingston, across the Cumberland Mountains.

Captain Walton died at his home in Smith County, March 6, 1816, leaving a handsome fortune and many descendants, all of whom have, up to this day, been useful and honorable citizens.

FRANK WEATHERRED.

Frank Weatherred was a native of Virginia; served in the War of Independence under General Lafayette, and was with that officer at the seige of Yorktown. He was one of that gallant band that stormed the Brittish works under command of the gallant French commander. He came to Sumner County, and settled near Bledsoe's Lick, on lands which belonged to the late Senator William B. Bate. He was a carpenter by trade, and some of the old houses still standing in that vicinity attest the excellence of his work. He did much of the woodwork on Cragfont, the home of General James Wnichester. He was a useful citizen; reared several sons, one of whom was the ancestor of the late Senator Bate. Two of his children married into the Colonel Anthony Bledsoe family. His wife was a sister of General Sumpter, of South Carolina.

THE WILSON FAMILY.

Prominent among the early settlers of Sumner county was the Wilson family. Zaccheus Wilson was one of three brothers who removed from Pennsylvania and settled in Mecklenburg County, North Carolina, about 1760. At the time of the Mecklenburg Convention, May 20, 1775, he was present and signed the Mecklenburg Declaration, pledging himself and his extensive family connection to its support and maintainence. He was a member of the Convention that formed the State Constitution of North Carolina in 1776. He was a man of liberal education, and very popular in the county in which he lived. His family were Scotch-Irish Presbyterians. His eldest brother, Robert, removed with him to Tennessee, and to Sumner County soon after the close of the Revolutionary War. Zaccheus lived to an advanced age, and lies buried in an unmarked grave about one half mile south of Gallatin on the old cotton factory grounds. Samuel Wilson married a Miss Knox, daughter of Captain Patrick Knox, who was killed at the battle of Ramseurs Mill. Major David Wilson, brother of Zaccheus, a native of Pennsylvania, was an officer in the War of Independence, and for his service received from the State of North Carolina, a track of land in Sumner County, Tennessee, where he settled. He was a member of the Territorial Assembly in 1794, and was the Speaker of the House of Representatives. He was a magistrate of Sumner County as early as 1787. His residence was about two miles east from Gallatin. He was a valuable member of the new settlement, and took an active part in all public affairs and in the Indian wars. Wilson County was so named in his honor. He married Sallie McConnell, sister of General James White the father of Hugh Lawson White. His remains lie in an unmarked grave near Gallatin.

Samuel Franklin Wilson was born in Sumner County in the month of April, 1845. In 1861 he left school and entered the Confederate Army as a private in Company I, of Colonel William B. Bates' regiment. He was in the battles of Corinth, Richmond Kentucky, where he was wounded; Perryville, and Murfreesboro, where he was again wounded. In 1863 he took part in the Tullahoma campaign. He lost an arm at Chickamauga, which ended his military career. After the close of the war he attended the University at Penfield, Georgia, and graduated from the University of Georgia with second honors, in 1868. In 1869 he graduated in law at Cumberland University, and commenced practicing at Gallatin. In 1871 he was elected a member of the Legislature, and in 1879 of the State Senate. In 1880 he was nominated for Governor on the "low tax platform," but was defeated. In 1884 he was an elector on the Cleveland ticket, and the next year was appointed by President Cleveland United States Marshall. In 1895 he was appointed one of the Judges of the Court of Chancery Appeals, and has served continuously since.

MAJOR GEORGE WINCHESTER.

George Winchester was a younger brother of General James Winchester. He was born in Maryland, and served in the war of the American Revolution, and afterwards came to Sumner County, and was a member of its first County Court. After North Carolina ceded the territory now known as Tennessee to the United States, Winchester was appointed by Governor Blount a justice of the peace, in 1790. He also appointed him Register of Sumner County, and Second Major of cavalry for Mero District. The next year he was appointed First Major of the cavalry of Mero District. He participated in nearly all the fights with the Indians; led several expeditions against them, and was active in all public affairs. He located the first permanent water mill in Sumner County, on Bledsoe's Creek, near where it crosses the Gallatin and Hartsville pike. He was greatly beloved by the people for his kindness of heart and for his many virtues. He was killed and scalped by Indians near the town of Gallatin, about the east end of what is now Water Street, on the morning of August 9, 1794, while on his way to the seat of justice to attend court. He was never married.

GENERAL JAMES WINCHESTER.

General James Winchester was born at White Level, Md., February 6, 1752. He received a liberal education, and in May, 1776, was appointed a Lieutenant in the Third Maryland in the War for Independence. He was a brave and gallant soldier, and participated in a number of engagements. He was taken prisoner by the British and held until 1780 when he was exchanged. After the close of the war he moved to Tennessee and settled in Sumner County on Bledsoe Creek, where he owned a large body of valuable land. He was a man of education, of culture and refinement, and was a very useful citizen. His military experience made him invaluable in repelling the attacks of the Indians. He directed the scouts and spies and frequently accompanied troops in their pursuits of the enemy. He was a member of the Territorial General Assembly in 1794 and Speaker of the first

State Senate in 1796. In the War of 1812 he was commissioned a Brigadier General and placed in command of one wing of the Northwestern Army. At the disastrous battle of the River Raison he was taken prisoner by the British and sent to Quebec, where he

GENERAL JAMES WINCHESTER

was held for more than a year. He was severely criticised for surrendering, but the criticism was unjust. While riding among his panic-stricken soldiers, trying to rally them he was surrounded and taken prisoner, and after he had surrendered, on the promise of the British commander that the men should receive such treatment as civilized victors accord to vanquished, he sent an order to his army to surrender. Most of the men surrendered, and many of them were treacherously and brutally massacred.

In 1814 General Winchester returned to his home in Sumner County, where he died July 27, 1826.

General Winchester was one of the original proprietors of Memphis, Judge John Overton and General Andrew Jackson being the others. They in partnership purchased the Rice grant of 5,000 acres on which the city was built. General Winchester's son, Major Marcus B. Winchester, who served on his staff, and was taken prisoner with him, was the first Mayor of Memphis.

General Winchester married Miss Susan Black, of Sumner County. His home, "Cragfont," a large, substantial stone building, constructed under his own personal supervision, and by workmen brought for that purpose from the East, is still standing and occupied, though it has passed from the possession of the family. He and his accomplished wife dispensed a liberal, old-time Southern hospitality. They were the parents of six sons and six daughters. The county seat of Franklin County was named in honor of General Winchester.

The old Winchester home, "Cragfont," is now the property and is the home of W. B. C. Satterwhite.

They had children: Maria, married Mr. Bendlore, of New Orleans; Selina, married William Lord Robinson, of New Orleans; Caroline, married Orville Shelby and moved to Lexington, Ky.; Louisa, married Edmund Rucker. Their son, General E. W. Rucker, a gallant Confederate soldier, now resides in Birmingham, Ala. Helen, never married. Almira, married Col. Alfred R. Wynne; Marcus B., moved to Memphis and was the first Mayor of that town, elected in 1827 and served two terms; Lucilius, married Amanda Bledsoe, daughter of Isaac Bledsoe, of Sumner County; Valerius, married Samuella Price, of

Nashville; James, married Mary House of Sumner County; George, married Malvina Gaines, aunt of Hon. John Wesley Gaines; Napoleon, no information.

COLONEL A. R. WYNNE.

Colonel Alfred R. Wynne was a son of Robert and Cynthia (Harrison) Wynne. He was born in Sumner County in 1800, and lived to be about four score and ten years of age. He received a good education at Hickory Ridge, Wilson County, then, at the age of 16 years, returned to his native county and became clerk in a store at Cairo, where he remained for several years, then commenced business on his own account at the same place. Three years later he sold out and engaged in the milling business at Stamps Mill. In 1834 he purchased a farm at Castalian Springs, where he continued to reside until his death. He was a Colonel of militia, having command of 1200 men under the old military laws. In 1866 he was elected a State Senator and served one term. He was for forty-seven years postmaster at Castalian Springs. In March 1825 he married Almira, a daughter of General James and Susan Black Winchester. Fourteen children were born to them, some of whom are now living in Sumner County at the old Castalian Springs farm.

Colonel Wynne had one sister, Cynthia, who married Albert Gallatin Donoho, of Trousdale County, and whose son, Dr. Donoho, has for years been a prominent physician of Hartsville.

Colonel Wynne's wife inherited from her father an interest in the property known as Bledsoe's Lick. He organized a company, which erected the large log buildings and occupied as a hotel during the summer months. He gave to the place the name "Castalian Springs." Later he purchased the other interests and became the sole owner. At his death the property passed to his three children, Winchester Wynne, of

Gallatin; Misses Sue and Louise Wynne, who reside at the old place. The two sons of Winchester Wynne, George and Edmond Wynne, reside with their parents in the old home.

THE PIONEER PREACHER

Dr. McDonald, in his "History of the Cumberland Presbyterian Church," paints a woeful picture of spiritual matters in pioneer times. He says: "Orthodoxy, the catechism, a deathless attachment to principles and to ecclesiastical rights, a holy horror of any innovations on the traditional methods of work, singing Rouse's Psalms, and hearing sermons three hours' long on election, made up the religion of many among the best citizens."

"But after the revolution, mainly through the influence of the French soldiers who had aided us in that struggle, infidelity swept over all this western frontier, and threatened for a while to carry all the population. All the historians are agreed in their testimony to this vast prevalence of infidelity. Some say that nine-tenths of the people were infidels. The general lack of preaching, and the bad character of many who did preach, helped to sweep faith away from the face of the country. . . Most of the preachers were bad men. Drunkenness, wrangling, licentiousness and heresy brought the most of them to grief sooner or later."

This may have been true of some sections, but not of the Cumberland country, where there was but little lawlessness, and few crimes committed against God or man.

Carr names several preachers who had arrived in the Sumner County settlements before 1795, calls them "eminent men of God," who "warned the people to flee the wrath of God." The pioneer preachers were, as a rule, good men, and they exercised an influence for good. They were not men of learning, but what they lacked in education they made up in enthusiasm.

The pioneer preacher was one of the people, one who, in early youth, was noted for his great piety, and for frequent and fervent prayers in public. He was the pride and the joy of his mother, the hope of his father, and the model to which all the mothers for miles and miles around pointed their sons. He was a general favorite with all the pious girls, and frequently the butt of the bad young men. He felt that he was called to preach. There could be no doubt of it, he had heard the summons and had no choice but to obey. He usually married while quite young, and the general verdict was that he had made a grave mistake in not marrying some other girl. But mistake or no mistake, in due course of time he was surrounded by a numerous brood of children, which, if rumors were to be credited, were the worst children in the whole settlement. And to this day we sometimes hear the same report of preachers' children. But it is not always true.

The worldly possessions of the Pioneer Preacher were few. They consisted of a horse, bridle and saddle, a pair of saddle bags, a pocket bible and a hymn book, the last two being well worn, dog-eared, thumb-marked and greasy from constant use. If he was married he also owned a meager lot of household furniture and fixtures, only such as was absolutely necessary for his family. More would have been extravagance and a burden to a man who had no permanent abode, a shepherd with a scattered flock. The preacher was extravagant in piety and prayer, but in nothing else.

The circuit embraced many settlements, some of which were many miles from the abode of the preacher. He traveled on horseback, sometimes on foot, from one appointment to another, stopping at night at any friendly cabin when night overtook him.

He sometimes camped in the woods, sleeping with his back to a tree, while his horse grazed about. Sometimes he was overtaken by storms, rain or snow, for which he was illy prepared. Swollen streams were frequently encountered, and the good man was put to great inconvenience, his health and even life being endangered. But he put his trust in Providence and landed safely on the other shore. He had a sublime faith in Providence. He trusted Providence to provide food for his family during his itineracy, and there is no authentic record of any member of such a family starving to death. Doubtless some of them at times went to bed hungry, but hunger is good for the soul. Providence also provided for the preacher and his faithful horse and supplied them with food at intervals. The Pioneer Preacher did not confine his preaching to Sundays, but he "dispensed" the gospel every time he found a few faithful souls gathered together in the name of the Lord. There were but few roads in those days, and the good man was forced to travel over mountains, across valleys and through trackless forests, without even a blazed tree to guide him on his way.

The Pioneer Preacher had no vacations with full pay, such as the modern preacher enjoys. If he had any leisure it was spent in wrestling with the Lord and fighting the devil back from his little flocks. Satan was abroad in the land, and he did not then, as now, take a vacation during the heated term, nor did the preacher.

In those days there were but few church edifices—they were called "meeting houses," and were constructed of logs, with puncheon floors and benches, the latter without backs or cushions. These buildings did duty as school houses as well as places of worship. Sometimes cattle, hogs and sheep resorted to them for shelter from the storm. One "meetin' house" sufficed for a whole settlement, all worshipped together regardless of church affiliations. The circuit riders, exhorter, prayer meeting and 'sperience meeting all attracted the saint and the sinner, the good and the bad. The congregation was usually limited by the number of settlers in the community. In sparsely settled districts, where there were no meeting houses, the people assembled at the cabin of some one of the neighbors for worship. There were no organs, pianos, nor violins in the churches of that day. The only music was the mingled voices of the multitude singing, often out of harmony, but vociferous, some in a high key and some in a low key, each doing his or her best for the glory of God.

The visit of the Pioneer Preacher was an event in the lives of the settlers. The fattest chicken was killed, and the best the cabin afforded was put upon the table. The good man said a long blessing before the meal, and held family prayer before retiring at night and before breakfast in the morning. He slept in the best bed, the family occupying the same apartment, as the cabin contained but one room. There was no privacy except in the forest.

The Pioneer Preacher was not paid a stipulated salary, as preachers now are, and often did not receive as much as $5 a year in the "root of evil." Contribution boxes were unknown at that day. Salvation was free. The gospel was not retailed at so much per and perquisites. The preacher and his family subsisted entirely upon perquisites; an occasional peck of meal, a pullet, a ham, a side of bacon, a saddle of venison, a pair of home-made socks or mittens, a few yards of home-made jeans or linsey woolsey and such articles as the people could spare from their limited stores; these were freely given and thankfully received.

The Pioneer Preacher was an oracle; it was through him that the news was spread, and this was another reason, aside from his holy calling, why he was always welcome. There were no newspapers, and the mails were irregular and uncertain, so the preacher was the bearer of the news from one settlement to another, and, too, he was the bearer of letters and messages. He knew everybody, and everybody knew him.

He commenced religious services by lining a hymn, in which the congregation joined lustily in singing. This was followed by a long and fervent prayer, then the text was announced and the sermon begun, and it was continued with unabated vigor for two or three hours. Everything in the bible, "from kiver to kiver," was accepted as literally true; it was the revealed word of God, and who did not accept it was an infidel and an outcast. There were no "higher criticism," and doubt did not disturb the minds of the people. All Christians believed the Bible, though different denominations had different interpretations for certain passages, and, as now, furious disputes and debates failed to settle the debatable passages.

Sermons had an extraordinary influence upon their hearers. They were solemn, earnest, and often approached the grotesque. The preacher taught the good, old-fashioned doctrine of hell, where fires of brimstone and melted pitch were never quenched, and where the wicked burned forever and were never consumed. Hell was a bottomless and shoreless lake of fire, into the immeasureless depths of which sinners were plunged headlong, that on its burning billows, tipped with flickering flames of damnation, souls were tossed and dashed through all eternity. They believed in a personal devil, with horns and claws and a forked tail, and who laughed with diabolical glee while he shoveled sulphur into the blazing pit of unquenchable fire. The good man held out no hope for those who died in sin. Their punishment would continue unchanged throughout all eternity.

These good old preachers vied with each other in picturing the torments of the damned, the agonizing screams and writhings of lost souls, the endless throbbing, burning anguish, the blistering fires of unconsuming wrath. Even now, after all these good and devout men have long gone to their reward, it makes one's flesh creep to recall the awful pictures they painted in such frightful colors in their efforts to turn men from sin to repentance. We can see the doomed soul the moment it leaves the body plunge into the depts of eternal perdition, into the lake of torment. It is seized by gloating demons with hooks of red hot iron and is thurst into flames a thousand times hotter than melted iron. A thousand devils scream with infernal delight at the sound and sight of its awful agony and hopeless despair.

"Imagine, if you can, yourself to be cast into a furnace where your pains would be as much greater than that occasioned by accidentally touching a coal of fire, as the heat is greater! Imagine, also, that if your body were to lie there for a quarter of an hour, full of pain and all the while full of quick sense, what horror would you feel at the entrance of such a place, and how long would that quarter of hour seem to you, and after you had endured the pain for one minute how frightful it would be to you to think you would have to endure it for the other fourteen! But what would be the effect on your soul if you knew that you must lie there enduring that agony to the full twenty-four hours! And how much greater would be the torment if you knew you must endure it for a whole year! And how vastly greater still if you knew that you must endure it for a thousand years! O then, how would your heart sink if you knew that you must bear it forever and ever; that after millions of years and millions of ages your torment would be no nearer to an end; and that you should never be delivered. Thank God for his tender mercies, and his loving kindness in providing such a place for unrepentant souls."

After all these years have come and gone that favorite text of the Pioneer Preacher still rings in our ears: "Depart from me, ye cursed, into everlasting fire prepared for the devil and his angels." A favorite illustration of eternity was: "Grind the world into sand, place the sands into an immense hourglass, let these grains of sand drop, one every million years, and when they have all passed through eternity will only have just begun!"

"How many years and centuries shall the lost soul be imprisoned? Forever. How many ages shall it groan in tears of regret and despair? Forever. How many years shall it burn in flames? Forever. Will there be no interruption of these torments? Never. Stretch your imagination, add years to years, ages to ages, multiply them by the leaves in the forests, the sands of the sea shore, the drops of water in the immensity of all the oceans, you will not conceive the meaning of ever, never! On the brazen arch of hell *forever* is written in letters of eternal fire."

Such were the pictures painted by these pious men, and they had their effect in a harvest of redeemed souls. Set the most hardened sinner on a puncheon bench where for two or more hours he must face a preacher with eyes in fierce frenzie rolling, while in stentorian voice he pictures such horrible scenes, and if it don't fetch him to the mourners' bench he is surely a goner. When the old-time preacher took off his coat, unbuttoned his collar and got down to business in this strain, he usually made the dry bones of sinners rattle. Strong men would groan, women would weep and little children shriek in agony of fright.

Death-bed scenes were favorite themes with the Pioneer Preacher, and here, too, he was an artist. The joys, the exquisite delights of the departure from the corrupt body of the soul of the Christian. The despair, the agony, the terror, the consternation of the dying sinner. They were awful pictures.

Heaven was painted as the very reverse of hell. But possible more souls were induced to flee the wrath to come through fear of torment than through hope of paradise. The Pioneer Preacher was endowed by nature with powerful lungs, and he preached his sermons loud enough to make the women cry and to bring from the male side of the house a sonorious and hearty "amen." Be it remembered that the two sexes did not mingle indiscriminately in houses of worship at that time. The women sat on one side of the house and the men on the other. The sheep were divided from the goats as it were. It was not considered bad form for a worshipper to light his cob pipe and enjoy a smoke during the sermon, nor for a mother to give her babe its natural food.

Many amusing incidents might be related of these meetings, but I will forbear. The Christians of that day were earnest and devout. They believed in the good book. If it was not in the Bible it wasn't so, and if it was in the Bible every word and every syllable was true, and he who doubted was damned. They hated cards and had a contempt for fine clothes. A fiddler occupied a low place in society. Silks and broad cloth were deemed worldly and a "biled shirt" was looked upon with suspicion. The preacher was usually a muscular man, and he not unfrequently found it necessary to enforce respect by the application of muscular energy. He was not a college-bred man, and his sermons were delivered in pioneer English without frills or Latin quotations. His dress was of home-spun, though on state occasions he donned an antique suit of broad cloth, well worn and threadbare and with brass buttons on the coat, which was cut with a forked tail and had an enormous collar. With this suit he wore a hat of uncertain age, probably inherited from a remote ancestor. It was tall, and made of fur, and was the wonder and admiration of all beholders. The gestures of the Pioneer Preacher were vigorous and violent. He would sometimes squat very low, then suddenly, like a jack in the box, rise on his tip-toes, fling his arms, roll his eyes heavenward and shout loud enough to be heard for a mile or more. No mortal could have doubted his earnestness and holy zeal. There was a good deal of hyperbole in his discourse, but he was in dead earnest. He wrestled with the Lord for the salvation of sinners and made the devil take to tall cane. He didn't know whether the world was round or flat, and he didn't care. It was only a place of temporary abode for weary souls where they were prepared for better or worse after the judgment. He knew that heaven was above and that hell was below, and that was enough. He was absolutely sure that the world was made about six thousand years ago out of nothing; the Bible said so, and no man could doubt it and be saved. Previous to that period the place where the earth had its orbit was an aching void.

In those days the family dog regularly attended divine service, and they often disputed with each other while the good man was warning sinners to flee the wrath to come. Crying babies did not interfere with the devotional exercises, other than to stimulate the preacher to renewed exertion. The children had souls to be saved.

The lot of the Pioneer Preacher was a hard one, but he never complained. He faithfully performed his duties until called by the Master, firm in the faith that he would wear a crown of glory on the other shore.

O.M

www.ingramcontent.com/pod-product-compliance
Lightning Source LLC
Chambersburg PA
CBHW071955220426
43662CB00009B/1137